P9-CFK-180

Praise for *Human Resources in the 21st Century*

"Ideally for effective organizational learning and change, the CEO and Head of HR should meet every Friday afternoon for a couple of hours over a period of three or four months—just the two of them—and discuss at least two chapters from this book. Since this book is loaded with rich ideas and many actual and useful case examples of learning and change, the two executives would quickly begin to change for the better their own organization especially the HR function."

> **W. Warner Burke, PhD,** Edward Lee Thorndike Professor
> of Psychology & Education Program Coordinator,
> Graduate Programs in Social-Organizational Psychology

"One of the best collections of readings by HR's best and brightest stars."

> **Warren Bennis,** Distinguished Professor Business, USC
> and Coauthor of *Geeks and Geezers: How Era, Values,*
> *and Defining Moments Shape Leaders*

"I believe in the value of professional HR support in changing our business. My experience over the past years has been that this is crucial in getting the changes we wanted in Unilever. This is a great book to demonstrate this and comes exactly at the right time to show you what we mean with professionalism in HR!"

> **Antony Burgmans,** Chairman, Unilever N.V.

"Fully engaging the 21st century workforce is the *only* way leaders can drive their organizations to their goals and missions. This book, reflecting the ideas and insights of dozens of leading thinkers, provides the road map for building and inspiring a winning team."

> **Hank McKinnell,** Chairman and CEO, Pfizer Inc.

"This is a valuable resource for all business people who think about the *people* part of their business. You cannot read this thought-provoking collection without entertaining a new idea, challenging an old belief, or learning something you can immediately put into practice. It is a useful tool for experienced professionals, managers at all levels, and students."

> **Deborah K. Smith,** Former Senior Vice President, HR
> for Merck and Bausch and Lomb, and Executive Vice President,
> HR for Coty Inc. and Chair of CAHRS at Cornell

"Never before have HR issues been more important and HR departments less relevant. Here's a book chock full of thought-provoking ideas, insights, and solutions for getting HR back on track."

> **Michael Treacy,** Author of *Double Digit Growth*

"A roadmap to the immediate future of human resource management."

Dr. Warren Wilhelm, President, Global Consulting Alliance

"People are essential in any endeavor. Good leaders have always understood this. The people challenges that we will face in the 21st century are immense . . . and this book provides insight and solutions from thought leaders in the field on how to address and overcome the hurdles that lie ahead."

James B. Adamson, Non-Executive Chairman,
Kmart Corporation

"In this comprehensive publication, HR and operational leaders are reminded how daunting and critical the responsibility of leading others is. With its answers, and, more importantly, its questions, *Human Resources in the 21st Century* reveals that Human Resources is dynamic, ever changing, ever on the edge, and enjoying the struggle in the 21st century. Thanks to the contributors . . . all of you have reconfirmed my passion for human resources."

Cheryl E. H. Locke, Vice President, Human Resources,
Brigham and Women's Hospital

"These times demand that leaders display the highest levels of ethics as they drive for business results in an economically challenging environment. *Human Resources in the 21st Century* provides valuable insight into the critical role the HR professional plays as part of the overall business agenda. This is a valuable tool for not only the HR community but for any executive who needs to bring out the best qualities of an individual and create an engaged workforce."

Mary T. McDowell, Senior Vice President and General Manager,
Industry-Standard Servers, Hewlett-Packard Company

"*Human Resources in the 21st Century* is an amazing collection of relevant and timely articles from leading-edge thinkers in the field. Like a Tiffany diamond, this book has many brilliant facets.

As a practitioner in the field of leadership development for well over a decade, I have been observing, with great interest, the critical shift in the role and value of human resources. It is fast becoming a discipline that helps capture the hearts and minds of the employees, and, in so doing, impacts the bottom line and the success of the firm. This book is a beautiful and compelling guide to understanding how HR needs to redirect the bulk of its work from transactional matters to transformational issues. I heartily recommend it as a must read."

Deepak Sethi, Vice President, Executive and
Leadership Development, The Thomson Corporation

HUMAN RESOURCES
IN THE
21ST CENTURY

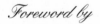

Editors

MARC EFFRON
HEWITT ASSOCIATES

ROBERT GANDOSSY
HEWITT ASSOCIATES

MARSHALL GOLDSMITH
ALLIANCE FOR STRATEGIC LEADERSHIP

Foreword by

ROSABETH MOSS KANTER

WILEY

JOHN WILEY & SONS, INC.

Published by John Wiley & Sons, Inc., Hoboken, New Jersey.
Published simultaneously in Canada.

The following authors hold the copyright to the chapters they contributed:
Rosabeth Moss Kanter; Jeff Brown and Lindy Williams; Beverly Kaye, Devon Scheef, and Diane Thielfoldt; Marshall Goldsmith and R. Roosevelt Thomas, Jr.; Jon R. Katzenbach, Niko Canner, and Marc A. Feigen; Margaret Wheatley; Stan Davis; William Bridges and Susan Mitchell Bridges.

For general information on our other products and services, or technical support, please contact our Customer Care Department within the United States at 800-762-2974, outside the United States at 317-572-3993 or fax 317-572-4002.

Wiley also publishes its books in a variety of electronic formats. Some content that appears in print may not be available in electronic books. For more information about Wiley products, visit our web site at www.wiley.com.

Library of Congress Cataloging-in-Publication Data:

Human resources in the 21st century / edited by Marc Effron, Robert
Gandossy, Marshall Goldsmith.
    p.   cm.
Includes bibliographical references and index.
  ISBN 0-471-43421-3 (cloth : alk. paper)
  1. Management. 2. Personnel management. 3. Corporate culture. 4.
Organizational change. 5. Leadership. I. Effron, Marc. II. Gandossy,
Robert P. III. Goldsmith, Marshall.
  HD31.H81247   2003
  658.3—dc21

                                   2002153112

Printed in the United States of America.

10 9 8 7 6 5 4 3

CONTENTS

111046

PART III   *Emerging Organization and Culture*

PART IV   *Leading Change: The Enduring Task*

PART V   *The HR Profession: Coming Demise or New Beginning?*

FOREWORD

HR is alive and well, central to the success of companies.
HR management is on the agenda and evolving slowly but steadily.
HR departments are aging and ailing.

T HAT'S MY CONCLUSION from years of working with companies, advising
CEOs, teaching managers and future leaders, reviewing the evidence, and
learning from the chapters in this book. The future of the "field" of human resources can only be understood by distinguishing those three issues: the importance of people, the attention to their management, and the organization and
tasks of specialist departments.

Can there be any question that people are more central to business success
and organizational performance than ever before? Evidence has mounted that
"intangible assets" play an increasingly large role in defining the value of a company in the capital markets, as several studies by economists at the Brookings
Institution in Washington have reported; intangibles such as brands, worker
skills, organizational routines, customer relationships, and the like can account
for nearly two-thirds of the marketplace value of manufacturing companies,
swamping the contribution made by physical assets such as facilities, equipment, and product inventory.

Intangible assets rest on human and organizational capabilities—to innovate,
share and maintain values (important to brand equity), learn and utilize skills,
and manage relationships. It is no wonder that some companies, such as the
Swedish insurance logistics firm, Skandia, started to measure "intellectual capital" and report it alongside financial capital. It is no wonder that companies
began to recognize that knowledge workers are knowledge nomads, as I reported in my book, *Evolve!*. Knowledge nomads feel free to move from company
to company taking the contents of their brains with them. It is no wonder that
the 1990s growth economy was characterized by "talent wars" in which companies dependent on innovation vied to provide the best workplace amenities to
attract the biggest brains—as they will again in every sector and still do in
high-tech and creative industries. So human resources—the idea that people
matter—is alive and well.

How people are developed and led—the substance of HRM, or human resource management—is definitely on the agenda. Not only are "best places to
work" lists increasingly common (and segmented by type, like working mothers
or minorities), but a variety of workplace and employment issues are reported to

social investors picking socially responsible companies, also a growing phenomenon, as social investment funds swelled to over $2 trillion in the United States by 1999, about 13 percent of investments under professional management, according to the Social Investment Forum. Having official policies and programs that get social responsibility credits is one thing, but what really makes a difference in the workplace experience is the quality of management; studies show that views of a company are heavily influenced by the behavior of bosses.

With that recognition, "leadership" is today's hot topic, one that is likely to be sustained throughout the decade and beyond. Much of the emphasis in burgeoning leadership development programs is leadership of people, not just leadership of the business. Bosses are to be turned into coaches, coworkers into teams. Managers are being made more conscious than ever of their role in developing, motivating, and retaining people. They are being held accountable not just for financial results, but for the quality of their relationships with the people around them. There is increasing attention to what I call the "3Ms" of motivation and morale (and not just the classic M of money): *mastery* (providing jobs with challenge and growth potential), *membership* (making the workplace a community of colleagues), and *meaning* (helping people make a difference in the external community and the world). So HRM is evolving slowly but steadily.

At the same time that HR assets and issues are gaining momentum, the professionals who feel that those assets and issues are their domain are losing ground. The HR function, the HR department, is aging and ailing, vulnerable to outsourcing to consultants or replacement by technology. In this book, some say that the HR department is an endangered species. They see it as endangered despite the fact that there are some stellar examples of flourishing, evolving practices introduced to companies by their HR staffs, and there are outstanding companies such as Southwest Airlines with influential top "People" people. Creative new approaches are bubbling up, but traditional administrative staffs are threatened. Clearly, we must separate innovation from organization, entrepreneurship from empire.

Quick! Name five famous leaders in the HR field. (A pause while you ponder.)

My guess is that your names are all external thought leaders. It's not just that consultants and business school professors write books, speak at conferences, and get their names around. There is something about the HR field as it gets connected to companies that shunt internal HR executives to the sidelines. What do we think about a function that operates behind the scenes when its role is powerful (whispering in the ear of the CEO), but is most visible when its role is trivial (announcing a new benefits information Web site)? What do we think about a function that has to hide its involvement in major initiatives (for example, a British company with a major culture change knows it "cannot be seen as another HR program," so it keeps the senior HR executive in the background as the "puppet master"—their words—to the line manager appointed to lead the effort).

Most of the articles in this book suggest that the HR department exists to serve people, to meet their needs, putting a happy face on the work of HR. But this hardly captures the wide sweep of sometimes contradictory roles that are often bundled in the HR department. There are watchdog and police functions—compliance to ensure, forms to fill out. There are adversarial situations in which the interests of top management and the interests of ordinary employees are not in alignment (even if we think they should be). Sometimes HR is involved in activities designed to change people's behavior and attitudes, whether they like it or not (e.g., diversity initiatives).

Moreover, the chapters in this book barely mention unions and labor relations, but unions serve as quasi-HR departments at times—looking out for the needs of their members, sometimes finding and grooming people through hiring halls and apprenticeships, a major track in countries such as Germany. While union membership has been declining overall in the United States, there has been some growth in areas in which people supposedly have "better" or "more pleasant" jobs (but also higher expectations): in the service sectors, the growing edge of employment.

Today's HR function covers a wide spectrum of activities requiring very different skill sets, from compensation and benefits administration (highly quantitative) to employee relations (highly qualitative). There are legitimate organization design questions about whether that bundle needs to be together in light of new realities and technologies.

Some people find hope for the future of the function in finally cracking the problem of making HR more "strategic" (sometimes shorthand for a desire to be included in top management business decision making). But that exhortation to make the HR department more strategic has been discussed endlessly for at least my professional lifetime. I recall a conference dedicated to that question in the early 1980s, with all the right people gathered and a special magazine issue dedicated to the conclusions. Every five years, same issue, new players. Has there been progress? Compare the recycling of the "strategic HR" issue with the success of the competitiveness issue. During that same era two decades ago, there were concerns about the competitiveness of American companies and the need to change their cultures and practices; many companies did make those changes, resulting in much improved performance and much better workplaces. Yet, we are still hearing that HR has to be more strategic. Why? Is it possible that this is a perennial conundrum as long as too many incompatible activities are grouped into one staff department?

Being "staff" rather than "line" (an old but useful distinction) carries its own problems. Evidence persists that, like many staff functions, the HR department can be conservative and risk averse, afraid to offend the powerful line managers whose support they need and whose favor they curry. When I recently invited a world-renowned CEO to speak at Harvard Business School, staff kept calling with lists of his requirements, most of which were unimportant to him when we actually spoke personally. Leadership development firms sometimes report that the HR representatives are extremely nervous about anything that looks like taking a risk in an executive program.

Speaking of risks, what role does the HR function play in the most important organizational issues facing companies, issues about workplaces, culture, or productivity? If the cutting-edge role is leadership for change, as this book asserts, it is not clear that HR departments are really with it. Jim O'Toole's chapter describes decades of important culture change at Corning and doesn't mention a single HR executive or HR move. Clearly, some of the most important internal issues facing companies have a strong HR component, yet sometimes the HR department is waiting to be told what to do.

Why did HR lose the "quality" cause to engineers, when TQM wasn't just about statistical process control, it was about training in problem solving and teamwork and empowerment? Where are HR departments in the process of due diligence in mergers and acquisitions? It is common knowledge that most mergers fail not because of bad strategy or undisclosed financial information but because of cultural, communications, and other people issues in the integration process. So where are HR departments? If they are to be found at all, they are rationalizing benefit programs, not speaking out on issues or taking a leadership role in integration. How about corporate citizenship/corporate social responsibility/community relations? Much of this involves, or should involve, mobilizing the workforce. When Yvonne Jackson was Compaq's HR vice president, before the HP merger, she was a strong advocate of community service and employee volunteerism, but Timberland assigned a marketing exec to run its community service activities.

And now for the biggest issue of all in the opening years of the 21st century, at least in the United States and parts of Europe: corporate governance and executive perks. Why aren't HR executives claiming this territory? After all, it's not just about accounting or board of directors' independence; it's about organization design, compensation policy, and other matters that should fall squarely in the HR domain. Will we look back to see another major business issue on which HR departments merely did what they were told?

There is often a connection between internal courage and external courage, internal reputation and external reputation. Unfortunately, with the exception of some professional associations such as Society for Human Resource Management (SHRM) and American Society for Training and Development (ASTD) that get involved in workplace policies, HR professionals tend not to be visible public advocates of the importance of people and investment in people. HR executives do not tend to lead on relevant public policy issues of training and development, higher education, or foreign workers.

Diagnosis of what ails the HR function raises important role questions about exactly who the professionals in HR departments are supposed to be. Issue advocates or administrators? Visionaries or implementers?

I'm not questioning the high importance of HR activities. There is no doubt that the responsibilities now bundled in HR departments are extremely important one by one. But some can be automated. Some can be outsourced. Some can be unbundled and returned to line business managers and to other staff functions (finance for compensation, IT for HR information systems and employee databases, etc.). Some can be located in fully owned subsidiaries that operate as profit centers.

One of my favorite examples of true change is Humanitas in Turkey; a company formed out of the HR department of Garanti Bank to be a service hub for the bank's parent, the holding company Dogus Group. Saide Kuzeyli, executive vice president of HR, truly was the partner of CEO Akin Ongor as he transformed Garanti Bank from a sleepy third-world organization to winner of Euromoney's "best small bank in the world" award in the late 1990s. But as the HR function grew in importance, it made more sense to make it a business serving many companies than to keep it as staff to one. Now Humanitas picks and chooses projects where it can have impact, brings in external contractors, and enjoys the credibility of a profit center.

If they can do it in Istanbul, we can do it in Illinois, . . . or New York, London, Toronto, and beyond.

I think all this change signals the end of the HR empire, not the end of HR activities. The senior HR executive is not endangered, but the HR department is; and that senior executive might not even be a "professional" or specialist in HR, just a savvy leader who knows how to connect people and strategy. There will continue to be high-level executives dedicated to people or to workplaces or to culture and values, but there will be a shrinking department under them, and a lot of specialists once in HR but now reporting to finance, IT, or corporate relations.

That's my best guess. But read the chapters in this book and draw your own conclusions. Or get aroused about the need for change, and shape a different future.

ROSABETH MOSS KANTER
June 2002

Rosabeth Moss Kanter is an internationally known business leader, best-selling author, and expert on strategy, innovation, and leadership for change. She is the Ernest L. Arbuckle Professor of Business Administration at Harvard Business School. She advises major corporations and governments worldwide and is the author or co-author of 15 books, including her latest book, *Evolve!: Succeeding in the Digital Culture of Tomorrow*. Other award-winning bestsellers include *Men & Women of the Corporation*, *The Change Masters*, *When Giants Learn to Dance*, and *World Class: Thriving Locally in the Global Economy*. In 2001, she received the Academy of Management's Distinguished Career Award (the association's highest annual award) for her contributions to management.

Considered one of the most prominent business thought leaders in the world and well-known as a dynamic speaker, she has shared the platform at major events with prime ministers and presidents as well as CEOs in many countries, and she appears often on radio and television. In addition to serving on company boards, she co-founded Goodmeasure Inc., whose consulting clients have included some of the world's best companies; Goodmeasure is currently developing electronic Web-based versions of Kanter's leadership and change tools to help embed them in the daily work of organizations everywhere.

Dr. Kanter's current research is on the development of new leadership for the digital age—how to guide the transformation of large corporations, small and mid-sized businesses, health care, government, and education as they incorporate new technology, create new kinds of alliances and partnerships, work across boundaries and borders, and take on new social responsibilities. In 1997–1998, she conceived and led the Business Leadership in the Social Sector (BLSS) project, under the auspices of the Harvard Business School's Initiative on Social Enterprise, which involved national leaders, including CEOs, senators, governors, and then First Lady Hillary Clinton, in dialogue about public-private partnerships for change, the launch of a BLSS video series, and a national call to action in collaboration with business associations, an activity she continues as senior advisor to IBM's Reinventing Education program. From 1989–1992, she also served as editor of the *Harvard Business Review,* which was a finalist for the National Magazine Award for General Excellence in 1991. She joined the Harvard Business School faculty in 1986 from Yale University, where she held a tenured professorship from 1977 to 1986.

She has received 21 honorary doctoral degrees and over a dozen leadership awards, and has been named number 11 on the list of the "50 most influential business thinkers in the world," and is on the list of the "100 most important women in America" and the "50 most powerful women in the world." She serves on many civic and nonprofit boards, including City Year, the 14-city national service program that was the model for AmeriCorps. Her public service activities span local and global interests. She has been a judge for the Ron Brown Award for Corporate Leadership given at the White House, a member of the Board of Overseers for the Malcolm Baldrige National Quality Award, is a fellow of the World Economic Forum, served on the Massachusetts Governor's Economic Council (for which she co-chaired the International Trade Task Force), and led the effort to establish a Year 2000 Commission for legacy projects for Boston. She currently serves on U.S. Secretary of Labor Elaine Chao's task force on the skills gap for the 21st Century Work Force Council.

PREFACE

CHANGE. SPEED. TECHNOLOGY. Complexity. Globalization. Demographics. Forces so profound they can wipe out or create new industries overnight. They are so profound that none of us can predict, with any certainty, the dominant industry in the worldwide economy in the next 25 years. They are so profound that it is quite likely that the world's largest company in the year 2027 does not yet exist.

As the new millennium progresses, many of us wonder what this ubiquitous change means for the future of the corporate world. Times have changed, and the forces that once worked within organizations regarding people, practices, culture, and leadership are different from those that will work going forward. The attributes of those who will succeed have yet to be defined. The Darwinian struggle in the business world will be won by the people and organizations that adapt most successfully to this new environment.

As organizations grapple with progress and change, the human resources function is once again under scrutiny. Will HR be able to sustain itself in the 21st century? Can it endure the challenges? Will it morph into something different? We travel around the globe and witness cutting-edge work accomplished by talented professionals and leaders in the field, but is this enough? Positioned at a challenging and dangerous crossroads, HR is confronted with determining its fate: coming demise or new beginning.

To address this topic most effectively and with the broadest of perspectives, we assembled contributions from a group of insightful, experienced academics and practitioners in the field. The book is organized into five parts that present critical areas of focus: People, Practices, Organization and Culture, Leading Change, and Future Challenges.

People are, indisputably, an organization's most important asset. While the concept that people matter is not new, the challenges of management today are different than even a decade ago. Yahoo!'s SVPHR and Chief People, Libby Sartain, imparts her knowledge on these challenges in the opening chapter. She draws on her experience in getting "extraordinary results from ordinary people" at Southwest Airlines and Yahoo! and outlines the key elements for attracting and retaining today's best talent. In their chapters, Michael Useem, Jeff Brown and Lindy Williams, Beverly Kaye, Devon Scheef, and Diane Thielfoldt, Neville Osrin and Francis Stickland, Marshall Goldsmith and R. Roosevelt Thomas Jr. discuss their ideas for action, addressing what employees want, the labor shortage, the role of HR and business leaders in employee engagement and impact, and the challenges of managing a diverse workforce.

To retain the best people, organizations must provide the appropriate programs and practices to continually develop employees and keep them engaged. Part II delves deeper into these emerging practices in HR. This Part includes the writings of Jon R. Katzenbach, Niko Canner, and Marc A. Feigen, Linda Sharkey, John W. Boudreau and Peter Ramstad, David Lewin, Adrian Furnham, Charles G. Tharp and Ben E. Dowell, D. Quinn Mills, and Elliott Masie. Each chapter provides solutions for implementing powerful programs and practices to engage, retain, and develop the ever-changing and demanding workforce of the 21st century. Building a sense of pride and viewing it as a motivator in the workforce, executive coaching, corporate learning and technology in the new millennium, and leadership development are addressed as well.

Given the importance of creativity and new ideas to corporate success, companies must work harder than ever to recruit and retain the right staff and to create a corporate culture that encourages loyalty, collaboration, and innovation. In this increasingly global world, how can leaders build the right organization and culture to accommodate the people and practices that will bring success? In Emerging Organizations and Culture, Part III, Lynda Gratton, Allan R. Cohen and David L. Bradford, Kate DCamp, Yvonne R. Jackson, Richard Kantor, Howard Morgan, and Robert J. Joy and Paul Howes examine the challenges of globalization, the importance of creating adaptation and flexibility in the 21st century corporation, and the new challenges entailed in understanding and meeting both business and employee needs.

Now more than ever, the credibility of leadership is being challenged, corporate reform is being crafted and debated, and corporations are under intense pressure and scrutiny to change their organizational culture. Part IV addresses Leading Change: The Enduring Task. Margaret Wheatley outlines the skills to successfully maneuver and survive in turbulent times. James O'Toole and Wayne Brockbank differentiate fact from fiction regarding organizational change and how it is managed. Arjan Overwater and Thomas W. Malnight reflect on an important leadership journey. Marc Effron helps us find the missing link between leadership and business strategy.

We conclude where we began: with the question that was the genesis for this book, "What's next for the HR profession?" The HR function has had an interesting history under many different guises. Stan Davis, J. Randall MacDonald, and Jeffrey Pfeffer chronicle this fascinating story and make some predictions for the future of HR and the challenges and implications the function will face in the coming years. Chapters from William and Susan Mitchell Bridges, David Ulrich and Norman Smallwood, and Jason Jeffay and Sandy K. Bicos make suggestions for the next phase in the annals of HR, and James B. Dagnon, Robert Gandossy, and Andrew Sobel close the book by looking at the importance of HR executives making a shift to a role as trusted business advisors.

As you read *Human Resources in the 21st Century,* you'll acquire a diverse perspective of what's ahead for HR. We encourage you to form your own opinions and ideas, as you catch a glimpse of the future. We hope you will find inspiration in these pages to aspire to a future that is filled with challenges and opportunities for every organization's HR leaders!

> MARC EFFRON, Hewitt Associates
> ROBERT GANDOSSY, Hewitt Associates
> MARSHALL GOLDSMITH, Alliance for Strategic Leadership

ACKNOWLEDGMENTS

WHEN WE FIRST considered the ideas for this book sitting at Marshall's dining room table in sunny Southern California, we made a list of our friends and colleagues who have influenced our thinking over the years. The list consisted of academics and practitioners with enormous insight, influence, and ideas about the challenges and the opportunities that lay ahead for human resources (HR). We were delighted when nearly everyone we approached for this book eagerly accepted. We'd like to thank all of these exceptional contributors for providing exactly what we had hoped—insights and ideas about the challenges and the opportunities for all of us in the 21st century.

We also want to thank those in the HR and business community whom we've learned from, and those who struggle every day with difficult and sometimes competing, complex demands. We hope that you find on these pages a source of inspiration and challenge.

Matt Holt and his team at John Wiley have been supportive of this project from the beginning. He patiently guided us through from idea to finished product.

We are thankful to leaders at Hewitt Associates. Dale Gifford, our chairman and CEO, for his support of the project, and John Anderson for his help in clearing the way for us to get this done.

Lauren Cantlon of Hewitt Associates and Sarah McArthur were a terrific help in editing, communicating with authors all over the world, and keeping everyone on schedule. This book would not exist without them. Julie Offord of Hewitt makes our everyday life easier, and we thank her for working her "magic" again here.

We would like to thank City Year and The Drucker Foundation for the strong, moral direction they provide to so many. In a world where there seems to be more wrong than right, it is refreshing to acknowledge these organizations for all of the good that they do. All royalties from this book will be donated to these nonprofit organizations.

This has been a very exciting project. We had an opportunity to share great ideas with each other, debate and challenge authors, and collaborate with clients and colleagues at Hewitt and the Alliance for Strategic Leadership. This book is stronger because of all of you.

M. E.
R. G.
M. G.

PEOPLE:
HR'S BOTTOM-LINE ASSET

PEOPLE ARE AN organization's most valuable asset and the only source of last-ing competitive advantage for businesses today. Everything else can be repli-cated—products, services, infrastructure—but not people. The great industrial leader of General Motors, Alfred Sloan, once said, "Take my assets, leave my peo-ple, and in five years I'll have it all back." This basic tenet of organizational life is heard time and again in corporate corridors. Yet, there are few organizations that are held up as models for others to emulate. While models in action are hard to find today, the challenges ahead suggest there will be fewer tomorrow.

The following six chapters challenge human resources (HR) and other busi-ness leaders to consider the key talent questions of the 21st century. What are the people challenges ahead of us? What will employees need and want? How can organizations engage their employees and inspire them to stay and succeed? What are the implications of a more diverse and ever-changing workforce? Can organizations get extraordinary results from ordinary people?

Insights for the future lie in experiences today. The authors of the chapters in Part I provide answers to these questions.

CHAPTER 1

≫◆≪

Getting Extraordinary Results from Ordinary People

LIBBY SARTAIN

OVER THE COURSE of my 25-year career in HR, I have had the good fortune to work for several organizations that were founded on the premise that ordinary people can accomplish just about anything. For example, in the 31 years since Southwest Airlines started, extraordinary initiative and spirit from its entire community of employees has been so integrally connected with the airline's culture and business success that wonderful, daily examples of breathtaking customer service are taken as a matter of course. This is one of my favorite stories: One day a Southwest reservations agent took a call from a Phoenix customer wanting to travel to Houston. According to practice, after booking the flight, he then asked her, "Would you like a rental car?" Now this posed a problem for our passenger. She explained that she was a recent widow, flying to Houston to undergo cancer treatment at MD Anderson Cancer Center. Already feeling emotionally and physically stretched to her limit, she didn't relish traveling alone, and she was especially afraid of driving in a strange city.

"How much do you think it would be to take a cab instead?" she asked.

"My guess is between $40 and $50," our agent replied.

She gulped, thanked him for the information, said she'd give it more thought, and then hung up.

While our Houston-based agent went on to booking more flights for more customers that day, this particular customer was never far from his mind. He soon came up with a plan. Trading his shift with another employee, he made sure he was standing at the Houston gate to meet his customer. There he was, holding a sign with her name on it. He drove her to the hospital himself, visited her during her treatment, and then drove her back to the airport when she was ready to return.

Other customer service groups might have severely disciplined this action. The lawyers would have thrown up their hands in dismay! What if there was an accident? The liability could have ruined Southwest, but this young man remains a heroic example of the relationship between the company and its customers. Southwest employees aren't there to sell tickets and fly airplanes. They are there to give people the freedom they need to live their lives to the fullest. Whether it's being able to afford to go to a wedding 3,000 miles away or being able to seek out life-saving cancer treatment 1,200 miles away, Southwest employees—whether they are a customer service agent or the CEO—know that they are providing freedom, hope, meaning, and joy, not just transportation. Everyone at Southwest Airlines knows not to confuse financial results with the overall mission, but by living certain core values daily, profitability follows.

As the former vice president of people, I'm often asked, "How does Southwest Airlines get such extraordinary results from ordinary people?" This implies that I had somehow discovered a miracle compensation program or the Holy Grail of learning and development. In response, I'm often tempted to begin my answer with a question of my own: "How would you define *ordinary*?" This isn't intended to be flippant. The first step to "getting results from the ordinary" is to realize that we are all ordinary and that, as we've entered the new millennium, we are surrounded by such heroic acts from the so-called ordinary people that no one should be tempted or allowed to dismiss the valuable, day-saving contributions of what we have come to call the "rank-and-file."

Legends and lore of most organizations include stories of how the actions of one employee can create a product that will be used by millions of people on a daily basis. For instance, most of us have heard about the celebrated scientist for 3M products who invented Post-it™ Notes (using a type of glue that had been rejected because it wouldn't stick), so that he could temporarily mark his place in his hymnal during choir practice. It is commonplace for the efforts of one person to impact many.

One employee single-handedly invented the most innovative marketing tool Yahoo! ever rolled out. He created IMVironments™, multimedia, viral-messaging environments for instant messaging conversations. This product, used by millions of Yahoo! users every day, not only provides a significant differentiation for Yahoo! Messenger, it also introduced a new and unique advertising and marketing medium that resulted in significant incremental ad revenue.

As I write this chapter in the summer of 2002, the newspapers and magazines are still filled with stories coming out of September 11, 2001. There are stories of how ordinary office workers took a few extra minutes before desperately evacuating their World Trade Center offices to gather up and encourage their coworkers to venture into the stairwells. The *New York Times* received a Pulitzer for its coverage of the extraordinary spirit and passions of the so-called ordinary people who perished. Months later, the construction and clean-up crews finished the job "ahead of schedule and under budget." Even now, when a few of those people we might call extraordinary (CEOs of multinational firms) are in disgrace, the headlines remain full of the heroic acts of ordinary people battling historic wildfires in Colorado and Arizona. So, perhaps we need to stop thinking in terms of ordinary.

Yet, as corporate leaders we have hundreds, if not thousands, of employees throughout the ranks, all of whom are capable of extraordinary results and want to give their best. It is through them that the cumulative impacts of passion, imagination, dedication, and results can be experienced throughout your company. While this perspective doesn't necessarily *exclude* the elite, the highly educated, the organizationally anointed leaders in the executive offices, it must absolutely embrace the many, many more who come to work every day to do the job. Maybe that job is a day-to-day, routine task. Yet, as we've seen in the last year, we never know when we're going to be called to rise to the occasion. To unleash the extraordinary efforts of the workforce, organizational leaders must first believe this to be possible. It is up to us to make sure our people have the resources, support, and freedom to meet the challenge—or seize the opportunity—when the occasion presents itself.

As we move into the future, with the employment relationship shifting again and again, HR is going to be forced to rise to this challenge not only by external market forces, but also internally by the people themselves. In 15 years, millions of workers have been eyewitness to the death of both the old conventional contract and the demise of many promises the so-called new economy may have held for the future. Our high performers weren't just sitting back wringing their hands. They've been actively researching the markets, the opportunities, or even themselves to determine which opportunities truly deserve their passion, imagination, intelligence, and energy. Our most desirable workforce is even more desirable than ever before. They're equipped to be true partners in helping our companies succeed. We had better have high-quality opportunities to offer them in return, or they will go to our competitors.

Create an Environment of Mutual Loyalty and Trust

There is unlimited potential when a healthy, high-performance culture is fostered. When the elements of a spirit of passion, innovation, and dedication are in place, the principles and values of your organization become self-governing. Then you can devote your attention to achieving your business's market and growth objectives. But that spirit must include a value of mutual loyalty. In his book, *Loyalty Rules!* Frederick F. Reichheld writes, "Loyalty is not dead; it rules in the new economy—just as surely as it rules in the old. Leaders who grasp its true nature and economic potential understand that loyalty cannot be a one-way street. They earn people's loyalty when they treat them in a manner that inspires their trust and commitment."[1] The word *loyalty* may make leaders nervous, as it can imply a blind expectation of cradle-to-grave employment. Most employees know better than that and are merely looking for an employment relationship they can depend on—that they can depend on being associated with a company that has meaningful values and that is consistently and reliably faithful to those values; that tells them the truth as early as possible; that would never give them cause to be ashamed or embarrassed. A loyal employee is not a naively committed individual. He or she is informed, rededicated again and again, and rationally chooses to stay engaged with the company through good and bad times. Loyalty comes from honest, two-way communications, adhering to the stated values, and clear expectations and rewards. The new loyal employees have every right to expect that their company is loyal to them in these terms. When you break that understanding, you can say goodbye to the right to hope for extraordinary results.

Trust fuels productivity much more effectively than any other motivational technique. Yet, our organizations are staffed by skeptics and cynics of our own making. Not adhering to our stated values, layoffs, poorly integrated acquisitions, and the latest fad in management science lead to an atmosphere of mistrust. According to Robert Levering and Milton Moskowitz, in the best workplaces there exists an atmosphere of mutual trust between management and employees. *Trust,* according to these experts, is defined by a partnership between employees and management and the recognition that employees add value to the organization.[2]

Trust may be especially difficult to cultivate in a team-based work environment in which interpersonal politics, ambition, laziness, and even greed cause otherwise wonderful employees to withhold their effort either out of self-preservation or anger. To establish mutual trust, organizations must share information, tell the truth, and treat employees as adults. Yet, ironically, publicly traded corporations cannot share much with employees that they are not willing to share with investors. In their book, *Built on Trust,* Arky Ciancutti and Thomas Steding wrote, "Many of today's leaders have not been training in the emotional aspects of high-performance team life. In business schools, the emotional content of teams is often given lip service but not effectively addressed. Yet emotions are at the core of any team. To produce extraordinary results, we need to understand how such emotional dynamics as trust, fear, dignity, and meaning operate on teams."[3]

Create an Energized Environment in Which Innovation Thrives

People need to be recognized and applauded for their individuality, their creative problem-solving abilities, their originality, and even for their willingness to break the rules or upset the proverbial applecart. The innovation-promoting environment celebrates the joy of work and effort, and it is connected to the future through constant discussion of how today's solutions serve tomorrow's needs. It runs on high energy and thrives on peak performance. In his book, *Peak Performance,* Jon R. Katzenbach wrote, "The most evident characteristic of any peak-performance workforce is the energy level it exudes. Walking into the workplace, you feel its energy, which is noticeably different from that of any average performing workplace. Activity levels are more intense, attitudes are more positive, interactions are less constrained, and formal positions are less evident. People work hard, but they have fun at work and take full advantage of a widespread sense of humor."[4]

There is no one-size-fits-all list of the specific qualities that create a culture promoting independent thinking and spirited engagement of the employees. It's not the silly games, the company song, the Mylar balloons, or the bright colors. All those things may work, but if they're not consistent with the company culture on a deeply intrinsic level, they will be received as meaningless juvenilia. The *behaviors* that are usually found in high-engagement companies, however, are almost universally humane. There is a systemic kindness, a sense of humor, a celebration of each person's individuality, even a tolerance for mistakes that are made by well-intentioned employees trying new ideas or just trying to do the right thing. While results are important, recognized, and rewarded, it's also important to remember that innovation breeds mistakes. In a sense, this approach carries risk and a price. But so does the "safe" approach of avoiding risk and punishing a failed, but authentic, experiment. That price is one that no future-oriented company can afford.

Hire for Attitude and Fit: Train for the Rest

Extraordinary results come from people with extraordinary attitudes—not extraordinary education or experience. I was asked several times during my tenure with Southwest Airlines, "How do you make your people be so nice?" or "How do you train your people to be so compassionate?" The answer was that we couldn't train or make people be that way. We hired nice, compassionate people and trained them for on-the-job skills. Then, our culture and leadership did the rest of the job. You can have the most highly educated, the most supremely experienced star candidate, but that doesn't mean that person will be a star performer. Energy, passion, curiosity, compassion, and independence are all characteristics of employees that Southwest Airlines and Yahoo! look for in their applicants. Those are characteristics that you can influence, promote, cultivate, and even propagate; however, they aren't characteristics you can effectively and time-efficiently build from scratch. At least you shouldn't have to. In the time it would take to instill those characteristics in a talented but poorly fitting employee, that person will be dragging the coworkers down as they experience what they would probably perceive as a breach of covenant between themselves and their spirited employer—you.

Don't be too quick to fall in love with the MBAs. As noted in *Business 2.0,* an MBA degree may not prepare candidates for the world of work.[5] Several studies, even those conducted by the business school professors, found that there is little evidence that an MBA makes a candidate more successful. Jeffrey Pfeffer, a management professor at Stanford, found there is almost no data to support the assumption that a business degree leads to business success.[6] If you have to choose between an educated, highly talented candidate who doesn't fit and a lesser-educated, highly talented person who does fit, always choose the latter. Profile or model what it takes to do the job (common sense, team player, intellectual capacity, self-confidence) and hire the people who will and can love their jobs.

Make the Work Meaningful

Believe it's possible to hire people who will and can love their jobs. People want to be part of something important, a cause, something bigger than they are. Understanding the larger meaning behind what your company does is a key step to finding and recruiting people who love their work. The very first step is to believe that it's possible to love your job. This principle may seem simple, self-evident, and naïve, but when you study the recruitment and employment practices of companies around the world, you will see that most of them have set up elaborate defenses against the indifferent employees that they assume will swamp their workplace like ants at a picnic. The only way that you can truly have faith that it's possible to recruit employees who love their work is first by making sure you see the value and meaning behind what you do and the company you do it for. Your company doesn't have to be researching the cure for cancer or flying patients to their cancer treatment. However mundane it may be, if there's a market for your business, it's filling a human need somewhere along the line. Therein lies the secret of identifying the meaning behind what you do and attaching your own need for loving your work to it.

If you don't find a way to attach compelling meaning to the nature of your company's business, you won't be able to attract and recruit those self-perpetuating, fueled-on-passion employees who commit extraordinary acts every day. First you have to believe you can, and that simple step requires a huge cognitive leap away from the commonly held assumptions that work is hell and employees must be aggressively managed and motivated in order to do that work.

Martha Finney, HR journalist and consultant specializing in employee engagement, points out that *as a society* employers and employees alike believe it's impossible to find that ideal match of talents, passions, and abilities with respectful, inspiring, and meaningful work. We tend to assume those kinds of experiences are reserved only for the rare, the extraordinarily lucky, educated, connected, talented, and/or wealthy. What engages employees is, she says, "the feeling that they are making a difference in the work that they care about; that they're working with people who share their mission and values; and that their company respects them as adults. From that simple starting place, anything can happen, for both the individual employee and the company itself."[7]

Identify and attach that intrinsic value of what your company does—and what your employees do within it—to your workplace environment and you will have a workplace of independent, creative, passionate, and dedicated employees who are capable of achieving extraordinary results on a daily basis. At Yahoo! our employees believe that what they do every day can help define the future of the Internet, and that our work will be viewed by millions of people worldwide who use Yahoo! every day. In effect, we can change the world.

As we continue moving into the 21st century, we must make our workplaces a celebration of the passion and effort that comes from all our employees. In the first two years of this century, we have seen how the mighty have fallen. We've seen how the everyday, the ordinary have risen to the challenges before them in absolutely heroic measures. All around us, we've seen hands reach out to lift each other out of rubble, out of ash, out of devastation, out of despair— ordinary, strong, dedicated hands: Hands holding up a sign with the name of a disembarking widow wondering how she can manage the trip to the hospital all by herself. Hands typing on computer keyboards changing lives through the messages they write.

Richard Barrett, author of *Liberating the Corporate Soul, Building a Visionary Organization,* wrote: "Organizations are becoming the new communities of the world, bringing together people around a common purpose with shared values that transcend cultural, racial, and national boundaries."[8] These are extraordinary days to be an ordinary person. I'm glad to be among them.

CHAPTER 2

≈►◆◄≈

Looking North on the Leadership Compass

Effective HR Management for the New Century

MICHAEL USEEM

TWENTIETH-CENTURY DICTIONARY DEFINITIONS of leadership served company managers well during the past century. The *American Heritage Dictionary* deems a leader to be "one who is in charge or command of others."[1] *Webster's* describes a leader as "a guiding or directing head, as of an army, movement, or political group."[2]

Conceived this way, the challenge facing a "directing head" in "command of others" was to mobilize and focus their collective energies. By extension, company managers would need to think strategically, communicate persuasively, and execute decisively. Leaders must make wise choices among plausible alternatives in each of these arenas, and then deftly mobilize subalterns to get the job done.

Building on this basic formula, informed observers added other ingredients. For management writer Peter Drucker, leadership required training followers to "do the right thing."[3] For political historian James MacGregor Burns, leadership must be embraced as a "calling."[4] For U.S. President Abraham Lincoln, leaders should appeal to the "better angels of our nature."[5]

We can see many of these defining elements in President John F. Kennedy's skillfully articulated vision for the American space program: "I believe that the nation should commit itself to achieving this goal before this decade is out," he declared in 1961, "of landing a man on the moon and returning him safely to Earth."[6] With this strategic goal and a federal agency that learned, with White House backing, how to do the right thing, astronauts Neil Armstrong and Buzz Aldrin did land on the moon five months before the decade was out.

11

We can see the same defining elements of leadership in Herb Kelleher's creation, in 1971, of Southwest Airlines to make flying affordable and a company profitable. With an unrelenting insistence on using off-beat airports and low-cost airplanes to achieve his twin goals, Kelleher went on for three decades to provide customers with some of the lowest fares and investors with some of the highest returns in the industry.

So far, so good. For mustering their subordinates, company managers everywhere have drawn on this leadership formula, and it became a 20th century prescription for effective human resource management.

Looking North, Not Just South

As long as those in authority understood what was to be done and those out of authority knew what to do, the formula furnished what managers required. Yet, for many organizations, such a precondition no longer prevailed as they entered the new century. For them, even adroit application of the dictionary definitions would no longer suffice: Directing heads found themselves less able to know precisely what strategies to pursue, how to promote them, or when to execute them. In other words, they were less "in charge" or simply incapable of "directing" others.

The challenge to top management's omniscience and omnipotence came from wholesale changes that companies had been making in their architecture during the closing years of the past century. Their organizational transformations had come in response to intensifying market competition and more demanding investors, both of which pressed companies to become more fast-acting and more performance-driven. Consequently, firms created autonomous teams, established business units, and otherwise devolved responsibility and accountability to the frontline, where decisions could be made rapidly and results would be measurable.

As a result, top-tier executives increasingly called on frontline managers to identify what worked, and then to report the solution up to the top. The job of manager has thus become more dependent on successfully persuading not only subordinates to act, but also one's superiors to do so. For this, the manager has come to need far more than the traditional leadership tools. The manager has to be more adept at guiding not only their direct reports, but also their bosses.

A useful way to characterize this second face of leadership without losing sight of the first is to view both as integral spokes of a "leadership-360." Akin to the "feedback-360" process, in which managers solicit evaluations from superiors and subordinates, the leadership-360 encourages managers to see their obligation as leading both subordinates and superiors, of looking north on the compass while still seeing south.

If the cultivation of downward leadership had become a defining element of effective human resource management during the past century, the development of bidirectional leadership is becoming a defining element in this century.

A Delicate Art

In looking north on the leadership compass, however, middle managers face a more daunting task than when gazing south: They must now exercise authority where they have none at all, in effect taking charge when they are *not* in charge. Their calling is not to seize power or even to question authority, but rather to offer up strategic advice or policy change before it is too late, suggestions that any superior should surely welcome.

However, leading up will certainly not be welcomed by all bosses. Some managers still report that they work for supervisors who micromanage everybody, communicate with nobody, and rarely think strategically. Worse, the supervisors may reject all suggestions from under to do otherwise, even when market demand and organization culture put a premium on learning from those closest to the customer.

Exercising upward leadership for many managers thus constitutes an inherently delicate art. To come forward when a superior does not welcome it will be risky, and it could prove little more than a career-shortening move for the audacious who attempt it, leaving both the subordinate and the company worse off for the try.

When undertaken well, however, upward leadership can help all concerned realize their aims and the firm its goals. To do it well and avoid its pitfalls, upward leadership therefore deserves as much explicit development among managers as has long been given its downward form.

Upward Leadership Is a Developed and an Acquired Capacity

Leading up is not a natural capacity, but it can be cultivated, and two mutually dependent components are essential: Subordinates must become better prepared to step up and superiors must be ready to embrace the upward step.

Moreover, two mutually dependent parties are responsible for building it: Superiors must help subordinates develop this capacity and subordinates must work to acquire it themselves. Behind them all are the companies themselves, whose cultures and actions can encourage both parties to exercise the upward leadership that is needed.

By way of affirmative example on both points, consider David Pottruck, chief operating officer of broker Charles Schwab, who faced a critical moment in 1997. Would he be able to convince his chief executive and the company's directors to support his urgent proposal to move the brokerage company fully into Internet trading?

Through its thousands of customer-service representatives, the company bought and sold shares for a million clients. The rise of the Internet threatened to undo all that and undermined a framework of trust painstakingly built between the service representatives and Schwab customers over many years. The Internet furnished free and fast access to company information that had long been the brokers' province, and it opened a way to trade stock at a fraction of the time and cost required to do it through a broker.

Pottruck had privately concluded that the company would have to create a full-service brokerage offering with Internet trading at a price of $29 per trade, far below the current price of $80 for full-service trading.

Pottruck prepared to make the case to his boss, CEO Charles Schwab. Pottruck knew that the firm's founder appreciated market trends, and as Pottruck explained his reasoning, Charles Schwab immediately affirmed his interest in the move. Charles Schwab was willing to take large risks and place big bets when the odds were known, and he pressed Pottruck to nail them down.

Pottruck instructed his staff to assess the effect of providing full service to everybody at $29 a trade. The strategists responded with a shocking conclusion: It would depress the company's revenue in 1998 by $125 million and its earnings by $100 million, more than a fifth of its projected pretax profits.

Although he was sure of the long-term merits of the new plan, Pottruck was less sure if returns from it would grow quickly enough to avert financial disaster. He knew that the plan would require vigorous support from the chief executive and board members if it were to succeed, and he also appreciated that they were prepared to learn of fresh ideas from below.

David Pottruck gave Charles Schwab the financial forecast of the low-price, full-service plan and warned of its effect on profits in the short term. The founder always insisted on putting customer service first and Pottruck had made that principle his guiding premise; Schwab had consistently stressed careful analysis, which Pottruck had done; Schwab had delegated much to those he trusted, and Pottruck had already earned his confidence. Following weeks of discussion, Schwab endorsed the plan.

Pottruck then carried the case to the company directors, whose wholehearted support would be essential as well. A prior boss and mentor at the company, Larry Stupski, had earlier provided invaluable coaching for what Pottruck was about to do. Stupski had urged Pottruck to become personally familiar with the directors, to listen carefully to what they said, and to avoid any appearance of "selling" ideas to them. With Stupski's mentoring, Pottruck came to appreciate that the board wanted a balanced, calm, and wise executive. He learned they wanted an upward leader.

When he brought his new plan to the board, some directors wondered why any change was needed since the year was already proving to be the best in company history. After-tax profits were nearly $270 million, and what Pottruck was proposing could reduce them by a third or more. Some questioned if the alternative had been thoroughly studied. Still others asked Pottruck if he was convinced that short-term downsides could indeed be weathered.

By the end of the board meeting, the directors agreed to back what would become the company's most fateful decision of the era. On January 15, 1998, Schwab announced it was offering Internet trading for $29 with full customer service, including personal consultation and advice.

The first quarter's results, as Pottruck had forecast, were devastating. Quarterly revenues had been growing at 6.5 percent per quarter in 1997; now they declined by 3 percent. Pretax income had been rising by 8 percent per quarter in 1997; now it dropped by 16 percent.

Yet, by the end of 1998, the number of Schwab customers with online accounts nearly doubled, and Schwab finished the year with 20 percent growth in revenue and 29 percent rise in profit. Pottruck's initiative, quickly embraced by his superiors, proved both prescient and profitable. It propelled the firm into the top ranks of the brokerage business, giving it a market value on a par with Wall Street mainstays such as Morgan Stanley and Merrill Lynch.

David Pottruck brought strategic insight and a reasoned capacity to pursue a risky but ultimately rewarding path before others had seen the way. His initiatives depended on a boss ready to be persuaded and a board ready to be moved. That readiness was not a given: Pottruck had conscientiously worked to build their trust in him by openly communicating with them, providing them with careful analysis and detailed forecasts, and then delivering on what he said he would achieve. That initiative itself was partly the product of the mentoring that he had received from Larry Stupski and of an open culture that had been fostered by the company.

It Takes Two

Leading up requires fortitude by those below, and it also requires responsiveness by those above. Charles Schwab & Co. benefited from both, but if either is missing, the consequences can be fatal. Consider two examples, one without fortitude (discussed next), the other without the responsiveness demonstrated by Schwab.

In 1994, Chairman Lee Kun Hee of the Samsung Group decreed that Samsung should invest $13 billion to become a leading car producer, aiming to make 1.5 million vehicles by 2010. Global auto manufacturing was already a crowded market, plagued by overcapacity, but Lee was a powerful chieftain and a passionate car buff, and none of his subordinates dared to question his plan.

A year after the first cars rolled off the line in 1999, however, Samsung Motors was failing, and it soon liquidated its assets. Many of Samsung's top managers had silently opposed the investment, and Lee later told them he was puzzled why none had openly expressed their reservations. By then, however, Lee had reached into his own pocket for $2 billion to placate his irate creditors.

If that was the cost of passivity, consider the cost of unresponsiveness. On August 14, 2001, Jeffrey Skilling resigned from his position as Enron Corporation's chief executive, citing personal issues, and Chairman Kenneth Lay resumed his post as CEO. A day later, Enron vice president Sherron Watkins sent an anonymous memo to the chief executive that bluntly outlined a host of accounting problems that she believed threatened to ruin the firm, presciently warning that the firm could "implode in a wave of accounting scandals." On

August 21, at the urging of her associates, she met with Lay to more forcefully communicate her dire appraisal.

In the rubric of upward leadership, Watkins was thinking strategically on behalf of the entire enterprise. She saw that the company was at risk, and she communicated her concerns persuasively. She told her chief executive in purple prose and then to his face that his company was on the precipice.

On that day in August, immediate intervention to root out the accounting malfeasance was essential. However, the chief executive chose instead to refer her memo to Enron's outside law firm, even instructing it not to be concerned with Enron's accounting practices. The law firm in turn responded that Lay faced a public relations problem and might best get rid of Sherron Watkins.

Lay had been given a warning by a manager who had foreseen the disaster that awaited him. Watkins had sought to save the company before it was too late. It was a bold effort to do what the boss should have been doing already. Yet, her unresponsive chief executive was not ready to think, communicate, or act, instead allowing the nation's seventh largest corporation with 20,000 employees to become the nation's second largest corporate disaster on December 2, 2001.

Sherron Watkins did the right thing, she appealed to the better angels of Enron's nature, and she had undertaken the task not as a job but as a calling. Watkins had applied all the qualities that define great downward leadership to an act of great upward leadership. But she learned, and Enron's employees, customers, and investors later came to appreciate in the wake of their enormous losses, that it takes two for upward leadership to work.

Upward Leadership When It Was Really Needed

A good test of an organization's capacity for upward leadership is the response of subordinates when a superior is momentarily absent or too far from the frontline to render meaningful assistance. It is then that we can see how important company development of both upward fortitude and downward responsiveness can be.

Many companies were so tested on the morning of September 11, 2001 when terrorists rammed airliners into the Pentagon and World Trade Center. Though headquartered on the other side of the continent, eBay and Cisco Systems, like so many other companies, were put to the test that day. Both found that it was up to them to exercise leadership at a moment when it was critically needed.

The world's largest online auction site, eBay prided itself on not only being the earlier mover in its market, but also being fastest in responding to competitors' moves and first in introducing new features. When Amazon.com and other firms entered the auction market, chief executive Meg Whitman immediately incorporated their best features, such as password retrieval and fraud insurance, onto eBay's Web site. She was also continuously inventing her own fresh features, whether it was a way for buyers to look for items in their own city or for them to be notified when an item they desired became available for bid. In an era and market that placed a premium on strategic thinking and fast action at the top of the firm, Meg Whitman brought much to the table.

However, on the morning of September 11, 2001, Meg Whitman was visiting Japan and her chief operating officer, Brian Swette, was in Florida. The remaining managers at eBay had no choice but to act that morning on their own. They quickly confirmed that all 2,500 employees were safe, secured the company Web site, and launched an online auction to raise $100 million for the disaster's victims. They did almost exactly what the CEO would have wanted done.

"By the time I was able to call in from Japan," said Meg Whitman, "our team was already thinking about and acting on the big issues." This was a created, not accidental, capacity. Since joining eBay in 1998 when it employed a mere 35 people, Whitman had invested mightily in recruiting the right lieutenants and molding them into a team that was able to lead its 2,500 employees even when she was a continent away. "I did not have to say anything," observed Whitman, "for the right thing to happen."[7]

Cisco Systems' chief executive John Chambers was also out of town on September 11th, and he too received the upward leadership that every manager should want. When he called his headquarters upon hearing of the calamity, he also learned that his subordinates had already swung into action in the ways he would have wanted.

Chambers asked for the creation of a crisis communications center, and he was told that a manager "already got that going." He urged that all employees and their families be located, and he was informed that another manager was "already leading that effort." He insisted that Cisco customers facing the biggest challenges be contacted immediately, and he was told, "John, we've already got the operational center going."

In an era when subordinates may be suddenly required to fill the boss' shoes and are expected to render great upward advice, such examples suggest how essential it is for seconds-in-command to master the leadership required to counsel or even become momentary firsts-in-command, and for the latter to embrace their seconds' advice and service when it is rendered.

Building Upward Leadership before It Is Needed

For upward leadership of the kind that we have seen at Charles Schwab, Enron, eBay, and Cisco to be effective, a supportive culture is required, and this must be built before it is needed. Once established, a company-wide emphasis on leading upward serves as a kind of inertial guidance system, continually reminding everybody that they are obliged to stand up without the need for superiors to ask them to do so.

Two underlying steps are important to foster that mind-set. First, if a company expects those in the ranks to step into the breach when needed, subordinates will need to understand top management's strategy, methods, and rules. Second, if a company wants subordinates to offer their best advice, top management must value and make timely use of it. Behind both steps must be a human resource agenda that defines great managers as looking not only south on the leadership compass, but also north.

CHAPTER 3

⟹•◦•⟸

The 21st Century Workforce
Implications for HR

JEFF BROWN AND LINDY WILLIAMS

IN ITS LATEST report on the subject, the U.S. Bureau of Labor Statistics predicted a shortage of approximately 6 million workers by the year 2008.[1] Studies project eventual shortfalls between 10 and 16 million workers, with a peak expected between 2015 and 2025, as the labor pool grows at a rate far below that of the job market expansion. Concurrently, the face of the U.S. workforce will be changing dramatically. The number of people between the ages of 35 and 44 is expected to decrease 15 percent by 2016 and, according to the U.S. Census Bureau, the average age of workers will be well over 40 by the year 2010. In addition, the make-up of the workforce will be drastically changing. Minority groups will be growing at unprecedented rates. For example, Asian/non-Hispanic workers, as a group, are anticipated to grow 40 percent, Hispanic growth is forecasted to be 37 percent and Black/non-Hispanic growth around 20 percent—all considerably higher than the overall growth rate of 12 percent and the White/non-Hispanic rate of 7 percent.

Underlying this shift is the impending exodus of Baby Boomers, workers born between 1946 and 1964, from the regular workforce. Although this generation is reported to have made limited plans for retirement and could, therefore, remain working longer than those before them, there will be a significant impact as some percentage of this large generation, as many as 60 million, transitions into senior citizen status.

What does this mean for human resources (HR)? Is the sky really falling? Well, the sky may not be crashing down, but the thunder you hear is real. The good news is that we have some time to prepare for the future. We have the past to learn from in order to not just weather the coming storm, but also to benefit from the challenges it presents. Organizations that seize this opportunity to plan and prepare will be well positioned to set themselves apart in the market-place, in the eyes of current and prospective employees as well as stockholders, and in the form of a best-in-class employer and enviable shareholder returns.

What Do We Do about It?

To use this time wisely and thrive as we move into the 21st century, there are three important questions that HR professionals need to be asking now:

1. What will the organization need and want?
2. What will employees need and want?
3. What will HR need and want?

It seems simple: Answer these three questions and the problem is solved. Unfortunately, it may not be that easy. When HR evolved from the shadows of personnel departments, responsibilities such as watching out for the interests of employees, anticipating the talent needs of the organization, and coaching and developing tomorrow's leaders were added to what were primarily administrative tasks. Although technology has helped to lighten some of the administrative burden associated with the past, many HR professionals continue to struggle with how to completely fulfill their new strategic duties. The impending labor shortage presents an open invitation for HR to make a monumental impact and to demonstrate true worth to the organization. The other scenario is that HR will once again face the fate of becoming the tactical and administrative center of the organization. To "step out" and seize the opportunity to forever change the perception of HR, we need to think about what we do and how we do it in a radically different manner. The successful HR of the future will push their organizations to marketplace success by anticipating and leading rather than reacting and managing.

What Will the Organization Need and Want?

As the competitive landscape intensifies, the role of HR to find, attract, engage, and retain scarce, top-level talent who can deliver on new and ever-changing customer demands will become increasingly critical to a company's overall success. To do this successfully, the traditional recruiting and development programs and processes of the past will not suffice. HR will need to create and facilitate new processes that help the organization identify the following:

- Future talent needs (based on the marketplace, competitive positioning, organizational mission, and business strategy).
- The desired makeup of the organization's human capital (subject matter experts versus broad industry generalists, team structure versus individual production specialists, etc.).

- Internal talent to be grown and leveraged.
- Competencies and skills that will have to be acquired from external sources.
- The organization's demographic profile will need to be engaged and energized.

When addressing the question, "What will the organization need and want?" the key areas of focus are continuity planning, talent management, and employee development.

Continuity Planning

Traditional succession-planning processes will not be sufficient in building a resilient organization for the future. HR must ensure that readiness exists to face the changes that are imminent for the company, and it can lead this effort by understanding what skills and abilities will be required to meet both short- and long-term objectives. Rather than focusing primarily on intended successors for a position, a comprehensive continuity-planning process also includes building corporate awareness of the following: (1) the organization's workforce demographics, (2) in-house talent potential and availability, (3) emerging key positions (some of which may not currently exist), and (4) talent gaps that may require external recruiting or accelerated development programs.

Talent Management

The responsive mind-set of recruiters, which has been to wait until a position opens before beginning the search process, will quickly become obsolete when recruiters are faced with the impending labor shortage. Instead, internal recruiters will be challenged to become more closely tied (through goals, objectives, and success measures) with the business strategy and, in turn, to become much more aggressive in their activities. Staffing departments that transform into mini-search firms, conducting name generation, identifying key talent outside their organization, building "passive networks" (to be called on in the future), and building contacts and goodwill by themselves will outdistance more traditional competitors. Databases full of contacts and information will need to be culled on an ongoing basis, turning staffing into an ongoing process rather than a reactive event.

Employee Development

The traditional practice of training employees after they assume new roles will not provide the organization with the ongoing talent needed to compete in the future. Proactive training strategies—building skills in anticipation of changing responsibilities—will become the norm. This means arranging learning opportunities for people on a purposeful and continuous basis, thereby creating competency pools and talent reserves for later use.

In addition, the new "technologically savvy" employees will have little tolerance for inadequate or outdated technology, including the systems and software used for training. Many employees in this group also have a strong desire for peer interaction and group learning, therefore traditional classroom training is quickly fading away (and *not* to online delivery!). Training and learning experiences that evolve from trainer/facilitator-led class or discussion to working sessions with subject matter experts (SMEs) will have a better chance of capturing the interest of these workers. Early efforts in this direction indicate positive responses to sessions that take the form of real-time learning labs in which everyone is a trainer and learner working on real-time, tangible business issues and actionable solutions for the organization.

Last, organizations have a golden opportunity to turn to flexible, "do-the-job" assignments (e.g., rotations and job swapping) that assist employees in building and cultivating new skills. Organizations will benefit from the productivity and new ideas generated while the "temp" employee is in the role, and the employee will benefit by building skills and extending their network of contacts.

What Will Employees Need and Want?

In two words: individual flexibility. The employees of tomorrow will be more business savvy than ever before. In addition, the expanded cultural diversity of the workforce will demand that HR tailor benefits to meet the "value levers" of each group and/or person. While monetary compensation will be as important as always, creating personal value will become a major factor designing processes to meet the various needs of these groups.

Benefits

Traditional, one-size-fits-all benefits will likely not be a market differentiator or employee motivator in the upcoming years. Employees will want more of a say in not only what is offered and what they do and do not participate in, but also in how their benefits packages are formed and funded. Individualization will be of key importance.

As an example, rather than a benefits-premium formula that is based on the number of people covered (single, spouse, dependents, and so forth), a shift to allow people to spend their benefit allocation according to their specific situation may occur. Factors could include the following:

- Individual risk tolerance.
- Anticipated need for services.
- Value for fee.
- Ease of use.
- Level of service desired.
- Desired level of coverage.

Another area in which HR can lead the way in combating the labor shortage is by offering graduated retirements to employees. Moving away from the "work today, retire tomorrow" mentality of yesterday, HR will have the opportunity to be creative in offering potential retirees a way to gradually exit the workforce, which will allow them to progressively adjust to a new life outside of work. While there may be legal hurdles to overcome, the benefits of having these experienced employees for a few additional years, to coach and mentor replacements for key positions, could be immense. These advantages would show themselves in terms of continued productivity, shortened learning curves, and employee satisfaction with the process.

Compensation

It's no secret that what motivated people 50, 25, even 10 years ago has changed dramatically for many. It's no longer enough to provide just an annual base-compensation increase; more and more people are downplaying salary and looking for more out of their employers. To meet the differing needs of employees, we suggest making a "rewards pool" available for people to choose from, depending on their interests. This pool need not consist solely of monetary rewards (such as merit increases and bonus or stock options), but could also include such things as more time off, access to outside performance coaching, or increased medical coverage (all of which would, at worst, have a neutral impact to the organization).

What Will HR Need and Want?

As we mentioned at the beginning of this chapter, human resources is on a journey. The call to transform ourselves from order takers to strategic thought leaders has launched us on a path to gain a "seat at the table." For some this has been a successful effort, for others there remains a distance to bridge. Regardless of where HR professionals find themselves at this point, it will be critical that we remain focused on the objective of adding value by growing, nurturing, shaping, and protecting the human capital that is essential to our organizations' success. The two key components for HR in accomplishing this mission will be: business acumen and reinvention expertise.

Business Acumen

It is not enough to simply know our profession; we must also know our organization and our industry. We must become experts at the business and be able to talk in operational terms. We need to master the fundamentals, understand and help shape the strategies, and appreciate both the challenges and opportunities of our business partners. By understanding our organization, we can ensure that the HR programs, policies, and procedures that we put in place will have a direct and meaningful impact on our organizations' success.

Reinvention Expertise

The ability to reinvent ourselves, as individuals and as organizations, will spell the difference between success and failure in the future. Although we may search for the comfort of stability, the reality is that change will not cease. In a world in which new markets emerge over night and the desire for products can disappear without warning, the individuals who pause too long or cling to out-dated answers risk losing the edge they fought so hard to gain. This is not to say that we should seek change for the sake of change. Our challenge is to remain in tune with the future, so that we can prepare to seize the opportunities that are presented and create opportunities where none seem to exist.

Conclusion

We feel that the impending labor shortage and demographic shift present a window of opportunity that will be open for just a short while. During this time, HR can show its ability to be creative and flexible in meeting both the organizations' and the individual employees' needs. By being proactive and strategic, HR can lead their organizations in preparing for this unique future. If HR misses this window, we may well find ourselves reliving the past—with hiring plans that are unreasonable if not ludicrous, performance issues created by poor hiring decisions, and unhealthy turnover for starters.

American anthropologist, Ruth Benedict, once said, "We grow in time to trust the future for our answers."[2] We do not have all the answers at this point, and we must begin to ask the critical questions. Our potential for success is boundless. Only if we continue to move forward will we realize the invaluable contributions that we are capable of making not only to our organizations, but also to our profession as a whole.

CHAPTER 4

━━━▷◆◁━━━

Engaging the Generations

BEVERLY KAYE, DEVON SCHEEF, AND DIANE THIELFOLDT

No LONGER JUST a problem for families, the generation gap has donned casual business attire and come to work. For the first time in modern history, four generations are working side by side in most companies. And, just like a multigenerational family, each age group has different motivators, communication styles, and work values.

See if this sounds familiar . . .

- Bill, a 61-year-old company veteran, watches the new crop of interns settle in at his division. He marvels at their selfish outlook and apparent lack of loyalty.
- Susan, a 48-year-old mother of two and caretaker for her aging father, looks at her in-basket and wonders how she'll ever find the time to meet the needs of both her family and her work team.
- Jennifer, a 30-year-old supervisor, chafes under the attention of her boss. "If he doesn't stop micromanaging me and let me do the job my way, I'm out of here," she thinks.
- Greg, a 22-year-old, fresh out of college, is ready to conquer the world. "I'm going to be a director by the time I'm 30," he tells his older coworkers, immediately alienating them.

What's going on in companies today? Why can't the generations get along? What used to be humorous grousing around the water cooler has turned into a serious corporate issue as demographics and company needs collide. It's likely your organization—if not your work team—has members of the Silent Generation (born 1933–1945), Baby Boomers (born 1946–1964), Generation Xers (born 1965–1976), and maybe even some Millennials (born 1977–1998). And that's only half the story. The prominent feature about the workforce in the first half of the 21st century is that it will grow much more slowly than in any other decade since the 1960s. In fact, researchers predict that we face a workforce shortage of somewhere between 15 and 25 million workers in the first 20 years of this century.

Engage the Generations: It Makes Good Business Sense

How can you engage each of these generations, inspire them to stay and succeed? Why is it important that you target each one? If your organization is expanding, your diverse workplace should mirror your diverse marketplace; if you need to attract and retain top talent, your company must appeal to high-quality candidates of all ages; if your company suffers from conflicting attitudes about work, misunderstandings over communication, and miscues about motivation, you need to narrow your generation gap; and if you see employees that have "quit" but are still at their desk every day, you need to not just retain them but also to truly engage them in their work.

Here are the top five reasons that organizations need to proactively work on engaging all four generations:

1. *Slipping away.* Is your precious knowledge capital walking out the door? Are you seeing an onslaught of Silents and Baby Boomers checking out their retirement options? If your workplace is built around Boomers, the average age of your employees is somewhere between the late 30s and mid-50s, which means that capturing their expertise is a high priority.
2. *Whining and walking.* Have you noticed that your Silent Generation and Boomers are inclined to whine when they're dissatisfied—and that Generation Xers and Millennials are inclined to walk? Retaining talented younger workers is a top challenge for many organizations.
3. *Quitting and working.* People can quit and still come to work. Some of your key talent may be physically present at work, but not psychologically there. It's worse to have them stay and do damage than to go and seek work fulfillment elsewhere.
4. *Competing and constraining.* Are you in a race to attract and retain top talent? Recruiting and retaining high-quality knowledge workers remains a core challenge as organizations compete for a smaller pool of workers.
5. *Clashing and complementing.* You've noticed that the people you work with have differences in work ethic, teamwork, expectations of you, and expectations of the organization, and you wonder if the differences are related to their generations.

To engage the generations, you must first understand them. Let's take a look at each generation's portrait.

Get to Know the Generations

The Silent Generation: Your Sagely Silents

Meet Bill and his cohort group . . . The oldest generation typically found in today's workplace was born between 1933 and 1945. These oldest members grew up in a time of economic turmoil in the aftermath of the Great Depression. They dealt with economic hardships by being disciplined and self-sacrificing. They lived and helped reinforce the American Dream. They have enjoyed a lifetime of steadily rising affluence.

There are 52 million Silents, and they defy generalization more than any other generation. So watch those stereotypes!

Employees from the Silent Generation are typically disciplined, loyal team players who work within the system. They have a huge knowledge legacy to share, and they embody a traditional work ethic.

There's a natural affinity between this generation and the young Millennials. It's a perfect match to have them mentor the youngest generation of employees, and the Silent Generation's natural civic-mindedness lends itself to this task.

Don't dismiss their technical skills as out of date: Del Webb, a major developer of homes for retiring couples, points out that the top requested feature in new homes for retirees is his-and-hers offices. Most Silents have a positive view of technology, so provide your older employees with proactive service and support for technology tasks and let them run with it.

Silents feel unappreciated, but they're open to returning to the workplace after initial retirement, as long as they have the flexibility to put their newfound freedom first. You might consider asking some of your retirees to return as part-time consultants and mentors, as well as instituting phased retirement to gradually ease older employees into retirement at a mutually agreeable pace.

Tips on managing this generation: Assure them that you value their work and that it's respected; ask them to share their knowledge legacy; and give them hands-on training and praise their mastery of new areas; don't take it for granted.

The Baby Boomers: Driven to Succeed

Meet Susan and her hard-driving colleagues . . . The most populous generation in the United States, 76 million Baby Boomers were born between 1946 and 1964. They typically grew up amid economic prosperity, suburban affluence, and strong nuclear families with stay-at-home moms. Boomers asked tough questions about social issues, civil rights, war, sexual freedom, and more. They took stock of their radically changing world and got to work with a vengeance.

Boomers tend to be optimistic, competitive, and focused on personal accomplishment. They work hard, maybe too hard. This is the generation that increased our workweek from 40 hours to 70 or 80 hours. As younger generations have entered the workplace, Boomers have waited for them to pick up this traditional approach to work. Some researchers divide the Baby Boomers into two groups: (1) those born between 1946 and 1954 (the "Woodstock" group, known for their idealistic endeavors and social conscience), and (2) those born between 1955 and 1964 (the "Zoomer" group, known for their preoccupation with self).

This generation has ruled the workplace for years and is comfortable in the culture they've created. They view changes as sometimes painful but inevitable. Many companies experience their biggest generational conflict when Boomer managers are confronted with younger employees who don't "fit the mold" that they themselves created.

Tips on managing this generation: Spotlight intangibles such as fulfillment and spirituality; redesign jobs to accommodate family demands of children and aging parents; and encourage them to "lighten up." Let them know how their contributions are unique and important.

Generation X: Declaring Their Independence

Meet Jennifer and her resilient contemporaries . . . The 51 million members of Generation X, born between 1965 and 1976, grew up in a very different world than previous generations. Divorce and working moms created "latchkey" kids out of many in this generation. This led to traits of independence, resilience, and adaptability. Generation X feels strongly that "I don't need someone looking over my shoulder."

At the same time, this generation expects immediate and ongoing feedback and is equally comfortable giving feedback to others. Other traits include working well in multicultural settings, desire for some fun in the workplace, and a pragmatic approach to getting things done.

Generation X saw their parents get laid off or face job insecurity. Many of them also entered the workplace in the early 1980s, when the economy was in a downturn. Because of these factors, they've redefined loyalty. Instead of remaining loyal to their companies, they have a commitment to their work, to the teams they work with, and to the bosses they work for. For example, a Baby Boomer complains about his dissatisfaction with management, but figures it's part of the job. A Gen Xer doesn't waste time complaining—she sends her résumé out and accepts the best offer she can find at another organization.

At the same time, Generation X takes employability seriously. But for this generation, there isn't a career ladder. There's a career lattice. They can move laterally, stop and start . . . their career is more fluid.

Tips on managing this generation: Create a "campus culture" environment that allows flexibility and independence—including flextime and/or telecommuting; mentor them instead of managing them; promote a participatory work environment; provide chances to compete; offer constant feedback; and assign a series of long-term, meaningful projects. Motivate them by eliminating as many rules as possible.

The Millennial Generation: Up and Coming

Meet Greg and his self-confident contemporaries . . . Just beginning to enter the workplace, The Millennial Generation was born between 1977 and 1998. The 75 million members of this generation are being raised at the most child-centric time in our history. Perhaps it's because of the showers of attention and high expectations from parents that they display a great deal of self-confidence to the point of appearing cocky.

As you might expect, this group is technically literate like no one else. Technology has always been part of their lives, whether it's computers and the Internet or cell phones and text pagers.

Millennials are typically team-oriented, banding together to date and socialize rather than pairing off. They work well in groups, preferring this to individual endeavors, and they're used to tackling multiple tasks with equal energy. They expect to work hard. They're good at multitasking, as they've juggled sports, school, and social interests as children.

Millennials seem to expect structure in the workplace. They acknowledge and respect positions and titles, and they want a relationship with their boss. This doesn't always mesh with Generation X's love of independence and hands-off style.

Tips on managing this generation: Provide a fun, friendly environment that still has structure and stability; personalize their work; help them become a specialized generalist, boost teamwork; offer flextime and/or telecommuting; and address them personally.

Bridging the Gap

"GEN-FRIENDLY" PRACTICES AND POLICIES

Use these ideas as a starting point for reviewing how generation-friendly your organization is now and for considering how to better engage all generations:

- *Rethink retirement plans.* Accelerate or shorten the vesting period of your 401K, pension plan, or other retirement program to accommodate career mobility, and make sure benefits are transferable between your units or divisions. This promotes flexible careers and provides a way for employees to establish their financial independence early in their careers.
- *Diversify.* This is a desirable hallmark for Gen Xers and Millennials who grew up surrounded by people of all types. They know when companies only give lip service to diversity. If you're known in your industry or community as a diversity-friendly employer, you're miles ahead of the competition in the race for Gen Xer or Millennial talent.
- *Shift your schedule.* The ability to manage work-life balance is the number-one need of all generations. Offering a variety of flexible hours, telecommuting, and options for taking time off will appeal to everyone from Silents transitioning to retirement to Boomers caring for aging parents and children to Gen Xers starting families.
- *Create a career lattice.* Not everyone wants to climb the corporate ladder. Gen-friendly organizations offer encouragement and flexibility for employees who want to ping-pong through the organization, picking up skills along the way. Create nonmanagerial career ladders, and offer promotions and raises tied to building expertise and not just position.
- *Customized career development.* Consider offering career development workshops that target the unique needs of each generation and what they want from work. For the Silents, offer a "Retreading" session on planning for a retirement career or switching to part-time. For Boomers, offer a "Retooling" session on how to acquire the skills to fulfill personal career goals. For Gen Xers, offer a "Reflection" session on taking stock of your career and setting and reaching goals. For Millennials, offer a "Re-Orientation" session to get their careers off to a good start.

Despite the seemingly radical differences between the generations, there are some core needs we all share, from the 60-year-old veteran behind the desk in operations to the 23-year-old college graduate who just started in sales.

Research shows that salary and benefits aren't the main reasons people choose to stay at a company. Rather, people stay if their work is exciting, focused on growth, and encourages their development. You can increase retention and morale for all your employees by working on the concept of *engagement*.

From a leadership perspective, engagement maximizes the contributions of every person in the workplace, creating a compelling, retention-focused atmosphere that addresses the unique needs of the generations in a way that creates bridges and common ground, not division and discord. From your employees' perspective, engagement means being motivated, fulfilled, and committed to one's work.

Have your managers emphasize specific areas of universal needs and interests, developing them to create strong common ground to engage all employees. We call these areas the "three C's of engagement:" career, climate, and communication.

Careers: Activate Them

Regardless of our view of work and our work ethic, we all want our work to be satisfying and to offer opportunities for growth. There are several ways that even the most time-stressed manager can act as a career coach. For instance, you can have frank, one-on-one discussions with employees about their career aspirations and options. Familiarize yourself with the career goals of employees, and encourage them to have multiple goals that may move them in directions other than straight up the career ladder. These simple practices are often as meaningful as a formalized career path.

Make it a habit to give prompt and useful feedback, letting each employee know what you see as his or her individual strengths and opportunities for improvement.

Share your own lessons of experience. Let employees know how you got to your current position, including any mistakes and missteps, career changes, and alternate paths.

Your company—or individual managers—can encourage informal mentoring to help employees gain new skills and insights. Remember that cross-generational mentoring is a two-way street; don't assume that the Silent Generation is the only age group with skills and knowledge to share. By having managers or, better yet, other employees who mentor individuals of all ages, you'll help build everyone's skills base and keep everyone involved interested, motivated, and engaged.

If your company is undergoing downsizing, a merger, or other stressful changes, don't forget to keep a focus on careers. Often in these circumstances, the attitude is one of "be thankful you're getting a paycheck," instead of focusing on individual growth. There are many things that managers can do to energize careers during corporate change: it may look different than business as usual, but it still works.

You can activate the careers of Silents like Bill by involving them as mentors, giving them a chance to share their wisdom, and assuring them you value their expertise. Provide job security and demonstrate your appreciation for the things they've learned the hard way and can still contribute. Finally, make sure they understand their future lifestyle needs and link them to organizational resources.

Help Boomers like Alice explore their next set of workplace options, including consulting or part-time work. When possible, redesign their jobs to accommodate multiple family demands. Encourage them to enrich their present jobs and grow in place if they need to slow their career pace.

Generation Xers respond to candid feedback and discussion about their careers. Tell them what they'll need to learn and look for in their current jobs to succeed. Acknowledge their ability to work independently and encourage them to leverage their entrepreneurial aptitude.

Engage the Millennials by demonstrating the stability and long-term value of your organization and of their jobs. Provide work schedules that help them build careers and families at the same time. Make groups and teams part of their work experience.

Climate: Create One

A good working climate is another value we all desire. Everyone wants a workplace that's trusting and open—and every manager has the opportunity to create his or her own "weather system," regardless of the overall climate of the organization.

Managers can create an ideal climate by delegating tasks to develop employees and shaping the work to the needs of each individual. Even members of the Silent Generation are interested in trying new things at work, so challenge each individual to learn new skills.

You should also celebrate individual and team accomplishments, whether through verbal praise or more tangible rewards (from a handmade certificate to a $100 gift allowance). Preferably, use as many different means of recognition as possible to appeal to all generations; Boomers prefer practical rewards like time off or monetary incentives, while Millennials actually enjoy more responsibility on the job.

To create an ideal climate, you must prove your openness to ideas and innovations from your employees. Don't just listen to them. Act on their ideas or let them know why you can't.

Consider adding or increasing camaraderie-building events for employees, such as a team breakfast or off-hours picnic. If possible, add or increase flexible work schedules. Nearly 80 percent of Americans of all ages report that having a work schedule that enables them to spend time with their families is one of their top priorities.

Create a microclimate for Silents by verbally and publicly acknowledging their experience. Provide proactive technology support services if they aren't computer savvy and use due process.

Encourage Baby Boomers to "lighten up" and send a clear message that long hours are no longer a badge of honor. Give them flexibility and spotlight personal fulfillment and meaningful work.

With Generation Xers, resist micromanaging and provide a flexible and participatory work environment. Give them more opportunities, such as jobs in different departments or new tasks.

And for Millennials, encourage group work, try to personalize their work (one size *doesn't* fit all), and communicate the civic side of your company, such as pro bono work for a local charity.

Communication: Emphasize It

Another way you can engage all generations is to communicate often and in as many different ways as possible. We all need feedback and different types of communication, but people of different ages respond to different methods of communication. The solution: Use them all: e-mail, voicemail, newsletters, staff meetings, and a favorite of the Boomers: management-by-walking-around.

Communication that engages others is seldom seen in a written memo. Most often it's direct and in person. Remember, managers don't have to know all the answers. They just need to listen to all the questions, respond with what they know, and be straight about what's unknown. Keep those lines open, especially during tough times.

Make it a personal goal to beat the rumor mill with proactive communication. When you get information, share it. Let your employees see the big picture of what's happening in your organization, especially regarding upcoming changes or events that will affect them. Don't forget to include long-term plans and outlooks in your staff meetings.

As straight shooters, Silents appreciate straightforward messages that are balanced and reasonable. Make sure your communications with them are "say what you mean and mean what you say." Summarize information for them. They grew up with newspapers.

Baby Boomers want to hear what's new, innovative, and different. They prefer a news magazine format for written communication. Be expeditious. They appreciate saving time.

Generation Xers need communication that's frequent, truthful, specific, and concrete. They want to know how the news impacts them personally.

With Millennials, emphasize your commitment to them as individuals. Personalize your communications. Share your vision and invite them to participate.

It is possible to bridge those generation gaps and engage employees of all ages, through understanding each cohort group and expanding the common ground we all share: The desire for meaningful work, a good climate to work in, and the desire for open communication. Add a positive and unbiased attitude toward employees of all generations, and you can build even greater unity. We need everyone's energy and ideas, and organizations that ignore this will lose in the competitive race for talent.

CHAPTER 5

<hr/>

Globalization

How Real Are the People Challenges?

NEVILLE OSRIN AND FRANCIS STICKLAND

The Globalization Debate

THE GLOBALIZATION DEBATE is gathering pace and the heat being generated is giving new meaning to the phrase "global warming." For some, it is the perceived menace of American popular culture trampling on the local version that touches a raw nerve. As one wry observer notes: ". . . the whole world is being taken over by McDonald's and Coca-Cola and have a nice day and high fives, health warnings, air punching, group hugs, the American dream, child-proof caps, cinnamon flavoring, Scooby Doo, comfy fit . . . and baseball caps."[1] In *No Logo,* the bible of the anti-globalization high priests, Naomi Klein wrote that "globalization doesn't want diversity; quite the opposite. Its enemies are national habits, local brands and distinctive regional tastes."[2] Greg Dyke, director general of the BBC, appears to agree. In a speech in 2000, he said: "We are told the world is globalizing. That's not true: it is Americanizing."[3] For better or worse we can debate, but are the effects of Americanization permanent? AA Gill thinks not, revealing his astonishment at what he calls ". . . the ephemeral impact of American cultural imperialism," he poses the question: What will be left from America's moment as global top dog? His response seems cruel and over simplistic, but not without some supporters: "Americans are in my experience enthusiastic at home but apologists abroad . . . [their] gift to the world is ideas, impermanence, the lure of the road, the new beginning and an heroic optimistic capitalism"[4]

However, there are also strong arguments that emanate from those in the other corner. Brink Lindsey argues that for much of the 20th century, the invisible hand of the market gave way to the dead hand of the state.[5] He presents a compelling picture of how the effects of state ownership, price controls, trade barriers, and other leftovers from the statist era still grossly impede the global economy. Put bluntly, local diversity and national habits can curtail economic growth and business expansion across borders.

In short, depending on your perspective, globalization is nearly always described as an irresistible new force that will either wreck or save the planet. What is indisputable is that global change has been a way of life in the latter years of the 20th century and will continue to be so as we boldly step out in the new millennium. As Stephen Rhinesmith puts it: "The forces of technology, political freedom, territorial dispute, ethnic rivalries, economic competition, and entrepreneurial ingenuity are stronger than all the centuries of social, political, and economic fabric that have woven the world into its current form."[6] However, these historic reflections are, for the HR practitioner, something of a luxury. The reality is that for most major corporations, globalization features prominently on their corporate agenda. Steering a path through the minefield of strategic rationale, cultural collisions, differences in work-related values, structural issues, and problems relating to the distribution of power and authority, is a stupendous challenge.

Developing a Global Mind-Set

Fundamental to success is the ability to create and develop an appropriate global mind-set. But what is a *global mind-set?* In his insightful analysis, Jean-Pierre Jannet defines the global mind-set as ". . . a state of mind able to understand a business, an industry sector, or a particular market on a global basis. The executive with a global mind-set has the ability to see across multiple territories and focuses on communalities that cross many markets rather than emphasizing the differences between countries."[7] This would imply that companies experiencing global pressures would need to recruit and develop a pool of executives with a global outlook, able to explore and exploit business opportunities across borders. Part of this global mind-set would involve an entirely new array of analytic and conceptual tools not required previously. As Christopher Bartlett and Sumantra Ghoshal have documented well, international corporate life has historically been replete with domestic exporters, shipping goods across borders and multinationals, replicating the entire domestic business structure in each new country they enter to ensure complete flexibility and match customer needs in the new environment.[8] Table 5.1 summarizes the main ways companies expand their business across the planet.

For Jannet, two strategic issues are crucial: (1) selecting the pathways to globalization, i.e., the route from domestic to international to multinational

TABLE 5.1   Expanding across the Planet

	Going Gobal: Characteristics/Attributes	HR Challenges
Extending the family business. "Tidying up the international scrapbook," for example, Kanach Beverages.	Fragmentation of international assets drives a desire to refocus the global strategy. Monumentally complex organization charts full of legacy roles. Often acquire smaller but stronger businesses than themselves to expand their international footprint. Cross-border expansion driven more by wider name/brand recognition than by solid strategic logic. Strong desire to export not just product/business model, but also family values and ethos as well. (Typically an Anglo-Saxon model.)	Resisting a "one-size-fits-all" approach to worldwide HR policies and programs. Role assessment and structure creation to manage overseas operations. Being confronted with more advanced HR programs and policies during post-merger integration. Trying to drive an international HR and talent strategy from a loose business case. Navigating the intercultural challenges of instilling the "family way" onto a foreign workforce.
Keeping pace with strong international demand. "Riding the Tsunami of Global Growth without Drowning" for example, Intelligent Communications.	Cracks starting to appear in joint ventures and strategic alliances around the world. Overseas businesses have wider product/service offer to market than the domestic company. Profitability of international asset base crippled by management and operations overhead costs. Local power bases beginning to develop outside of the domestic business. Classic headquarters versus subsidiary power issues: process ownership, degree of local autonomy, corporate function location, and so on.	Keeping management development curriculum fresh to ensure that executives have relevant skills to match global growth. Tailoring domestic HR policies to fit different local business needs and human capital needs. Managing global mobility, expatriot and international pay costs effectively. Finding challenging new roles at home for returning wave of original ex-patriots. Creating unambiguous organizational designs, in which roles and accountabilities are tight enough for performance management and loose enough for market flexibility.

to global, and (2) leveraging the global logic that is driving the need for globalization. He identifies seven logic dimensions that drive globalization:

1. *Competitive logic.* Are we meeting the same competitors around the world?
2. *Global size logic.* Is critical mass a major factor for success?
3. *Regulatory logic.* Are different regulatory forces a potential barrier to growth?
4. *Purchasing logic.* Is the supply chain a source of competitive advantage?
5. *Information logic.* Are speed and dissemination of information and knowledge within and between markets truly critical to the success of the business?
6. *Customer logic.* Do our home-market customers expect us to deliver similar products and services seamlessly across the globe?
7. *Industry logic.* Is the whole industry "going global"?

In Rhinesmith's *A Managers Guide to Globalization,* he describes the *global mind-set* as ". . . a predisposition to see the world in a particular way that sets boundaries and provides explanations for why things are the way they are, while at the same time establishing guidelines for ways in which we should behave. In other words, a mind-set is a filter through which we look at the world."[9] A mind-set, for Rhinesmith, is a way of being rather than a set of skills. It is an orientation to the world that allows one to see certain things that others do not see. A global mind-set means that we scan the worlds from a broad perspective always looking for unexpected trends and opportunities that may constitute a threat or an opportunity to achieve our personal, professional, or organizational objectives. The challenge for executives is to develop broader, more flexible mind-sets and to back these up with a personal ability to deal with less structure. This demands more openness to unfolding complex events, many of which cannot be planned for in advance.

It is fascinating to note that in Jannet's scholarly work of some 220 pages, less than one page is devoted to the question of ways in which culture may impact globalization, and in the index there are no references to specialists in this field. Similarly, while Rhinesmith explores comprehensively and in great depth the cultural, human resource, and organizational dimensions, he is less acutely focused on the strategic rationale which underpins a company's commitment to going global. There is a similar uni-dimensionality in most of the literature on globalization: a tendency to focus on one or two primary facets rather than to explore globalization in a more systemic way. Given the complexity of the subject and its numerous facets, this is inevitable and it would be beyond the scope of this modest chapter to remedy.

Rather, our aim is to draw from our personal consulting experiences the crucial issues that companies face as they seek to implement their vision of self-transformation by extending global reach. Specifically, we will focus on the vital and often mission-critical interplay between the strategic rationale and the people dimension.

Where Does HR Fit in the Globalization Debate?

For the HR practitioner often charged with facilitating the process, issues of globalization rarely emerge in the neat categories suggested in the literature. The reality of globalization suggests that implementation can be effective only if a systemic approach to change is adopted. This is not theoretical; in our experience, emerging realities are wholly interrelated and revealed as complex and deep-rooted problems for which linear or piecemeal solutions serve only to make successful implementation increasingly remote. See "The World Is Not Enough" (box on pp. 40–41) inset for a graphic example of how fundamental people issues are, if success in globalization is to be achieved.

From our consulting experience with large-scale acquisitions, postmerger integration, and the creation of cross-border joint ventures and strategic alliances, we have encountered three common scenarios, each of which has demanded a response from HR. Doubtless there are others, and we do not hold these three up as comprehensive or the most frequently occurring. Rather, they provide a means to highlight some of the common people-related challenges to international business expansion and the associated key HR questions to focus on. (See Table 5.1.):

1. *Domestic market leader ventures abroad.* Establishing the first international beachhead. Trying to take a successful local business model outside the home market.
2. *Extending the family business.* Tidying up the international scrapbook. Consolidating international assets through a large acquisition overseas in an attempt to perpetuate the family brand around the world.
3. *Keeping pace with demand.* Riding the tsunami of global growth without drowning. Responding to quantum growth in early years due to massive product demand across multiple countries, and the strain this places on the domestic country infrastructure to nurture the rest of the organization.

As industries and market sectors mature and product and service differentiation becomes increasingly difficult, many companies are left with little option but to "reinvent" themselves. Such transformation invariably involves a range of different activities and competencies that are required to underpin an emerging new business model. Even more challenging is the realization that even though it may have little ambition outside its home market, the incursion into its territory of new competitors from abroad may well force the company to see its future in a far more global context. Thus, for many firms, the link between transformation and globalization is almost axiomatic. Indeed, in some cases the need to establish a "center of gravity" outside its home country becomes a cornerstone of its transformation strategy. The

"The World Is Not Enough"

For James Bond's adversary in the 1999 MGM film *The World Is Not Enough*, world domination through industrial espionage and the theft of a nuclear device was the rather less benign version of globalization envisioned by the mysterious terrorist known as The Anarchist. Thanks to Bond and the ever-vigilant "M," The Anarchist's plans are thwarted and the world is free to await its next global combatant.

In the real world, of course, it's not that simple, and it may take a little longer and require the combined forces of stock markets and shareholders to unseat those narcissistic CEOs whose ambitions will ultimately be thwarted by the realities of globalization. To observe the actions of the Lays, the Messiers, the Ebbers, the Kozlowskis, and others of similar ilk, one might be forgiven for assuming that for them, truly, the world is not enough.

In January 2001, *Fortune* magazine published an article profiling the movers and shakers for the forthcoming year entitled "People to Watch." Bernie Ebbers headed the cast of those we were advised to watch. How closely they needed to be watched became apparent only much later! Ebbers failed, followed closely by later revelations about Worldcom that left investors reeling and the telecom sectors in even worse shape than before. Another casualty of an overworked ego was ironically named Global Crossing, which suffered a 99.7 percent fall in its share price over the first six months of 2002 and subsequently filed for bankruptcy.

Yet, in terms of sheer *folie de grandeur* one would be hard-pressed to locate an ego larger than that of Jean-Marie Messier, whose autobiography is entitled "J6M.com" J6M stands for Jean-Marie-Messier Moi-Meme-Maitre-du-Monde: Jean-Marie-Messier-Myself-Master-of-the-World. Messier's rise and fall would have done justice to the Roman Empire. In 1996, he became CEO of Vivendi and over the next five years turned Vivendi from a largely utilities giant into a global multimedia giant with debts of $19 billion. To do this would require Messier selling off some of the assets he acquired, in effect admitting that his vision and strategy were flawed. For a while it seemed like the French establishment (often the subject of Messier's scorn) would stand by him after appointing a corporate governance oversight panel to supervise him. But in June, shares plunged to a 14-year low; fellow board member and erstwhile ally Bernard Arnault resigned from the board. Without Arnault's support, Messier could not survive. The reign of J6M had come to an abrupt and ignominious end.

Some of Messier's problems were of his own making. His love of the limelight set him apart from the more low-key profiles of his French CEO contemporaries. A French shareholder activist, Colette Neuville, was quoted in the *Wall Street Journal* as saying: "It has become like a drug for him. Seeing his name and his face in the media every day is his daily fix."[a]

There are many global realities; one of these is that the synergies that ego-driven CEOs are quick to claim in order to convince investors often fail to materialize in practice. This happens frequently because those whose jobs it will be to generate those synergies are often neither included in the due diligence process nor sufficiently involved in postacquisition integration planning.

AOL Time Warner suffered the biggest quarterly loss in corporate history, pushing its share price to a new low. Viacom absorbed a $1.1 billion loss for the first quarter of 2002. While there seems to be no inherent reason why such acquisitions should not create additional shareholder value, these write-offs reflect the view that the companies paid too much for their acquisitions, based on overly optimistic expectations that synergies could be achieved. A further problem is that investors and analysts tend to understand portfolio management, rather than the psychological, leadership, and organizational challenges of postmerger integration. This integration is fundamental to the attainment of synergies. Consequently, the more heterogeneous a company is, the more difficult it is for the city or Wall Street to evaluate its performance.

Barry Diller, CEO of United States Networks, merged his television company with Vivendi. He was reported in the *International Herald Tribune* as saying: "To impose synergistic behavior on separate entities is ill advised. You're far better off developing businesses on their own—in their own silos, if you will—then letting some natural things occur when good management enables it."[b]

For HR, this perspective encapsulates very neatly the perceived realities and the challenge of globalization.

---

[a] J. Carreyrou, B. Orwell, and M. Peers, "Column One," *Wall Street Journal*, May 29, 2002.

[b] Frank, Ahrens, "Dealmaker at Helm of AOL, *International Herald Tribune*, August 8, 2002.

underlying rationale of this scenario is not complex; yet, the issues involved yield a bewildering array of dilemmas and contradictions, many of them having a strong people dimension at their core.

Domestic Market Leader Ventures Abroad: Establishing the First International Beachhead

Consider, for example, the case of Empiric Mutual, a long-established and venerable life insurance company and the dominant force within its market for over 100 years. The company had an unblemished record of solid performance and was a byword for financial stewardship and probity. Nonetheless, in a world of high-profile global players, it became clear to the board of Empiric, and especially to its chairman and CEO, that the company had to transform from a huge, but largely domestic, life insurance business to a global financial services company. The move toward globalization was accompanied by a process of demutualization and listing the company on one of the major stock exchanges of the world. Organic growth clearly was not an option; the strategic rationale of demutualization demanded significant acquisitions within the major financial centers of the United States and the United Kingdom. Suddenly, Empiric found itself a fish in several strange ponds, some of which were substantially larger than the one in which it was accustomed to swimming. However, the company has prospered. It has acquired a solid reputation in the markets within which it now operates. Its products are well rated; it has a growing brand profile; its share price holds relatively firm; analysts' reports are broadly positive; press comment is generally favorable; and the companies it has acquired are household names with solid reputations. It has succeeded in attracting the top-level executives it sought to recruit. The transformation appears to have gotten off to a flying start.

Yet, the reality of globalization is not always what it seems. Some of the key high-profile human assets Empiric acquired (and that were seen to be critical to future development) have not been retained. Newly appointed senior executives have moved on after a relatively short tenure. Many structural changes have taken place, and in some areas the baton has been passed with breathtaking speed from one leader to the other. Postmerger integration has been slow and has not generated impressive shareholder value. Multiple acquisitions have built a core of new businesses that were not significantly represented in previous incarnations of Empiric. The business models that drive these acquired businesses do not necessarily align well with the skills and mind-sets of a corporate leadership raised in a different tradition. Several intercultural collisions are evident and vexing power issues have emerged between business units and the corporate center. Some key staff, at first delighted at the prospect of being part of a major global financial group with significant resources, are now disenchanted by what they perceive as a lack of vision and strategic direction.

Acquirer and acquisition do not appear to have passed Michael Porter's "better off" test for successful diversification.

Where does HR fit into all this? Almost without exception, the issues outlined here have people as their common denominator. Responding effectively to the following questions may well have resulted in more positive outcomes for Empiric:

- Are we absolutely clear about the strategic rationale of these deals and the people issues that need to be resolved for this rationale to be translated into an executive agenda?
- When making new executive appointments, are we looking at the type of leadership required (as revealed by the growth/return—transactional/transformational matrix) as well as individual psychological assessments?
- Are we able to articulate the nature of the cultural differences between Empiric and the organizations we are planning to acquire (beyond the "we got on well together in our discussions" level) and the extent to which these could compromise the deal?
- Have we made a formal assessment of the capability of the combined organizations to actually deliver the synergies on which the investment was based?
- Have we considered how the differences in national culture between Empiric's home country and those which feature in the global strategy would affect the execution of our strategy? How should these differences be managed and leveraged to secure a competitive edge?
- Above all, have we constructed an HR strategy specifically designed to support the complexity of this restructuring, particularly in relation to the multiplex of globalization, demutualization, and acquisition issues?

The reality of globalization makes the provision of answers to these questions an absolute imperative, rather than falling into the "nice-to-have" category as is so often implicit in the actions of those who are accountable for achieving the outcomes that determine success or miserable under-performance.

Extending the Family Business: Tidying Up the International Scrapbook

Another common globalization scenario is the international business with a mixed portfolio of overseas assets and operations, which is looking to make more of a global brand and market impact. Ponder the case of Kanach Beverages.

Background

Kanach Beverages (KB) is a North American-based beverages business. Family owned and controlled for over 100 years, KB still has a strong culture rooted in the founding family's values. From how the raw materials are sourced, converted into drinks, bottled and canned, and distributed to the market, the personal influence and iron will of J. D. Kanach III is paramount. This approach has allowed KB to dominate some North American markets and to achieve a top-three brand presence in the United States. Attempting to export this model overseas has for the most part been profitable, entering into joint ventures in some countries for manufacture and bottling. However, the most lucrative international market is in Latin America where drinks are shipped directly from the United States to ensure product quality. With the global beverage market going through radical consolidation, KB needed to grow fast through acquisition to keep up with the big players, or it risked being marginalized as a domestic exporter stuck in the past. The other more fundamental shift facing KB was the need to become more marketing and brand-led to counteract a century of being a supply chain and distribution-led business. The latter had stood them well and generated competitive advantage for many years. However, with 21st century advances in technology and many types of beverage fast becoming a commodity, taste has become a competitive norm and no longer a basis for differentiation. As a way of increasing sales and securing loyal customers, the importance of supply chain fades in the shade under the hot glare of powerful brand marketing.

The solution for KB came with an opportunistic acquisition of a very similar beverage business in Europe. On the face of it, the deal gave them several things, including:

- A cash-cow platform from which to build a sizeable European market share.
- Strong European brands to add to the portfolio and managers who had already navigated the jump from a distributor-led to a brand-led organization.
- Size and scale from which to continue in the beverage game with the bigger players.

The Business Challenge

However, within 90 days of owning the new business, it became clear that this brick in KB's global wall was not going to fit snugly. In the usual rhetoric of "best-practice exchange" and "value the differences" that follows any acquisition, KB management realized that they had purchased a business that was light years ahead of them. Its organizational structure simple and market aligned, it suffered none of the functional complexity, lumbering processes, and odd legacy roles from yesteryear at KB. Protected from the cold winds of commercial reality by family cash, KB had never been forced to rationalize its organization from the outside in. In contrast, the European acquisition had been through several changes of ownership in recent years, which had stripped away much of the organizational dross that slowed its progress through European commercial waters. KB was encrusted with a century's worth of barnacles—structure, roles, and family dogma—and was barely making a bow wave.

HR's Challenge

The core issue for HR was how to use the overseas acquisition as a catalyst for change to revitalize the domestic business—without allowing an internal "reverse acquisition" attitude to set in. Some of the key human resource and people questions that HR set about tackling included:

- How to transfer commercial savvy and brand management expertise from Europe to North America without the transferred managers quitting in frustration after six months due to the resistance they encounter at KB.
- How to develop more of an international outlook and mind-set among emerging North American high potentials. Thirty years of "going-global-means-we-export-the-domestic-model" attitude has resulted in a cadre of parochial senior leaders within KB with almost no international experience.
- How to create a more streamlined KB organization design and how to dismantle the 100-year-old structural edifice that currently exists.
- How to reassign key talent from the bloated "International Division"—a scrapbook of overseas equity stakes, distribution agreements, and wholly owned sales offices—and redeploy that resource back into the business to drive more focused global growth.
- How to set up and staff a slim corporate center to support further global expansion.
- How to align the executive compensation and benefit arrangements across two continents into a common framework that permits flexible resourcing and incentives and retains vital high potentials.
- How to build further internal HR process expertise to deal more quickly and proficiently with the next acquisition and postmerger integration without the need for expensive consultancy support.

For KB, the future looks daunting, but they have the will to survive another 100 years. The family recognizes that the only way to build out globally is to address the legacy of domestic business methods and allow business leaders the freedom to drive right choices locally without interference. This meant tackling HR challenges head-on in a coordinated, not piecemeal, manner.

Keeping Pace with Demand: Riding the Tsunami of Global Growth without Drowning

Our third scenario is from the technology sector. This was a common situation for many companies during the mid-1990s that had to respond to exponential growth-in-market demand in different parts of the world. The challenge was to do so in ways that did not stretch corporate resources too thin or irreparably abuse the loyalty of their employees.

Background

Intelligent Communications was founded in 1992 by a young Swedish entrepreneur who was disillusioned by the lack of innovation displayed by blue-chip IT employers. She saw a niche in the crowded IT product market for intelligent document management and printing software that was aimed at large corporate businesses that rely on massive and frequent mailings to their customer base, such as banks, utilities, telecoms, and insurance sectors. Having secured some early exclusive distribution and sales rights for the leading products available at the time, she proceeded to build a multicountry, sales and support business across Europe and Asia. Within five years, IC was operating in more than eight countries, barely keeping up with demand. Having expanded the product portfolio and set a new standard for customer service in the IT services sector, IC was riding a tidal wave of growth that showed no signs of abating.

The Business Challenge

The competition was closing in quickly. The blue-chip companies that the entrepreneur had abandoned smelled the opportunity and moved in with big money. So, IC decided to reposition its core business and move from a product offer to a solutions offer (a transition many IT services firms seek to undergo when their core product is threatened with commoditization and oversupply). Introducing "solutions selling" and beginning forays into the consulting world were natural next steps. At the same time, the company expanded its core product portfolio to include Web-based document management and electronic bill presentation offers. The business model and value chain were expanding well. Not short on strategic vision, the young Swede thought she had all the bases covered. Indeed the growth curve was classic and worthy of a Harvard case study. However, the strains of quantum early growth were beginning to show. As the international expansion continued, attrition rates crept up. Sales professionals were promoted into country manager roles with no general management experience. The corporate services of finance, legal, HR, procurement, and vendor management needed dedicated attention that the current structure and talent mix could not deliver. Almost everybody shouldered multiple roles: CFO on Monday, country manager on Tuesday, salesman for the big pitch on Wednesday, and so on. IC's infrastructure and talent mix could not cope anymore and required a complete overhaul.

HR's Challenge

As with many firms that grow quickly, there was no dedicated HR support. Country managers wore a personnel hat when necessary, but this was largely event driven. For instance, if an employee became pregnant, a maternity policy was quickly developed; if an employee resigned, a retention strategy was immediately created; and so on. An HR committee was formed comprising of the Global CEO, the country manager for Germany (the biggest operation), and the COO. Working with an outside consultant, this trio began the arduous task of rewiring the architecture, culture, and talent mix of Intelligent Communications to stay ahead of the closing pack. Translating the needs of global growth into focused HR strategies and plans was at the heart of their transformation goal. The six essential challenges tackled by the HR committee in the first eight months were:

1. *Challenge.* Stop the talent hemorrhage across the international operation.
   Solution. Develop a combination of new performance-management processes, employee listening, and management-development programs.
2. *Challenge.* Restructure the business from a "product selling" to a "solutions delivery" proposition.
   Solution. Develop a new organizational design that moves the company from functional silos (sales, technical services, and customer support) to a new structure built on lines of business (customer relationship, management support, consultancy services, communication solutions, and research and development).
3. *Challenge.* Make key central functions such as finance, purchasing, HR, legal, and research and development less of a part-time job for senior managers.
   Solution. Establish an embryo corporate center for shared services needed by each country (staff gradually as needs arise). This, coupled with removing day-to-day financial processing from country managers, unleashed a bigger Intelligent Communications impact on the fledgling competitors in each country.
4. *Challenge.* Rapidly construct a credible and professional HR system that deals with most of the big employee events in the business cycle.
   Solution. Bring standard solutions and basic HR policies in from the outside that satisfy local statutory requirements in each country.
5. *Challenge.* Develop new manager cadre to release the business founders into further entrepreneurial activity.
   Solution. Hire experienced operations managers for each country and move staff with strong sales competencies back into the field.
6. *Challenge.* Motivate (with incentives) star product-sales staff to make the transition to solutions selling and consulting.
   Solution. Introduce a phantom stock plan and reconfigure the commission-based reward scheme.

In this case, HR issues were dealt with in a pragmatic and nonbureaucratic manner by senior-line professionals. Basic, technical HR solutions were outsourced, but the communication and implementation of the solutions was owned passionately by the line managers. Herein lies a key for HR leaders to effectively manage a company's growth from local to global: Know what you can and can't do at the center and equip those in the field. Globalization then becomes essentially a process of decentralizing headquarters' power, and this applies to HR as much as any other function.[10] IC made this work for them. They got the balance right between HR prescriptive policy and local autonomy.

Conclusion

What does this tell us about the future of HR? In short, there are several emerging lessons we can learn from Empiric Mutual, Kanach Beverages, Intelligent Communications, and Vivendi:

- Industries will continue to consolidate. As the pond shrinks, large acquisitions will continue to be the preferred globalization vehicle for many companies. This means HR professionals will never be far away from the next deal, and they must be equipped not just to cope but thrive on mergers and acquisitions.
- Global brands will be necessary, but not enough to achieve a global presence. Building an "in-country" presence and infrastructure will be as important as brand, even if this is achieved through joint ventures or strategic partners. This means strong HR sourcing and workforce alignment strategies must be in place and working efficiently.
- The HR agenda must acknowledge the shift from domination to collaboration and release HR expertise from the center to equip the line to deliver.
- HR administration will increasingly need local solutions, while its strategy will need region/land-mass solutions (not "global" solutions).
- Developing a management cadre with a global mind-set is not just about a revamped leadership development curriculum. It requires an integrated response from the organization to assess, identify, and develop people through the structure into broad, participative thinkers and interculturally sensitive implementers.
- HR must be more of a gate keeper on leadership excesses: whether it be ego-driven strategy (Vivendi); naive preparation for global expansion (Empiric Mutual); not getting your own structural house in order before buying someone else (Kanach Beverages); or too-fast-too-soon (Intelligent Communications).
- As we move into the 21st century, the potency of power and territory issues in "going global" remains undiminished. From our experience, they are becoming even more critical to success or failure of international expansion. As a result, HR professionals, so often at the forefront of political correctness, need to get tougher and develop more robust ways of effectively dealing with power and empire dismantling as part of the globalization process.
- As this century begins, it is clear that international growth will increasingly bring with it more complex business structures and matrix organizations.

This means more ambiguity of roles, multiple reporting relationships, blurred accountabilities, and general uncertainty as lines of business operate across territories.[11] Now more than ever, HR must face business architecture issues to ensure that they can shape the disruption to the people environment that result from this.

In summary, HR's response to a "go-global" agenda must be multifaceted, integrated, and sufficiently complex to mirror the issues it faces. Piecemeal, project, or policy-based solutions are inevitably suboptimal and cost organizations a small fortune.

CHAPTER 6

Understanding Referent Groups and Diversity

A Key Challenge for Human Resource Leaders

MARSHALL GOLDSMITH AND R. ROOSEVELT THOMAS, JR.

A s OUR ORGANIZATIONS become more global and more diverse, it becomes critical that leaders in human resources understand how different referent groups can impact the behavior of people in their organizations. The concept of *referent groups* can be a useful tool for understanding diversity in organizations, on both a global and local scale. It can also help us understand behavior that may otherwise appear to be illogical or irrational.

A referent group can be defined as any group that an individual sees as a source for his or her identity. Our referent groups define a large part of who we are. While we all have multiple referent groups, our *primary referent group* can be defined as the group that is the major source of our identity.

Referent Group Dynamics

We all tend to judge others as being "right" or "wrong" from the perspective of our own referent group. More specifically, members of different referent groups are inclined to define *ethics* and *morality* from the perspective of their group. It is critical that leaders in human resources are able to *understand* others' perspectives without necessarily having to *judge* them.

The size of our referent group may range from "the world" to "me" and almost anything in between. For example, some people see themselves as "citizens of the world." They may even be willing to sacrifice what is good for most living humans to do what they think is right for the long-term survival of the planet.

They might see sacrificing the organization or even other individuals (including themselves) as something that is highly ethical. Some see the organization as a key referent group. In Chapter 7 of this book, Katzenbach, Canner, and Feigen discuss building *pride* in the organization. They suggest a positive approach to making the organization an important part of the individual's identity. At the other extreme, some people are focused on "me." They are willing to sacrifice what is good for the world to benefit themselves. Adrian Furnham discusses this phenomenon in Chapter 11, "The Icarus Syndrome." In most organizational life, either extreme—excessively global or excessively individual—will usually produce problems.

Some major referent groups include: gender, philosophy, country, geographic area, ethnic group, race, sexual orientation, work team, extended family, and nuclear family. To assume that the organization is anyone's only referent group is naïve. For each of us, varying parts of our identity are connected with multiple groups. This may vary with age. For example, *family* is a major referent group for children ages 6 through 12, while *peer group* becomes a more important referent group between the ages of 12 and 15. Younger people tend to have less identification with the organization as a referent group, while older, more tenured employees tend to have more corporate identification.

Historical events can change our referent groups. In the United States, the 9/11 attacks caused many young people to strongly identify with America; whereas the Vietnam War caused many young people to identify less with America. Before World War II, identification with race was much more common; after World War II, primary identification with race has become much less acceptable. We in human resources need to be sensitive to these changes and know how they can impact the perceptions of employees.

There may be major differences between the referent groups with whom we *pretend* to identify and those with whom we *really* identify. For example, in the 1950s American corporate world (of Sinclair Lewis), it was "politically correct" to pretend that the corporation was more important than "ourselves" or even "our family." Ironically, while the essence of capitalism is self-interest, it has often been considered inappropriate to overtly demonstrate any self-interest when working for a major capitalist corporation. Jeffrey Pfeffer (Chapter 31) puts forth a brilliant analysis of how this pretense "plays out" in daily corporate life.

The need to pretend that the organization is the only referent group is changing. For example, many of the highest-potential knowledge workers now define themselves as "free agents."[1] Free agents, "while interested in pursuing many different goals, are more interested in pursuing what *they* want to pursue."[2] They are not interested in sacrificing their lives for the "good of the organization." Organizational leaders and those in HR (who have more of an organizational identity) may perceive these workers as "selfish"; however, we need to understand that these high-potential knowledge workers can be great "team players" in an organization that recognizes their perspective and builds win-win relationships. An effective HR person "must build partnerships with top performers that recognize their needs and keep them motivated to stay with the company (rather than join the competition)."[3]

One of the best ways to understand the power of referent groups is to focus on *behavior* more than words. By observing behavior and then asking ourselves, "Which referent group is the person *really* serving?" we can begin to understand the deeper rationale for behavior that may have appeared illogical.

Many of the differences that exist among people are easily understood when we know their different referent groups. If you believe that the encroachment of the western world will lead to the demise of your "pure" religion and your primary referent group is this pure religion, it is perfectly acceptable (or even noble) to do almost anything to stop this encroachment. From this perspective, killing "nonbelievers" is not only acceptable, it is "holy."

In a corporate setting, if you believe that your family is your most important referent group, it can be perfectly logical to go home early and not "worship the corporate God." It can be noble to turn down promotions (even though this may show a "lack of ambition" to others). In Chapter 4, Beverly Kaye, Devon Scheef, and Diane Thielfoldt provide some creative solutions for motivating workers from different generations who may have different referent groups.

Recently, several executives in major U.S. corporations seem to have made "the executive team" a more important referent group than "our company." This focus has led to behavior that is designed to benefit executives at the expense of the stockholders, employees, and customers. While these executives may have "failed" from one perspective, many "succeeded" in acquiring millions (or even billions) of dollars while avoiding prison.

This opinion piece is not designed to say that cultural relativism is an inherently good philosophy. In fact, cultural relativists can be just another form of a referent group. They can define themselves as "intellectually superior" to people who have a well-defined set of core values. Many organizations have clearly defined values that relate to key referent groups. It is important for those in the human resources field to understand that multiple referent groups (that may not be on the values statement) can also be a key part of an employee's identity. This is especially true outside the western world. It is also critical for HR leaders to understand that when *any* referent group requires behavior that damages "our organization" potential problems may well arise.

Our suggestion is that we can all increase our own interpersonal effectiveness by better understanding the powerful concept of referent groups. We can better understand that perfectly logical people have very different views on the world. We don't have to agree with these views (or even respect them) to see how they can dramatically impact behavior. By understanding our own referent groups and the referent groups of others, we can often "agree to disagree" without wasting our time trying to convert each other. Even more important, people in our organizations can more easily disagree with each other without having to judge each other. By having a deep understanding of the impact of referent groups,

HR leaders can help organization members communicate more efficiently and more effectively. We can also better motivate employees to work together without having to have the same beliefs.

Implications for Managing Diversity

Multiple referent groups add to the complexity and diversity faced by HR leaders. As referent groups become more diverse, the challenge of effective integration becomes greater. This will become even more the case in the future. The catalyst in driving the importance of referent groups is not that referent groups have proliferated in number, but rather that people are more comfortable in being different and open about their various loyalties and identities. The need to "pretend" to be like everyone else is declining.

So much is said today about differences, that we forget how unacceptable it was to be different a few years ago. To be different meant you were lacking or inadequate in some fashion. Only recently have we in the United States endorsed the notion that differences are not necessarily bad.

This shift in attitude can be attributed to several factors, including:

- The increasing ease of global communication and travel has made it easier for immigrants to retain their identities with their national and geographic origins, while simultaneously meeting their responsibilities as U.S. citizens.
- The Civil Rights' Movement said to people of color that one does not have to be white to be okay.
- The Women's Movement said to women one does not have to be male to be okay.
- Changes in family authority patterns legitimize the expression of differences by children. Years ago, in many families, to question parental decisions indicated a lack of respect; today, doing so is more likely to be viewed as a healthy sign of independent thinking or the inquisitiveness necessary for effective learning.
- The growing prevalence of "knowledge workers" gives rise to a group of employees who, because of their expertise and experience, expect to have the freedom to be different.
- In the context of globalization, it is becoming apparent that the American Way is not necessarily always the most viable option.

As a consequence of the more openly expressed commitments to referent groups, today's HR leaders and those of the future, unlike their counterparts of the past, must achieve coherent and productive effort from individual contributors with varied agendas. Stated differently, those in HR must preside over a sea of conflicting loyalties. If they cannot generate consistent, focused results from this complexity and diversity, the viability of their enterprise will suffer.

A major challenge is deciding whom to include and retain, and whom to exclude. For many, a strong temptation will be to pursue less diversity, and thus, more workforce homogeneity. However, this should not be the emphasis. The goal should be the attainment of consistent, high performance. If identification with a referent group will inhibit performance, this should be a factor to consider in HR decisions. If identification will not impact performance, it (generally) should not be a factor in HR decisions. In this context of results, HR does not evaluate or judge associates on the basis of their referent group memberships and loyalties, but rather on their ability to deliver the required results.

HR must be unrelentingly mission-, vision-, and requirements-driven. At first glance, this sounds straightforward. It is not. Most of us often, if not typically, base our decisions on personal preferences, traditions, and conveniences that may not be requirements. We may be inclined to evaluate people from the perspective of our referent groups, not from the perspective of the job and our organization.

Not too long ago, a group of managers discussed a scenario about "foxhole diversity":

A soldier had to decide who would occupy his foxhole with him. The enemy presented challenges on all sides. As the soldier considered his colleagues from whom he would select his foxhole mates, he asked several questions:

- Does each candidate have all of his faculties?
- Does each have a gun?
- Does each have the ability to shoot?
- Does each have the will to shoot?

Nothing was asked about their race, ethnicity, gender, sexual orientation, education, or geographic origin. The deciding soldier stressed requirements.

In response to this scenario, one senior executive raised his hand and said, "Be clear, in my foxhole, I do want someone who has his faculties, has a gun, but also has the ability and will to shoot—and who also meets my personal preferences." When queried as to whose preferences count, he added, "I know what I am saying: I am not ready for a requirements-driven company."

No one challenged the executive; primarily because he candidly expressed what most of the people in the room were thinking. They all wanted someone in their foxhole who satisfied their personal preferences. These managers, and others unable to be requirements-driven, will have difficulty dealing with the sea of conflicting loyalties.

Effectiveness in the midst of individual contributors with a multiplicity of referent groups will call for HR leaders to be comfortable with *diversity tension*—the stress and strain that accompanies mixtures of differences and similarities. If you have diversity, you will have diversity tension. With respect to referent groups, the task of human resources is not to minimize this tension, but rather to make quality decisions in the midst of identity differences, similarities, and tensions.

For us, diversity tension is not synonymous with conflict. Tension may exist between two parties indefinitely without evolving into conflict. The issue becomes that of maintaining a sufficient comfort level with the tension, so that high performance may be achieved.

Finally, those in HR who wish to be productive in the context of referent groups must also prepare and empower their associates to understand without judging, to be requirements-driven, and to be comfortable with referent group diversity tension. It is not enough for HR, managers, and leaders to possess these capabilities; they must also develop these capabilities throughout the organization.

Conclusion

In this chapter, we have argued that an understanding of the referent group concept, along with the ability to be requirements-driven and to be comfortable with diversity tension, can enhance our interpersonal and managerial effectiveness. Further, to the extent that we can nurture these attributes in our associates, the effectiveness of our enterprises will be enhanced. In tomorrow's complex world, understanding the impact of varied referent groups and managing the diversity tension that will invariably come from these differences will become a requirement, not an option, for HR leaders.

II

EMERGING PRACTICES

—≫•◇•≪—

W E ALREADY SEE the challenges of today's workforce. The different needs, fears, and goals of the Boomers, Busters, and Xers create havoc on traditional HR systems and practices. In our efforts to meet these challenges, we often create unnecessary complexity and lose sight of what really matters. The chapters in this section provide clarity and some intangibles of high-performing companies. The authors discuss using pride as a strong and essential motivator in today's high-performing companies. They provide tactics for moving away from the traditional models of work and suggest how HR leaders can tap both the emotions and the minds of employees at all levels to cultivate "institution-building pride."

What can organizations do to help managers and their teams get and give the coaching they need? The authors explore this question and outline the importance of coaching and feedback. Through first-hand best-practice examples, they provide answers to this and other questions, such as: How can organizations demonstrate with data that their human resource strategies significantly enhance competitive advantage? What can organizations do to address talent management and ensure that employees succeed? How will technology influence learning and development in organizations as we progress through the 21st century?

CHAPTER 7

—⟫◆⟪—

Putting Pride to Work

Recapturing the Power of the Most Effective Motivational Force

JON R. KATZENBACH, NIKO CANNER, AND MARC A. FEIGEN

INCREASINGLY, THE MAJOR, long-term achievements of organizations depend on hundreds or thousands of small, daily achievements by individuals who are frontline employees. That is why the ability to instill pride is becoming so important to corporate success and a critical challenge in human resources management; pride is the emotional expression of individual commitment that motivates most people.

If you want to get a clear sense of the importance of pride as a force to motivate higher levels of employee performance in the 21st century, start by comparing today's work environments to the one that Henry Ford devised at the beginning of the 20th century. In the Broadway musical *Ragtime*, Ford shows up as a character, describing the genius behind his assembly line. While this scene is whimsical characterization, it does epitomize the traditional production line model of that period. Today, however—and most certainly going forward—our economy is based less and less on one person tightening, ratcheting, or reaching to pull one cord. More and more, it is a matter of men and women performing a very broad spectrum of rapidly changing tasks, who are guided by an understanding of their employer's constantly evolving competitive needs and aspirations. To meet this challenge, human resource leaders of the 21st century must find ways to tap the emotions as well as the minds of employees at all levels.

This chapter is adapted from *Why Pride Matters More Than Money,* copyright by Katzenbach Partners LLC and Jon R. Katzenbach to be published by Crown Business in March 2003.

Under traditional production models, efficiency demanded compartmental-
ization of each link in the supply chain. The most important quality a worker
could bring to his job was a willingness to work hard at repeating the same routine task over and over. Employees were motivated by piece work compensation systems and job security. As we move into the 21st century, this traditional
model fits fewer and fewer situations. Instead, goods and services have to be
tailored to individual consumer desires. *Information* is replacing oil and steel
as the most precious commodity. The most important qualities workers can
bring to their jobs are initiative, responsiveness, and commitment. They need
to develop the ability to shape and share information, to devise better ways of
doing things, and to connect the results of their work to the performance of
the enterprise.

These factors elevate the importance of pride as a factor in managing people
and driving organizational success. More than any other motivator, it is pride
that fosters cooperation and collective effort as well as individual initiative. It
is pride in your fellow workers that encourages information sharing. It is pride
in how you carry out a task that prompts a desire to perform it as efficiently and
effectively as possible. And, it is pride in working with respected colleagues
that leads to team performance.

There is another important distinction between Ford's era and our own.
Henry Ford engendered loyalty among his employees by virtually guaranteeing
a job for life at a decent wage. Today, few people believe their job is guaranteed
for any extended period, much less for life. Thus, commitment to a job well
done can seldom be driven by the desire for job security. Nor can it be driven
by monetary rewards alone. Pay levels are typically a function of mass labor
contracts and formal compensation structures that have little to do with individual employee responsiveness or commitment. While money can attract the
better employees or retain them, it is much less likely to motivate them.

Given the demise of the job security and piecework compensation paradigm,
employee commitment and performance must be motivated by other factors.
The most important of these is pride in some aspect of the job itself, such as, the
work product, the working environment or approach, and the worker's immediate supervisor and workplace companions. The growing importance of pride as a
spur to responsiveness, productivity, and creativity in the workforce increases
the importance of developing a cadre of *pride-builders,* frontline leaders who
are able to instill pride in those who work for or with them, focus it on priority
areas (strategic and operating), and marshal it to achieve results. Seldom do the
pride-builders rely on money to achieve these ends.

Throughout the course of history, there have always been people skilled at
the art of pride-building. Indeed, that was a strength of many of the founders
of our largest institutions, both public and private. Today, however, as
customer-focused, time-based strategies demand increasingly decentralized
decision-making, pride-building capabilities must be broadly extended. Increasingly, building pride is not just the responsibility of the CEO and other

senior executives; it is also the daily task of the line managers and frontline supervisors. It matters most in segments of the workforce that are closest to the actions that deliver performance results, for instance, where the product is crafted, the sale is made, and the service is rendered. Without the emotional commitment of people in those critical spots, you cannot expect to sustain a competitive advantage for long.

Managers who excel at instilling pride in their workers also deliver higher levels of both economic and market performance over their peers. For example, as a part of an ongoing research effort to explore case experiences of pride-builders in different organizational settings, we recently asked the manufacturing managers council at General Motors to identify 20 of the best pride-builders in the company's North American manufacturing organization. Our case studies of these managers confirmed their reliance on pride as a primary source of motivation. When we examined their performance against several important metrics, their results consistently exceeded that of their peers. Pride-builders demonstrated an advantage in the primary determinants of manufacturing performance at GM— namely safety, productivity, people, quality, and cost.

While it is always difficult to separate the chicken from the egg—Does performance drive pride or does pride drive performance?—we find little doubt in the minds of the best motivators that instilling pride is what enables them to get higher levels of performance from their people. Of the more than 50 pride-builders we have studied during the last two years, most deliver superior performance results for their enterprise, and all attribute their success to an ability to instill pride among their people *before the fact.*

Pride: It Adds Up to More Than Dollars and Cents

If pride is a critical determinant of lasting organizational success, how then do we harness it? That question underlies one of the biggest investment challenges faced by organizations and their HR departments today: How do we build a stockpile of pride and deploy it over time to motivate higher levels of employee performance in the most important segments of the workforce?

The most significant thing to learn about motivation from the experience of high-performing organizations is the importance of cultivating institution-building pride as opposed to self-serving pride. Enterprises that excel at engaging the emotions of their employees pay enough to attract and retain good workers, but they rely much more on nonmonetary approaches to motivate those workers to higher levels of performance.

Feelings of pride based on self-serving or materialistic gains work fine when the winds of fortune blow favorably, but they disappear as soon as storm clouds gather. On the other hand, an intrinsic feeling of pride based on the relentless pursuit of endeavors that matter for enterprise success is a lasting and powerful motivating force. It is an institution-building form of pride.

Institution-building pride is based on largely intangible values and basic human emotions, rather than tangible compensation and crystal-clear logic. It is the most important motivational element in a company for several reasons, including:

- Institutional pride stems not just from achievement, but from the *anticipation* of achievement. Pride is more than an emotion that people experience only when they do something well. The U.S. Marine Corps, for example, has sustained their remarkable culture and 200-plus year record of winning critical battles for their country on a very simple insight: Be proud of doing the right thing in the right way for the right reason. It is a Marine's definition of courage. Yet, most Marines wait several years before an actual battle experience. Their pride is based on always being prepared to do the right thing when it counts.
- What is required to instill institution-building pride is mostly teachable. It is not simply a matter of experience or instinct. The attitudes, approaches, and disciplines that instill pride comprise a managerial capability that can be made as fundamental as managing by the numbers.
- Institutional pride is based on a self-reinforcing cycle, in which workforce performance builds on business success, that feeds back into workforce performance. The powerful "closed-loop of energy" links pride to workforce performance and business success. Each element in the loop feeds on the others in a mutually re-enforcing cycle that results in higher and higher levels of business performance over time.

Motivating Pride: The View from the Top and from the Frontline

Before going on to describe how to build pride, it is important to recognize that the factors that motivate pride differ between top managers and frontline employees. At the very least, they rely on different words and mental images.

The top levels of any organization are made up of people well schooled in the fundamentals of business economics, competitive dynamics, market share, and global positioning. Broad economic and market factors are more directly related to what upper-level managers are responsible for and not related to what they are paid. Hence, they take pride in applying and measuring against those standards.

It is an oversimplification to argue that managers and executives are motivated by logic rather than emotion. Emotion plays a role in motivation at every level of an enterprise, as does logic. Nonetheless, rational factors like those mentioned previously are more likely to influence the managerial and executive ranks of a company who understand the economic and market forces and see them as relevant to decisions and actions they must take.

Simple emotional factors drawn from local situations become more important to lower-level employees, and actually tend to dominate among the highest performing workers. These factors include:

- What do my friends and family think about my company?
- What do people I know think about the products and services I make?
- How do the customers whom I serve (personally or directly) regard the usefulness and value of what I do?
- Do I respect the skills, values, and behaviors of the people whom I work with most closely?
- Do people whom I work with and admire respect what I do and how I do it?
- Are we winning against the competitors I know because of what I do?

Do's and Don'ts of Pride-Building

While there are many potential sources of institutional pride, and no magic formula for instilling it, practical experience has yielded a portfolio of techniques that have worked for the pride-builders in a wide range of organizations. These techniques fall into four fundamental themes that we discuss next.

1. Always Have Your Compass Set on Pride

The objective of pride-building is to achieve emotional commitment rather than rational compliance. That is why successful pride-builders ensure that their corporate compass always points to pride. In other words, they never lose sight of the need to instill pride. They are continually working to foster pride among people based on the activities they are engaged in every day. Most importantly, they do not wait on achieving major, breakthrough goals.

Some of the more useful techniques they pursue include the following:

- *Clarify exactly what matters and why it matters.* Employees need to understand what is important about their job—and why it matters for them to excel at the little as well as the big things. Real change leaders employ visions that touch people's emotions as well as capture compelling images of the destinations being pursued. These are *working visions*—a picture that can be envisioned by the typical employee.
- *Stimulate people's memories, both real and vicarious.* Since people can seldom feel the pride of arrival at the beginning of a difficult journey, it is critical for them to remember what it will feel like and keep that feeling in mind along the way. Recalling their own experience along earlier successful journeys, or vicariously relating to the analogous experiences of others can be extremely motivating.
- *Celebrate the "steps" as much as the "landings."* Instill pride in the little things, one step at a time, as well as in the major accomplishments. Tom Peters and Robert Waterman reminded us all of the importance of "early wins" in achieving "excellence."[1] Celebrating an early, seemingly not so significant, "win" has the same effect on adults that cooking and eating the first fish she ever caught has on your five-year-old daughter.

- *Focus on "containers" that are never empty/never full.* Michael Jordan and Tiger Woods are sports examples of this philosophy. Neither of them is ever content with a victory that most of us would regard as "the ultimate dream." Conversely, neither of them ever sees a loss as a disaster.

2. *Pride-Building Starts in Your Own Backyard*

Despite the impressive leadership systems that characterize peak performance organizations, it is apparent that the best efforts to instill pride are localized. They stem from frontline managers who know their people, their market situation, and the practical realities of their work environment.

While local circumstances vary, a few techniques are worth emphasizing:

- *Tap into family, community, and union events.* Pride-builders invariably go outside the workplace to find sources of pride that will be relevant to the workplace. Hector de Hoyos in Ramos, Mexico, deliberately reinforces the connection between GM and employees' families through Christmas parties and a summer camp for everyone. He draws on the values and attitudes that matter to the people who work at his plant. For example, he points out that "mothers matter most in Mexican culture." During summer vacations, the plant hosts a day camp for wives and children with daily educational activities, entertainment, and daycare for small children.
- *Trigger the "anticipation" of local pride.* When you are trying to instill pride in future performance, it is much easier to get your people to anticipate those motivational feelings by drawing on experiences and heroes that are local and well known to your people. Triggering feelings of pride that must anticipate future performance is easier to do when the trigger mechanisms are familiar and credible.

3. *Turn a Complex Idea into a Simple Message*

The more diverse and dynamic the activities, the more important it is to have two or three themes that can tie it all together. It is important to integrate multiple sources of pride around a few simple messages. A couple of techniques that have proven successful are worth mentioning here:

- *Develop and repeat your most compelling stories.* People seldom tire of good stories that stir up feelings of pride. Pride-builders find ways to stimulate people's memories of prideful experiences and their desire to repeat the experience.
- *Seek out "leading indicators" to simplify and sequence your task.* All of us like to be sure that we are covering all the bases, but remember the old adage: "Keep it simple, stupid." When confronted with a comprehensive framework designed by some consultant and promulgated by top management, the best pride-builder invariably "cuts it down to size." If several

metrics and priorities are involved, the pride-builder will pick one or two to emphasize for his or her people.

4. Avoid the Common Pitfalls

The techniques described above are the staple of pride-builders. It is important to take a look at the mistakes of "pride-eroders" and avoid them:

- *Don't inadvertently break up a winning team.* The planned rapid rotation of leaders who are on the fast track is a characteristic of many companies. Few recognize the negative impact of this kind of rotation on the motivation, trust, and commitment of the workers. Without consistent continuity across these leadership transitions, the pride that one leader instills can be lost. An aligned leadership team that remains at the helm during the transition can make a huge difference.
- *Rules can't always be rules.* Equally as frustrating as the rapid rotation of leaders is the across-the-board enforcement of top-down methodologies or arbitrary insistence on "consistency" across diverse units. These practices often constrain local flexibility. While a clear vision and strategy are essential, leadership mandates that inhibit local initiative and flexibility are likely to work against balanced pride over time. Even focused performance metrics require local interpretation and adjustment to fit the realities of different competitive situations and work environments. Like the Marines, you want to create self-discipline around the leadership intent, not mindless adherence to a set of inflexible rules.
- *You can't buy pride.* A common pitfall, of course, is over-relying on monetary incentives. The time-honored focus on stock ownership as a primary motivational tool works only when things are rosy. When the ship hits rough waters, stock values only distract the broad base of employees. What workers do in their everyday jobs seldom reflects itself directly in stock performance. While compensation and stock opportunity can provide important "attraction and retention" value, you need to look well beyond financial incentives to take advantage of the motivational power of pride.

Conclusion

One of the greatest challenges for managers has been to inspire the workforce to identify with its organization and make its raison d'être its own. Inspiring pride is part art, but it is also part science. Granted, it is a largely underdeveloped science.

The most commanding form of pride is the kind that is hard to express, in dollars and cents, or sometimes even in words. As much as anything, it is a feeling in our guts. It is the feeling we get when our spouse asks what we did at work that day, or when our children ask us to speak to their class on career day. It is the feeling we get when we see the product of our labor and come face-to-face with the people who benefit from it.

For a corporation that seeks to lead in the 21st century, pride is a form of investment currency, and it is one that is growing in importance. The challenge is to capture its value, deploy its power, and multiply its benefits throughout the organization.

CHAPTER 8

Leveraging HR

How to Develop Leaders in "Real Time"

LINDA SHARKEY

W E HAVE KNOWN for many years (through a variety of research projects, such as those conducted by James Kouzes and Barry Posner, at the Center for Creative Leadership, and Chris Argyris) that leadership is not primarily learned in the classroom—it is learned on the job.[1] Action learning, feedback, and coaching have all been used to help leaders develop through practical experience. Individuals can become better leaders by facing challenges and learning from their experiences. In fact, most leaders prefer to learn in "real time," in the business setting, rather than in a classroom. From reading leadership literature, we also know that when discussing their leadership journeys, leaders will very often cite a strong mentor or coach as a key component of their personal development.

Many successful leaders *understand* that coaching and feedback are important. They know how meaningful it was to them in their career growth. Though leaders understand the importance of coaching and feedback, they often don't do a great job of providing coaching and feedback themselves. Reviews of 360° feedback summaries from major corporations almost always indicate that "provides effective coaching and feedback" is one of the lower-rated items for most managers. With the demands of today's workplace and the global nature of today's workforce, many managers do not feel they can find the time to provide effective coaching.

What can organizations do to help managers get and give the coaching they and their teams need? One answer is to hire external coaches. However, organizations usually hire external coaches for individuals with uncommonly difficult interpersonal challenges. External coaches are often reserved for the most challenging cases and not used to help "good talent" get better. External coaches can be costly, and few organizations can afford to provide this service to "next generation" leaders. Additionally, it is difficult to document and measure the impact that external coaches have on the effectiveness of leaders over a sustained period of time. Another approach is to build coaching into the culture of the organization by developing internal coaching capability. And, who better to be coaches than HR professionals? Who better to get coaching from than those who see you in your daily work context? This is precisely what General Electric Financial Services decided to do.

Developing HR Coaches at General Electric Financial Services

At General Electric Financial Services, we tapped into three key competencies: (1) our fierce focus on growing top-notch leaders, (2) our solid human resource expertise, and (3) our learning culture. With these ingredients, it seemed natural to use the organization's HR professionals to develop leaders in "real time" and in their own context. We believe that as our fast-paced business environment becomes increasingly global, coaching must be provided in the cultural context of the organization and the locality. We developed a process that enabled leaders to coach others within their organization and (because HR professionals are essential players in keeping the corporate culture) obtain personal coaching from the HR community. Our process utilized a proven model for coaching. It also provided a framework for HR professionals to use in coaching others and in teaching others how to coach.

Developing the Need and Creating the Buy-In

General Electric Financial Services has long focused on growing its leaders. One of our leadership development activities is an experience for executive talent called the Executive Leadership Development Symposium (ELDS). This is an opportunity for leadership talent to attend a weeklong event that assists them in continuing to develop their leadership skills in preparation for their next career move. The symposium gives participants time to spend on their leadership development needs. They receive feedback through a number of survey instruments, and they are assigned a personal coach who works with them throughout the week. Each coach is assigned a team of participants. The coach holds one-on-one meetings with each team member, observes team behaviors and dynamics, and provides team feedback. Originally, we used coaches who were external to General Electric Financial Services, but participant comments about the coaches were less than positive. Then, we tried an experiment. With the next group, we used internal senior human resource managers (HRMs) as coaches, and we received great feedback. The HRMs loved the experience, and the coaching was seen as extremely helpful. When we followed up with the ELDS participants three months after the program, we asked them what additional support they would need to continue on their leadership journey. The answer was more coaching and a solid method for them to coach others. Bingo! The door was open to take leadership development to the next level and to continue to leverage HR in the process.

What We Did

Behavioral change expert Marshall Goldsmith and I spent time talking about an approach. Outside coaching was not an option for us. The experience of using our HR talent as coaches in ELDS was so powerful that we wanted to build on that success. I contacted the HRMs to see who was interested in continuing to coach on an ongoing basis. The response was overwhelming. The HRM's experience of the process was as positive as their coachees'.

We devised an approach that would teach the Behavioral Coaching Model to our senior HR managers and also prepare them to apply the model with our ELDS grads (see Figure 8.1). We modified the model to focus on two key issues: (1) getting personal coaching and (2) teaching others how to coach. Additionally, there is the supposition that to be a good coach you can benefit from the personal experience of being coached yourself. With that philosophy in mind, we designed a half-day seminar during which senior HR managers learn the model and also provide coaching to each other. They loved the approach.

Another powerful component of the model and its approach is that the coachees, rather than a manager or the coach, have total control over the issue on which they wanted to work. Research that supports this approach is very clear. Successful people are much more likely to change when they are involved in the change process and "buy in" to the behaviors that they choose to change. The coachees like the model because it is simple, easy to use, and very time efficient.

Next, the ELDS graduates attended a one-day "Best-Practice Forum" on coaching. With the HRMs leading the coaching process, coaching triads were built into the forum. The HRMs helped the triads on two levels: (1) providing and modeling coaching using the process and (2) helping the triad plan how to use the process to coach others in their business. The response was terrific, and, by popular demand, we ran the forum again in Europe using the same approach. The two-pronged model is illustrated in Figure 8.2.

At this juncture, it was clear that there was a strong desire for coaching and that HR saw this as a critical competency for serving their clients. The challenge was to spread this process further in our organization. With Marshall's permission, we developed a train-the-trainer program for HR professionals and rolled it out worldwide. We began incorporating the model into our leadership programs and using HR people consistently as coaches. The approach is now widely used throughout our businesses.

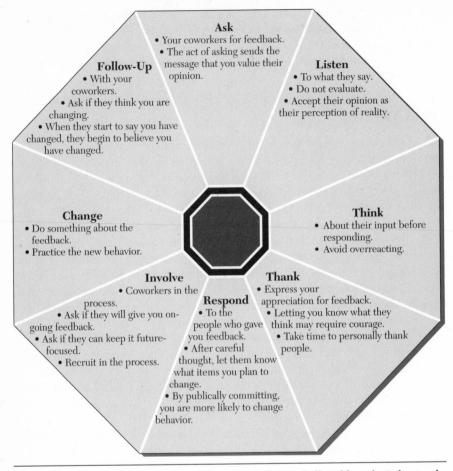

FIGURE 8.1   THE Behavioral Coaching Model. Marshall Goldsmith, Behavioral Coaching Model, 2002. Used with permission.

The Results

What were the results? We decided to use the mini-survey methodology (again designed by Marshall) to see if we were documenting consistent improvements. First, let me explain the mini-survey process. Three months after a coachee identifies a behavior to improve and goes through the steps of the model with a coach, he or she then follows up with five to seven people who can provide feedback on his or her behavioral change. The survey is completed electronically, similar to a full 360° assessment, but applies to only the one or two specific behaviors selected by the coachee. We devised a way to administer this mini-survey internally: Two weeks prior to sending out the survey, we notify

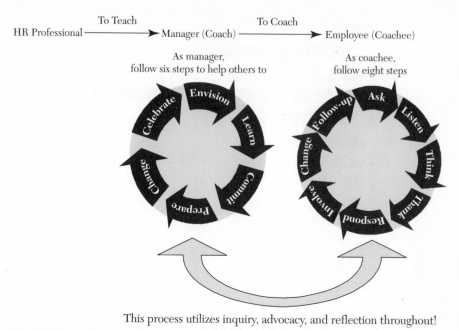

To Teach

To Coach

HR Professional ──────────► Manager (Coach) ──────────► Employee (Coachee)

As manager,
follow six steps to help others to

As coachee,
follow eight steps

This process utilizes inquiry, advocacy, and reflection throughout!

FIGURE 8.2   Behavioral Coaching: The Process

the coachee that the survey will be sent out. Unless we hear otherwise, we then send the survey to those who have been designated by the coachee. Once the surveys are completed and tabulated, the results are sent to coachees. The coachees then have specific data on the degree of their improvement. The first round of mini-surveys showed a great success: We had a 99 percent improvement rate. Building on this experience, we incorporated this approach into our leadership development process.

Figures 8.3 and 8.4 illustrate that we consistently showed leadership skill improvements in the three years that we have been using this process. (The mini-surveys use a −3 to +3 scale to measure improvement, with 0 indicating no change.)

Our other observation is that *follow-up* is key to improvement. As part of the behavior change process, coachees were instructed to discuss what they wanted to change with their preselected coworkers. They were asked to follow up with coaches and coworkers to get ongoing progress reports on how they were doing (as well as suggestions for further improvement), and Figures 8.5 through 8.9 on pages 74–76 show the degree to which the coachees followed up with their coaches and selected coworkers. The follow-up rate correlates strongly with the coachee's degree of improvement—another key element of success.

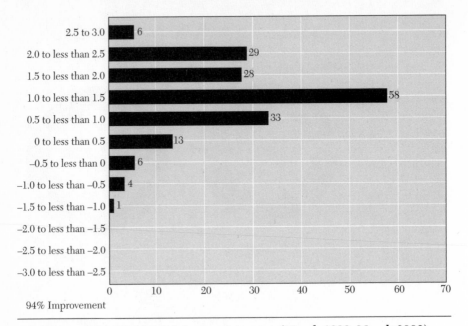

2.5 to 3.0	6
2.0 to less than 2.5	29
1.5 to less than 2.0	28
1.0 to less than 1.5	58
0.5 to less than 1.0	33
0 to less than 0.5	13
−0.5 to less than 0	6
−1.0 to less than −0.5	4
−1.5 to less than −1.0	1
−2.0 to less than −1.5	
−2.5 to less than −2.0	
−3.0 to less than −2.5	

94% Improvement

Figure 8.3　ELDS Mini-Survey Summary (March 1999–March 2002)

As you can see from Figure 8.5, coachees who did no perceptible follow-up showed little more improvement than random chance. Even a little follow-up produced a clear positive trend. Note that 20 percent of the coachees were seen as improving at the +2 to +3 level.

Participants who were credited with some follow-up showed a clear positive trend. Over 38 percent were rated in the +2 to +3 categories. This is nearly double the percentage in these categories when compared to "little follow-up."

Participants who were seen as engaging in frequent follow-up were rated as clearly increasing their effectiveness in selected areas for improvement. Over 74 percent of raters scored them at the +2 or +3 level.

Participants who were seen as consistently (or periodically) following up were rated as dramatically increasing in effectiveness. Over half were seen as improving at the +3 level.

Next Generation

Realizing the power of internally applied coaching, we decided that an organization-wide 360° process would further support our efforts to keep our managers on the top of their leadership game. A consistent 360° process was launched for our leaders starting at the top of the company and spanning around

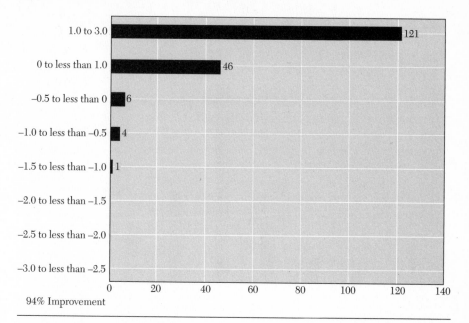

the world. Here again, we leveraged our HR community to drive the process and provide coaching. However, a unique twist was added. We provided all our leaders with a list of HR professionals from which they could choose their coach. Having the leader *select* the coach is another way that we built *ownership* into the process. Each leader selected a coach and spent time "ebriefing" their 360° feedback with him or her and, in many cases, with his or her direct reports who also went through the 360° feedback process. This was a massive effort, but proved to be very useful. We now have solid data on which to continue to drive our leadership efforts, and we have our key global players aligned with an internal coach to work on personal development. This will go a long way to help build open organizations in which people in the organization see helping others improve and grow through feedback and coaching as part of their job.

This data from the global 360° feedback process has provided another platform to continue to leverage HR at a strategic level within the organization. Because all of our leadership teams participated in the 360° survey feedback process, they now work as teams to help each other improve. When the leadership teams share their development needs with each other and use the coaching model, they often find three things: (1) they have similar issues, (2) they get great improvement suggestions from each other, and (3) they get support from

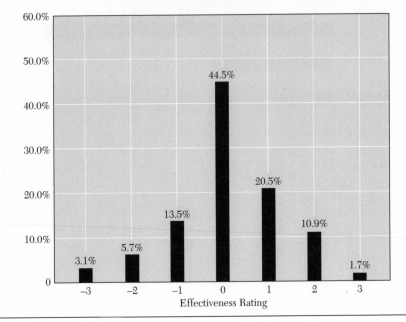

FIGURE 8.5   No Perceptible Follow-Up

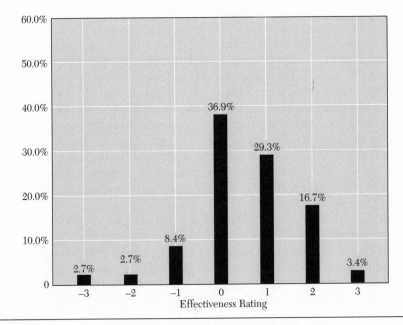

FIGURE 8.6   Little Follow-Up

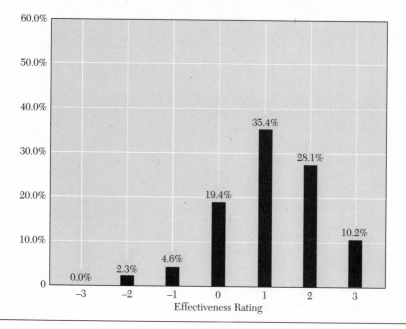

FIGURE 8.7   Some Follow-Up

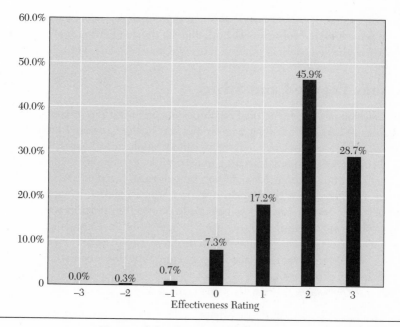

FIGURE 8.8   Frequent Follow-Up

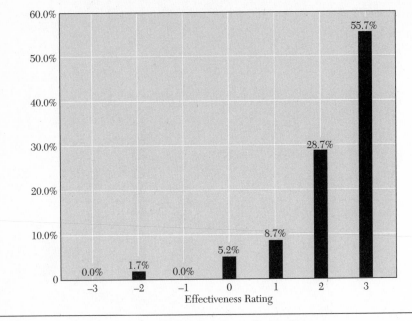

FIGURE 8.9   Consistent (Periodic) Follow-Up

each other to improve. Human resource professionals played a key role in driving this approach. HR professionals both taught the teams the approach and led them through the coaching process. This was another clear win.

Lessons Learned and Advice

HR professionals can be critical resources for organizations as they continue to globalize. While HR has long been important in the General Electric culture, there is no reason that our learnings cannot apply to other organizations. In global companies, the need to drive consistent leadership behaviors and organizational culture will be critical. Who else can raise the tough issues relative to culture and people but the human resource professional? Leveraging HR to be the corporate conscience and to help raise personal leadership issues will continue to be essential in the 21st century. Leadership development can't be confined to the classroom. It must also be "real time" in the day-to-day work experience. Who better to be the beacons for raising leadership development issues than HR professionals?

In our experience, there were some critical lessons learned:

1. Use a consistent 360° assessment tool across your business that accurately reflects the leadership behaviors required for success.

2. Link coaching to the 360° process to ensure that actions are taken beyond the usual action plan.
3. Use your internal human resource professionals as coaches.
4. Ensure confidentiality of your HR coaches.
5. Drive an internal follow-up process through the mini-survey approach.
6. Cascade the 360° assessment and coaching model through the organization.
7. Make sure each HR professional has coaching responsibility for his or her teams.

CHAPTER 9

Strategic HRM Measurement

From Justifying HR to Strategic Talent Leadership

JOHN W. BOUDREAU AND PETER RAMSTAD

"NOT EVERYTHING THAT can be counted counts, and not everything that counts can be counted." Albert Einstein.

The beginning of the 21st century reveals both the promise and the curse of human resource management (HRM) measurement. The good news is that the accounting and management professions recognize that traditional corporate measurement systems must be enhanced to account for intangibles in a knowledge-based economy.[1] Greater corporate accountability for human and intellectual capital is now a constant drumbeat.[2] Concepts, such as *knowledge, intellect, creativity, innovation, capabilities, commitment,* and even *fun,* have become part of the language of business in strategy, finance, operations, and marketing. People issues are "at the table." In other words, tough questions from shareholders, investment analysts, communities, employment candidates, and employees are answered. Questions such as:

- Is decreasing cost-per-hire good or are we tapping pools of less-desirable applicants who are easier to attract?
- If our employees complete 40 hours of training per year, are we building essential capabilities or just filling seats in classes?
- Do we have the talent needed to succeed?

Organizations must increasingly demonstrate, with data, that their human resource strategies significantly enhance competitive advantage, not simply that they are efficient or "best-in-class."

This unprecedented attention to human capital has been matched by an explosion of human capital data and measurement approaches. HR information systems accelerate the trend, continually lowering the cost and increasing the speed of data storage and delivery. It is now quite feasible to obtain hundreds of human capital measures in an eye blink and to conduct equally dizzying "cuts" and trends. Individual managers can choose to examine everything from head-count to the number of resumes received, from turnover to employee attitudes, broken down by division, time, region, or diversity category. The managers can then customize the information in any way they wish, often 24-hours-a-day, through a Web portal. As one manager jokingly remarked to us, "Our future data systems can analyze employee satisfaction by eye color if we wanted . . . but why would anyone want to?"

The potential bad news is that the explosion of measurement technologies and HRM data poses a significant risk: information overload, naivete, and unmet expectations could stifle the 21st-century evolution of the HRM profession before it begins. This dilemma is not intractable, but it is obviously not solved by developing more measures. The problem is more fundamental. This next evolutionary stage for HR is to develop a true decision science for talent, built on today's HRM professional practices.[3] In this chapter, we suggest the implications of such a decision science for HR measures.

Measures Must Support *Talentship:* A Decision Science for Talent

There are at least three markets that firms must compete within to be success-ful: the capital market, the customer/product market, and the talent market. Each of these markets has a wealth of measures associated with it. However, in each of the other markets, there is a clear distinction between the professional practices associated with the market and the decision science that supports it. Within the capital markets, the decision science tools of finance support the practices of accounting. Likewise, the decision science of marketing augments and supports the professional practice of sales. As we have noted, HR has a rich set of professional practices, but lacks a decision science.[4] We have proposed that now is the right time for such a science to emerge, and we call the new sci-ence *talentship*.

What does a decision science do? It provides a logical, reliable, and consistent—but flexible—framework that enhances decisions about a key resource, wher-ever those decisions are made. A decision science does not rigidly prescribe actions, but rather it provides a system to guide, identify, analyze, and enhance key decisions.[5] A decision science has particular implications for information systems and measurement techniques.

Consider the decision science of finance, perhaps the most pervasive organi-zational framework. The Dupont model we are familiar with today emerged in the early 1900s. It used the data from accounting processes and provided a frame-work to allocate financial capital to diverse business units using more than the traditional accounting measure of profit. This decision framework showed that business units with lower profit margins could easily have higher returns on invested capital, and it showed how business units could improve their return on capital even without increasing profit margins. Making decisions by allocating financial resources to the areas of highest return on investment, not necessarily the areas of highest profit, was revealed as a superior way to use financial capital for strategic success. Marketing is similar. Customer segmentation, for example, is a 20th-century development that allowed organizations to allocate their resources not just equally to all customers, or to the customers with the highest sales, but to the customers with the greatest impact on the organization's competitive success.

Thus, finance creates organizational value by enhancing decisions that depend on or impact *financial* resources. Marketing creates organizational value by enhancing decisions that depend on or impact customer or product resources. Finance and marketing provide reliable and deeply logical frameworks that show how financial and customer capital connect to sustainable strategic success for the organization (i.e., frameworks that support *strategic decisions* about financial and customer capital). Paradoxically, the most important decisions were *outside the profession itself.* Managers, employees, shareholders, and others learned how to reliably and consistently improve *their own decisions about the financial and customer resources wherever they are made.* Finance and marketing provide a "teachable point of view,"[6] and they are ultimately evaluated not so much by the quality of their programs, or even by the quality of their measures, as by the quality of decisions about financial or customer resources throughout the organization. Accounting and sales measures are inextricably linked with these decision sciences. The decision science asks key questions that challenge existing measures. This produces better measures, which lead to better decisions and more sophisticated questions. This synergy is not built by measurement or science alone; it is built through measures that reflect a powerful and consistent logic and vice versa.

For example, the accounting systems are powerful because they provide a decision framework for the accounting data, a framework that guides and enhances the quality of decisions that affect financial capital. Most of these decisions are made by leaders who are not in the accounting department. HR will never have measures that are equally significant so long as they focus on the activities or benefits of the HR function or programs. To be strategically significant, they must focus on and help improve talent decisions *wherever* they are made.

The contrast between the markets that have a decision science and HR is striking when you consider the rapid rise of information technology. The explosion of the Internet and information technology has had much deeper impact in finance and marketing, because it was accelerated by sophisticated decision frameworks. The logic of customer segmentation now allows organizations to tailor products and services (even specific service encounters) to specific individual needs. The logic of global currency trading has created financial markets today that adjust to arbitrage opportunities virtually instantly, making markets much more efficient. By comparison, information technology applied to HRM has resulted in significant efficiencies and enticing Web-portal interfaces. Yet, the promise of such things as "mass-customization" in rewards and remuneration, or the evolution of a true talent relations management system to rival the customer relations management systems of marketing, has been largely unfulfilled. The emergence of a talent decision science is a key to unlocking the potential of information technology in HRM.[7]

The lessons of marketing and finance teach us that the goal of a talent decision science should be *to increase the success of the organization by improving decisions that impact or depend on talent resources.* Decision support is different from professional practice. It means shifting the primary focus from "providing practices, programs, and services," toward "supporting strategic talent decisions." It is a key requirement for HR professionals to achieve true strategic impact and a useful touchstone in charting the future of HRM measurement. We have coined the term *talentship* to describe the new decision science.

Decisions: The Key to Strategic HRM Measurement

It is common to assess HR customer satisfaction by asking key decision makers if they like the HR measures, or if the measures seem "businesslike." It would seem ludicrous to assess the financial analysis framework by asking whether business leaders liked it. The finance decision system is so logically connected to key organizational outcomes and so able to improve important decisions about financial resources that it is accepted, even when its message is unpleasant. The key consideration in any human capital measurement system is its ability to *enhance decisions* by articulating the logical connection between talent and organizational outcomes. Measurement is an essential building block of such a decision framework. The explosion of HR measures is a necessary condition for developing talentship, but today's measures often lack a logical framework that articulates the key connections between talent decisions and organizational strategic success.

For example, Sears, Roebuck & Co.[8] adopted a relatively simple model of the retail value chain (i.e., making Sears a compelling place to work will affect store associates' behaviors, who will then create a compelling place to shop, which will affect customer spending patterns, which will create a compelling place to invest) that guided the choice and interpretation of hundreds of measures combining attitudes, employee behaviors, customer satisfaction, and financial success. Many of the measurements had existed for years, even decades, but were never linked in a compelling way until a clear mental model was established.

The HC BRidge™ Framework

We use the metaphor of a bridge to describe the linking elements between investments in HRM programs and sustainable strategic success. The HC BRidge™ Framework (a trademark of the Boudreau-Ramsted Partnership) is also useful for analyzing HRM measures (Figure 9.1).[9]

We chose impact, effectiveness, and efficiency as the anchor points, because they are key components in virtually all highly developed business decision sciences, and most measurement systems strive to address them. With regard to talent, they can be framed in terms of three key questions:

1. Impact asks, "What is the relationship between the changes in the quality of the talent pools and our competitive success?" We find that most HR research and systems focus on the average value of talent, with questions such as "Is the contribution of this talent important?" However, it is often the change or difference in talent quality that is significant. In the HC BRidge™ Framework, we call roles with high impact "pivotal roles," to capture this idea.

2. Effectiveness asks, "What is the relationship between our HR practices and the quality of our talent pools?" This includes how HR programs affect capability (Can employees contribute?), opportunity (Do employees

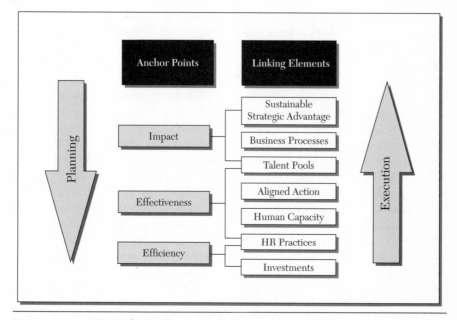

FIGURE 9.1   HC BRidge™ Framework. Copyright © 1999 by Boudreau and Ramstad (PDI). All rights reserved.

get the chance to contribute?), and motivation (Do employees want to contribute?), which are the elements of "Human Capacity" in Figure 9.1.

3. Efficiency asks, "What is the level and quality of HR practices that we produce from the resources that we spend?" Figure 9.1 shows that there are linking elements within each of these anchor points that further define the connections between HRM investments and strategic success.[10] Each linking element can be used to define HRM measures.

In this chapter, we focus on the broader anchor points to map today's measures and then those of the future.

Today's HR Measurement Options

Table 9.1 shows four key categories and examples of today's HR measurements that will help us illustrate the state of today's HR measures.[11] The last two columns of the table describe the primary appeal of each category of measures and the "tough questions" that reveal potential limitations or assumptions of each method.

HRM Operations: Measuring Efficiency

The first category, or row, describes measures focused on *efficiency*. These measures are usually expressed in *input-output* ratios such as the time-to-fill vacancies, turnover rates, turnover costs, and compensation budgets compared to total expenses.[12] These approaches are compelling because they connect HR processes to accounting outcomes (dollars), and also because they can show that HR operations achieve visible cost reductions, particularly when compared to other organizations. They are frequently a significant motivator for HR outsourcing. Many applications of Six Sigma to HR focus on such measures to detect opportunities to improve costs or speed. One of the major limitations of these types of measures is that they are not really HR measures at all. Rather they are efficiency ratios that can be used to monitor overhead costs in nearly any staff function. As a result, efficiency-focused systems can omit the *value of talent*. Fixating on cost reduction can reject more expensive decision options that are the better value. For example, cost-per-hire can be reduced by cutting the number of selection activities, but this may well reduce validity and subsequent workforce quality. Efficiency-based measures alone, no matter how "financially" compelling, cannot reflect talent value. Finally, they focus almost exclusively on the HR function, and not the decisions made within the rest of the organization.

Measuring Effectiveness: Demonstrating the Effects of HR Practices

The next category, "HR activity and best practice indexes," directly measures the association between the reported existence of human resource activities

TABLE 9.1   HR Measurement Alternatives

Measurement Approach	Example Measures	Primary Appeal	Tough Questions
Efficiency of HRM operations.	Cost-per-hire, time-to-fill, training costs, ratio of HR staff to total employees.	Explicit currency-value calculations. Logic of cost-savings is easy to relate to accounting. Standardization makes benchmarking comparisons easier.	"Wouldn't outsourcing cut costs even more?" "Do these cost savings come at the price of workforce value?" "Why should our costs be the same as the industry?"
HR activity, "best practice" indexes.	Human capital benchmarks, human capital index.	HR practices are associated with familiar financial outcomes. Data from many organizations lends credibility. Suggests there may be practices or combinations that generally raise profits or sales, and so on.	"What is the logic connecting these activities with such huge financial effects?" "Will the practices that worked in other organizations necessarily work in ours?" "Does having these practices mean they are implemented well?"
HR dashboard or HR scorecard.	How the organization or HR function meets goals of "customers, financial markets, operational excellence, and learning."	Vast array of HR measures can be categorized. "Balanced Scorecard" concept is known to business leaders. Software allows users to customize analysis.	"Can this scorecard prove a connection between people and strategic outcomes?" "Which numbers and drill-downs are most critical to our success?"
Causal chain.	Models link employee attitudes to service behavior to customer responses to profit.	Useful logic linking employee variables to financial outcomes. Valuable for organizing and analyzing diverse data elements.	"Is this the best path from talent to profits?" "How do our HR practices work together?" "What logic can we use to find more connections like this?"

(such as merit pay, teams, valid selection, and training) and changes in financial outcomes (such as profits and shareholder value creation).[13] In terms of the model, this approach attempts to directly associate two linking elements, HR practices and financial measures of strategic success. Some results show strikingly strong associations between certain HR activities and financial outcomes, which has been used to justify investments in those activities. However, most existing research cannot prove that investing in HR activities *causes* superior financial outcomes.[14] Another limitation of such measures is that they use one description of HR practices to represent an entire organization, yet HR practices vary significantly across divisions, geographic locations, and so on. This may partly explain why managers in an organization might inconsistently report HRM practices. Also, such systems typically only measure the existence of practices, but not if such practices are implemented well.[15] Even when there is an actual relationship, simply duplicating others' best practices may fail to differentiate the organization's competitive position.

These limitations can be illustrated with an analogy to advertising. It is quite likely that studies would show an association between financial performance and the presence of television advertising activity, perhaps even that advertising activity rises before financial outcomes rise. This would suggest that among organizations that compete with advertising, advertising decisions relate to financial outcomes. Would it mean that every organization should advertise on television? Obviously not.

Thus, these approaches shed some valuable light on the important question of whether HR activities relate to financial outcomes, and they have made important contributions to HRM research. However, even their strongest advocates agree that they do not measure the connections that explain why HRM practices might associate with financial outcomes, and they do not reflect other key elements of strategic success. Because they focus on large publicly traded companies, they may also fail to reflect different strategic environments. In terms of the HC BRidge™ Framework, they leave unanswered whether and how groups of employees significantly affect key processes and outcomes.

HR Scorecards

The third category of Table 9.1 describes HR *scorecards* or *dashboards*. These are inspired by Kaplan and Norton who proposed adding measures of "customer" (such as customer satisfaction and market share); "internal processes" (such as cycle time, quality, and cost); and "learning and growth" (systems, organizational procedures, and people) to traditional financial measures.[16] HR scorecards include procedures designed to align and arrange measures into each of the four perspectives.[17] Such approaches tie HR measures to a compelling business concept and, in principle, can articulate links between HR measures and strategic or financial outcomes.

Today's scorecards or dashboards, built on data warehouses, allow users to "drill down" using a potentially huge array of variables customized to unique personal preferences. For example, HR training costs can conceivably be broken down by location, course, and diversity category, and then linked to attitudes, performance, and turnover. While impressive, in the hands of the unsophisticated, such approaches risk creating information overload, or, even worse, a false certainty about the connection between talent and strategic success. As Walker and MacDonald observed in describing the GTE/Verizon scorecard, "the measures taken in isolation can be misleading."[18] They describe one GTE/Verizon call center where, "when HR reviewed the call center results from the HR Scorecard . . . the HR metrics showed a very low cost per hire, a very quick cycle time to fill jobs, and an average employee separation rate . . . the staffing metrics showed a high efficiency and cost control." However, the call center accomplished this by "changing talent pools and reducing the invest-ments in selection methods [which] kept costs low while bringing in applicants who were ready to start quickly but were harder to train and keep . . . a bad tradeoff." GTE/Verizon was fortunate to have HR analysts who discovered this logic flaw, but the example shows that even the best scorecards and drill-down technology alone do not necessarily provide the logical framework users need to make the best talent decisions.

HR scorecards are often limited by relegating HR to measuring only the "learning and growth" category, or by applying the four categories only to the HR function, calculating HR-function "financials" (e.g., HR program budgets), "cus-tomers" (e.g., HR client satisfaction surveys), "operational efficiency" (e.g., the yield rates of recruitment sources), and "learning and growth" (e.g., the qualifi-cations of HR professionals). Both lead to measurement systems with little link to organizational outcomes.

When we work with scorecard designers, they note that the majority of scorecards measure only HR operations and activities, the elements of effi-ciency and effectiveness in Figure 9.1. Scorecards admirably draw attention to impact, but the actual measurement strategic logic is often superficial, such as linking the organizational goal of "speed to customers" with the HR scorecard measure "faster time-to-fill," or linking the strategic goal of "global integration" with the HR scorecard measure of "number of cross-region assignments com-pleted." Still, the scorecard design principle of connectedness has promise, as we shall see.

Causal Chains

The last category of Table 9.1 describes *causal-chain analysis,* which focuses on measuring the specific links between HRM programs or individual charac-teristics and business process or outcomes. For example, the large U.S. re-tailer, Sears, Roebuck & Co., used data to connect the attitudes of store associates, their on-the-job behaviors, the responses of store customers, and the revenue performance of the stores.[19] This measurement approach offers tangible data and frameworks that actually measure the intervening links be-tween human capacity (in this case, store associates' attitudes reflecting their commitment or motivation) and business outcomes (such as store revenues). In terms of the HC BRidge, causal-chain analysis comes closest to mapping all the linking elements.

The drawback is that all causal chains simplify reality. Yet, they are so com-pelling that they may motivate oversimplification. Finding that employee atti-tudes predict customer responses, organizations may invest heavily to maximize employee attitudes. Yet, at some point other factors (such as employee knowledge of products) become more important. Continuing to raise attitudes can actually be suboptimal, even if it still produces small additional changes in business outcomes. It's important to have a logical framework that can reveal the new paths as they emerge.

HRM Measurement in the 21st Century

Future HR measurement systems must be more than merely logical, attractive, or even valid and reliable. It will not be enough merely to demonstrate that HRM programs have good effects, after the fact. Future measures must tangibly improve decisions about the talent that most affects strategic success. Future HR information and measurement professionals should become experts at identifying key talent decisions and the needs of those who make them, not just creating, improving, and tracking the HR measures. The HR data warehouse team we worked with in one large multinational said, "We have built the most sophisticated turnover tracking data and interface in the world. Now, we'll put it out there and see what our managers do with it." Future HR professionals will more often start by analyzing how managers should use data and make decisions, and only then devise frameworks and systems that effectively improve them.

From Strategy Reflection to Strategy Integration

Today's HR measurement systems commonly reflect strategic or business outcomes, but do not integrate talent with them. For example, in organizations that must grow profits, HR measures efficient HR operations; the organization must embrace digitization, so HR measures the number of HR transactions on the Web; or the organization must increase solution-selling, so HR measures the amount of solution-selling pay bonuses for salespeople. Certainly, such measures reflect the strategic concepts, but true strategy integration requires identifying the "pivotal talent pools" that have the largest strategic effect, and then measuring the changes in their actions that "move the needle" on key processes. For example, salespeople do affect solution-selling, but often the key bottleneck is a lack of sufficient product integration to offer the solutions that customers want. No amount of salesperson bonus-payments can fix a lack of integration. Future HR measures will better identify such bottlenecks and how improving the talent that affects them enhances success all along the value chain.

From Outsourcing for Efficiency to Informed Collaboration for Impact

If trends continue, a legacy of the 21st century will be significantly greater HR outsourcing.[20] Paradoxically, the more HR is outsourced, the more important are the HR measures we describe here. Outsourcing contracts are governed by measures. If the contract stipulates cost-per-hire or number-of-employee-calls-handled, that is what will be delivered. Today, HR outsourcing contracts typically emphasize efficiency measures because they are the most measurable. However, measurement availability does not equal measurement usefulness. As we noted at the beginning of this chapter, "not everything that can be counted counts." Future HR measures will have to do better. In our work, we find that decision-based, strategy-connected measures redefine the nature of the outsourcing relationship from providing efficient services to collaborating for maximum impact. For example, the outsourcer becomes accountable for key process outcomes for which talent makes a big difference, and the client's HRM professionals become the designers of the unique and logical connections that identify and evolve the measures as conditions change. This is only one example we have seen, and this transition often requires an objective third party to help develop and ensure consistent and logical measurement frameworks to define the outsourcing collaboration.

Toward Organization Contribution and Transparency

The 21st century began with earthshaking events that have irreversibly reshaped the role of corporations, governments, and the employment relationship. We are entering an era when measuring profits, shareholder value, or even competitive success is insufficient. Emotions, global diversity, values, affiliation, significance, balance, meaning, and integrity are increasingly prominent organizational goals. Organizational leaders will increasingly be expected to provide greater transparency regarding the logic of their decisions. Accounting scandals such as Enron didn't occur because the numbers weren't there, but because analysts could not or did not hold decision makers accountable for explaining the connection between the measures, key business processes, and shareholder value. The principles we have described here are consistent with this new focus. A logical connection framework, such as the HC BRidge™, will articulate the key connections between talent and organizational success. As "strategic success" is redefined to include more constituents, "talent decision makers" will increasingly include employees, governments, communities, and families. As the objectives become ever more diverse, measures that articulate logic and support decisions become ever more important. Measurement will take us beyond simply justifying HR practices or making the HR function seem more businesslike. HR measurement will fulfill the promise of improving talent decisions throughout organizations, which was the ultimate goal of measurement in the first place.

CHAPTER 10

Human Resource Management and Business Performance

Lessons for the 21st Century

DAVID LEWIN

RECENT STUDIES OF human resource management (HRM) and business performance find that certain "high-involvement" HRM practices are, in research parlance, "significantly positively associated" with such measures as market value, rate of return on capital employed, revenue growth, revenue-per-employee, productivity, product/service quality, and even organizational survival.[1] This conclusion is at least partly global; data in the component studies are drawn from business entities in Europe, Asia, and Central America as well as North America.

While there is not complete agreement among researchers or practitioners about precisely what constitutes high-involvement HRM practices, the following are most often cited: employment security; targeted selection; workplace teams and decentralization; high pay contingent on organizational performance; employee training; reduction of status differentials; and business information-sharing with employees.[2] Often, such practices are said to reflect an HRM strategy of managing people as assets. From this perspective, expenditures on high-involvement type HRM practices should be considered investments in human capital that will (ultimately) yield net economic return (value added) to the entity making the investments.

Given this reasoning, as well as the aforementioned research evidence, we would expect most, if not all, business entities to have adopted high-involvement HRM practices, yet only about one of every eight businesses has done so.[3] Some businesses don't believe the evidence about positive effects of high-involvement HRM practices on business performance; some businesses adopt only one high-involvement type HRM practice; and still others adopt the full complement of

91

high-involvement type HRM practices, but abandon them after significant effects on business performance do not materialize in the short run. Alternatively, others contend that knowledge of the positive effects of high-involvement HRM practices on business performance is only slowly becoming known to business practitioners and is therefore in the early stage of diffusion.[4] This argument implies that rate of adoption of high-involvement type HRM practices by business entities will increase over time as these entities learn more about the positive effects of such practices.

A different line of reasoning, however, and the one advanced here, is that high-involvement HRM practices constitute only one way of managing human resources to enhance business performance. Another way of achieving this objective is to manage human resources as an expense that must be contained or reduced. For this purpose, "low-involvement" rather than high-involvement HRM practices fit best.

A Dual Theory of HRM and Business Performance

To frame this issue more sharply, consider that a business's workforce is comprised of two distinct segments, namely, a *core* and a *periphery*.[5] The core workforce consists of those who are employed full-time and paid a regular salary or wage. This workforce is covered by fringe benefits; they have training, development, and promotion opportunities along well-defined career paths; and they participate in decision making through organizational decentralization, workplace teams, and other arrangements. Typically, this core workforce is also carefully selected, has employment security, has some pay-at-risk dependent on the performance of the business or a unit thereof, and partakes in the sharing of business information. By contrast, the peripheral workforce consists of part-time, temporary, contract, vendored, and outsourced "employees" who are generally paid a fixed wage, salary, or, in the case of outsourced employees, a lump sum (project-based) cost; are partially or not at all covered by fringe benefits; have little or no training, development, promotion opportunities, involvement in decision making, pay at risk or employment security; and do not partake in the sharing of business information.[6] Recognizing that most businesses have both core and peripheral workforce segments helps to explain why businesses do not widely or uniformly adopt high-involvement type HRM practices. Further, while the core workforce may be managed primarily as an asset or investment (in human capital), the peripheral workforce is managed primarily as an expense (to be contained or reduced).

Herein lies the foundation of a "dual theory of HRM and business performance." Expenditures on the core workforce should (accounting conventions aside) be treated as an investment intended to increase the value added to the business by employees in this workforce segment. Expenditures on the peripheral workforce should (following accounting conventions) be treated as an expense that the business seeks to contain or reduce and, in this way, also add value to the business. In both instances, the optimization problem facing the business is maximizing the return, or value, over cost. In the ideal, both sets of HRM practices should result in larger profit margins (i.e., revenue less cost) than would occur by following conventional HRM practices in which there are few or no distinctions between core and peripheral employees. Empirical evidence that supports this dual theory of HRM and business performance is summarized in this chapter.

High-Involvement HRM Coverage of Core and Peripheral Employees

If the distinction between core and peripheral employees (and the HRM practices applied to them) is valid, then high-involvement HRM practices should be applied largely to the former, not the latter. A recent study of HRM and business performance that focuses on businesses' use of part-time, temporary, contract, vendored, and outsourced employees sheds light on this matter.[7] The multilevel samples for this study totaled 289 companies, 313 business units (of companies), 457 manufacturing plants, and 249 sales and service field offices of a national insurance company.[8] As shown in Table 10.1, high-involvement type HRM practices are used significantly more for core employees than for peripheral employees in these business entities. Indeed, among the eight high-involvement practices—employment continuity, selective hiring, training/development, teams/participation, variable pay, performance management, promotion opportunity, and business information sharing—that provided the basis for this comparison, each is far more widely used for core employees than for peripheral employees. Collectively, the use of this set of high-involvement HR practices is two-and-one-half times greater for core than for peripheral employees (with means of 4.1 and 1.5, respectively, for "all practices" on a 1 = low, 5 = high rating scale). Therefore, and despite the variation in usage of high-involvement HRM practices by the sampled businesses, these data support the proposition that peripheral employment is low-involvement employment—and that core employment is high-involvement employment.

Low-Involvement HRM Practices and Business Performance

This same study attempted to determine if low-involvement HRM practices (applied largely to peripheral employees) are significantly positively associated with business performance. For this purpose, an index of low-involvement work practices (LIWP) was constructed that measures the proportion of an organization's workforce consisting of part-time, temporary, and contract employees, as well as employees who have been placed with vendors and employees leased from outsourcing firms.[9] The data for determining the LIWP index score at a point in time, 1998, and changes in the score over time, 1995–1998, came from

TABLE 10.1   Extent of High-Involvement HRM Practice Usage among Core (C) and Peripheral (P) Employees, 1998 (Mean Values on a 1 = Low, 5 = High Scale)

Variable	Companies		Business Units		Manufacturing Plants		Sales and Service Field Offices		Total	
	C°	P°	C°	P°	C°	P°	C°	P°	C°	P°
Employment continuity	3.4	1.5	3.2	1.4	3.0	1.6	3.3	1.3	3.3	1.5
Selective hiring	4.3	1.7	4.4	1.8	4.2	1.8	4.1	1.4	4.3	1.6
Training/ development	3.9	1.4	4.0	1.5	3.8	1.3	4.2	1.6	4.0	1.4
Teams/ participation	4.2	1.3	4.3	1.4	4.0	1.6	3.8	1.3	4.1	1.4
Performance management	4.5	1.6	4.4	1.5	4.1	1.8	4.2	1.6	4.3	1.6
Promotion opportunity	3.9	1.2	4.2	1.4	3.6	1.2	3.8	1.3	3.9	1.3
Variable pay	4.6	1.4	4.5	1.3	4.2	1.3	4.5	1.7	4.5	1.4
Business information sharing	4.0	1.5	4.2	1.6	4.5	1.5	3.8	1.4	4.1	1.5
All practices	4.1	1.5	4.2	1.5	3.9	1.5	4.0	1.4	4.1	1.5
N =	289	289	313	313	457	457	249	249	1308	1308

° All differences between means within pairs of columns significant at $p = < .01$.

surveys administered to each company, business unit, manufacturing plant, and sales and service field office. Business performance data were obtained from secondary sources in the cases of the company and business unit samples, as well as from the surveys in the cases of the manufacturing plant and insurance company field office samples. The variation in performance among each of the four sets of business entities was then subjected to multivariate analysis in which the LIWP index served as the main independent variable and several control variables (as examples, organizational size, capital-labor ratio, and unionization) were also included.[10] The main findings from these regression analyses are summarized next.

For the company sample, the LIWP index is significantly positively associated with return on capital employed; market value; revenue per employee, in the cross-sectional or single-year analysis; and changes in each of these business performance measures in the longitudinal or multiyear analysis. These findings imply that a one standard deviation increase in the LIWP, or proportional peripheral employment, is associated with a statistically significant 1.5 percent increase in return on capital employed, a 2.7 percent increase in market value, and a 3.2 percent increase in revenue per employee. For the business unit sample, the LIWP index is significantly positively associated with return on capital employed and revenue per employee, both at a point in time and over time. These findings imply that a one standard deviation increase in the LIWP, or proportional peripheral employment, is associated with a statistically significant 2.2 percent increase in return on capital employed and a 4.1 percent increase in revenue per employee in these business units.

For the manufacturing plant sample, the LIWP index is significantly negatively associated with total labor cost as a proportion of total operating cost (LABORCOST) at a point in time and with the change in this operating performance measure over time. These findings imply that a one standard deviation increase in the LIWP, or proportional peripheral employment, is associated with a statistically significant 5.8 percent reduction in manufacturing plant labor cost as a proportion of total operating cost. Equally notable, the LIWP index is not significantly associated with productivity or product quality at a point in time or over time. In other words, and contrary to expectations, these manufacturing plants apparently do not experience lower productivity or product quality as a result of employing peripheral workers and managing them with low-involvement work practices.

For the insurance company field office sample, the LIWP index is significantly negatively associated with the ratio of payroll cost to sales revenue, both in the cross-sectional and longitudinal analyses. These findings imply that a one standard deviation increase in the LIWP, or proportional peripheral employment, is associated with a statistically significant 4.8 percent decrease in the ratio of payroll cost to sales revenue in these field offices. By contrast, the LIWP index is not significantly associated with revenue growth, quality of service, or customer satisfaction. Consequently, and again contrary to expectations, these insurance sales and service field offices apparently do not experience lower revenue growth, service quality, or customer satisfaction as a result of employing peripheral workers and managing them in a low-involvement fashion.

High-Involvement HRM Practices and Business Performance

Because high-involvement HRM researchers have generally ignored low-involvement HRM practices, this research on low-involvement HRM practices should not do the same in reverse. Consequently, a high-involvement work practice (HIWP) index consisting of the eight practices shown in Table 10.1 was constructed and measured for each company, business unit, and manufacturing plant included in this study. The insurance sales and service field offices were excluded, because high-involvement work practices in the insurance company are standardized across the entire organization and therefore do not vary among field offices. The main findings from analyzing relationships between the HIWP index and the various business performance measures for the three other samples of business entities are summarized next.

The HIWP index is significantly positively associated with long-run (that is, changes in) company financial performance, short- and long-run business unit financial performance, and short- and long-run manufacturing plant operating performance. These findings confirm the results of other studies showing that high-involvement HRM practices "leverage" business performance. More to the point, however, the LIWP index remains significantly positively associated with the various measures of business performance when these businesses' use of high-involvement HRM practices is taken into account. Therefore, low-involvement HRM practices can also be said to "leverage" business performance.

Cumulatively, these empirical findings provide strong support for a dual theory of HRM and business performance, especially because high-involvement and low-involvement HRM practices are typically used by a business simultaneously. To illustrate, among all the business entities included in this study ($n = 1308$), more than 95 percent reported having some peripheral employment (in 1998); such employment averaged about 32 percent of total employment. Among these businesses, the mean score on the HIWP index, which ranged from 8 to 40, was 25.5, and less than 5 percent of them had HIWP index scores of less than 15. Hence, most businesses make use of core employees to whom high-involvement HRM practices are applied and peripheral employees to whom low-involvement HRM practices are applied.[11] Both types of HRM practices have been shown here to "leverage" business performance, and the positive effects of low-involvement HRM practices on business performance are not vitiated when the effects of high-involvement HRM practices are considered. Thus, it is possible for a business to manage one segment of its workforce by investing in high-involvement HRM practices and obtaining net value added, and to manage another segment of its workforce through low-involvement HRM practices that serve to "add value" by containing or reducing labor expense.

Balancing Core and Peripheral Employment

In light of this conclusion, it is appropriate to ask, "Is there a proper or optimal balance of core and peripheral employment for a business?" To answer this question, additional multivariate analyses were undertaken in which the ratio of peripheral employment to total employment for each business entity in each of the four samples served as the dependent variable, and the various business performance measures served as independent variables—in effect, "reverse" regression analyses. (Control variables were also included in both sets of analyses.) The main findings from these analyses are summarized next.

Better performing companies, that is, those with relatively higher return on capital employed, market value, and revenue per employee, make greater use of peripheral employment than poorer performing companies, and also increase their use of peripheral employment significantly more than poorer performing companies. The same may be said for business units, that is, business units with relatively higher return on capital employed and revenue per employee make greater use of peripheral employment than poorer performing business units, and also increase their use of peripheral employment significantly more than poorer performing business units.

In the case of manufacturing plants, those with a relatively lower ratio of total labor cost to total operating cost make relatively greater use of peripheral employment than poorer performing manufacturing plants, and also increase their use of peripheral employment significantly more than poorer performing manufacturing plants. Similarly, better performing sales and service field offices, that is, those with a relatively lower ratio of payroll cost to sales revenue, make greater use of peripheral employment and increase their use of peripheral employment significantly more than poorer performing field offices.

These findings do not mean that business entities should simply or linearly continue to increase their ratios of peripheral employment to total employment, however. This is because when the company, business unit, manufacturing plant, and sales and service field office samples were separated into quartiles based on changes (during 1995–1998) in one or another measure of their financial or operating performance, the top-performing quartile in each sample had a significantly higher ratio of peripheral employment to total employment than the bottom two performing quartiles, but a significantly lower ratio of peripheral employment to total employment than the second (best-performing) quartile. Specifically, the top-performing quartile of business entities had an average ratio of peripheral employment to total employment of .34 compared to ratios of .17 for the bottom or poorest performing quartile, .26 for the third or second-worst performing quartile, and .40 for the second or second-best performing quartile. Stated differently, on average, the gain in business performance associated with increasing use of peripheral employment is sharpest when the ratio of peripheral employment to total employment rises from about one-quarter to one-third. Increases in the ratio beyond this point are associated with declining business performance. Thus, from a business performance perspective, a balance of one-third peripheral employment and two-thirds core employment seems "optimal."[12]

Implications for Globalization, Organizational Change, and the HR Function

When added to extant high-involvement HRM-business performance research, the findings from this study have some implications for globalization, organizational change, and the HR function. Regarding globalization, there are many countries in which certain high-involvement HRM practices apparently don't fit because they run afoul of cultural values, custom, history, and legal constraints.[13] Variable pay, business information sharing with employees, and decentralized, team-based work are among such practices. Similarly, certain low-involvement

HRM practices, such as part-time, fixed contract, and outsourced employment, don't appear to fit well with many nations. Yet, it was only a short time ago that these (and other) high-involvement and low-involvement HRM practices were virtually unknown in the United States, where individually designed work for a fixed rate of pay in a high control organization predominated. The lesson here is that these historical U.S. practices were substantially altered by market globalization (among other factors) and that further globalization will, in turn, alter HRM practices elsewhere—especially if business practitioners pay closer attention to research findings about the effects of high-involvement and low-involvement HRM practices on business performance.

Regarding organizational change, researcher and practitioner attention has focused predominantly on external environmental factors such as technology, deregulation, customers and competitors as key drivers of change—global drivers, to be sure.[14] But from time to time, new ideas and new evidence about human behavior at work can drive organizational change. Historical examples include the emergence and expansion of "free" labor markets in the 19th century, the scientific management and Hawthorne-inspired human relations "movements" of the early 20th century, and the total quality and work process re-engineering innovations of the late 20th century.[15] Each of these developments brought about major changes in the design of work and the management of people at work, that is, major organizational change, both in the United States and abroad. From this perspective, the dual theory of HRM-business performance and its supporting evidence should cause executives and managers worldwide to rethink the doctrine that, when it comes to managing people, "one size or set of best practices fits all."

Regarding the HR function, its dominant role in the business enterprise has frequently changed to emphasize, as examples, social welfare services, union avoidance, organizational rule enforcement, compliance with regulation, and record keeping.[16] Only relatively recently has the HR function's principal role been characterized as a business partner or change agent.[17] The capability of the HR function—of HR executives and professionals—to serve either or both of these newer roles, however, is called into question by the creation of organizational learning functions and executive positions by several prominent businesses. In these businesses (and perhaps others), the HR function is viewed not as a key business partner or change agent but, instead, as largely fulfilling one or more of its older, traditional roles. For the HR function to turn around in the 21st century and fill the role of business partner and/or change agent, HR executives and professionals would do well to master the dual theory of HRM-business performance and the supporting evidence presented here. By doing, so they will be better able demonstrate how it is that certain HRM practices positively affect business performance, and to significantly influence their organizations in determining the balance between, on the one hand, high-involvement HRM practices and core employment and, on the other hand, low-involvement HRM practices and peripheral employment.

CHAPTER 11

⇒·◆·⇐

The Icarus Syndrome

Talent Management and Derailment in the New Millennium

ADRIAN FURNHAM

V ARIOUS SOCIODEMOGRAPHIC FACTORS have combined to make many HR directors particularly interested in attracting, managing, and retaining talented young staff. All organizations want and need *high-fliers:* talented, able, motivated, and creative people.

However, changes in the demographic profile of many western countries mean that there may well be a significant reduction in the number of young people and thus in the number of high-fliers. Further, many young people are "portfolio" managers who consciously plan their careers and stay with an organization only as long as it suits them. In addition, mobility and market forces mean that talented people may be easily lured away by organizations in other sectors that provide a better package. Thus, there is, and will no doubt continue to be, a "war for talent." Organizations have to fight for a small and perhaps decreasing pool of talented young (or even not so young) people.

Many human resources (HR) professionals have *talent spotters* at business schools; they may have close relationships with career counselors, academics, professionals, and head hunters who believe they know how to spot talent. Yet, talent spotters admit to a particular problem: A number of the people that they so carefully seek out later fail and derail. Because it is a taboo subject, there are few figures to back up any claim. However, many HR professionals suggest that a third of these high-fliers derail. This is more serious than not realizing their potential. It often means coming "badly unstuck" or "missing the plot," and causing considerable team and/or organizational turmoil. These derailed high-fliers might be termed *victims of the Icarus Syndrome*.

The Icarus Syndrome

In Greek mythology, Icarus was the son of the inventor Daedulus. Cretan King Minos locked the father and son up in a high tower. The talented Daedulus made two sets of wings of feathers and wax, which they would use to escape; he told his son that the only "design fault" was that the wax might melt if he flew too close to the sun. Icarus ignored the good advice of his wise father, flew too high, melted his wings, and crashed into the sea and drowned.

It is not clear from the myth precisely why Icarus disobeyed his father. Was he a sensation seeker prone to accidents? Did he do it out of boredom? Was he a disobedient, rebellious child? Was he simply beguiled by his own hubris?

We don't know the answers. Indeed, it is the function of myths and case studies that they allow for multiple interpretations. We do know that the modern derailed high-flier bears an uncanny resemblance to Icarus. But how and why are they chosen? What did the assessors miss? Or was the problem in the way they were managed?

The first section of this chapter discusses the major problems, selection, and what factors to watch for. We then consider some universally important characteristics in high-fliers who do not derail. Next, the problems of narcissism in management are considered. We briefly consider the idea that virtues at extremes (too much or too little) lead to derailment. The toxic boss is described and the impact he or she may have on others. Finally, the possibility of farming or growing high-fliers is considered.

Errors in Selection

Can we assess a person's potential for success? This is problematic because we are not talking about a specific job with assigned tasks, but about "potential." Because it is likely that the workplace, tasks, and style of even the short-term future will be surprisingly different from that of today, we are attempting to select for a job that does not currently exist or that cannot currently be described. The selector is attempting to assess the potential of the individual for a number of future, possible, "virtual" jobs. To do so, there are only three important questions to ask and answer.

What Personal Characteristics Change over the Individual's Lifespan?

Despite the fact that self-help books and workshop presenters tell us that personal change is common, possible, and desirable, most of the evidence is against them: Once you have attained a certain age, very little changes. Try going to a school reunion to see, apart from the wrinkles, how your classmates have changed over the years.

Intelligence levels decline modestly but, in effect, change little over the working life. The same is true of abilities, be they language, numbers, music, or lateral thinking. High-fliers are bright and they stay that way. Most people like to think that personalities can change, particularly negative features such as anxiety, low self-esteem, proneness to depression, impulsivity, or a lack of emotional warmth. However, data collected from individuals over a span of 50 years, both in terms of ability and personality, reveal that this is not so.[1] Extroverts become marginally less extroverted; the acutely shy appear a little less so, but the fundamentals remain much the same.

Major personal crises can change personal coping strategies. We might take up or drop drink, drugs, religion, or relaxation techniques, and these can have dramatic effects. However, the bottom line for those at about 30 years of age is "what you see is what you get." Skills can be improved, and new ones introduced, but at rather different rates. We find evidence of the Icarus Syndrome in the personality traits and disorders that do not change.

What Is the Cost of Development?

People can be better groomed for a job. For instance, politicians can be carefully packaged and repackaged through dress, hairstyles, and speech lessons, just as professionals can take training courses, earn diplomas, and learn from experimental weekends. However, there is an organizational cost to this development that may be more than the upfront price. Therefore, it's better to select for what you see than attempt to change it. (How many brides who believe not "Aisle, altar, hymn," but "I'll alter him" are disappointed by their lack of success?) Define the desirable traits, abilities, and values and find them in candidates. Acquiring and retraining skills is expensive and difficult. The cost may not be worth it. On the other hand, long-term development is important . . . even for high-fliers. Bright, optimistic, balanced people learn fast, embrace change, and adapt to circumstances. Dim, neurotic, pessimistic people do not and they are also very difficult to change.

What Characteristics Should High-Fliers Have?

Most people have few ideas about what to look for in selecting others. Sir James Blyth of Plessey looked for raw intellect, forthright honesty, determination, and physical durability. He also suggested that the selectors ask themselves: "Is the candidate a shit?" He noted that if the answer was yes, the candidate should be rejected. "Why work with too many people you don't like?" he reasoned. "As it is, you are likely to inherit more than enough, so why hire more?"[2]

What Should Selectors Look For?

Three things are vital for nearly all jobs:

1. *Intelligence or ability.* Intelligence and/or ability are sometimes called capacity, cognitive potential, or educational attainability. Since the turn of the 20th century, we have known about general intelligence. Despite the hype concerning idiot savants, bright people are pretty good at most things and dim people are pretty bad. On average, bright people learn faster and adapt more quickly. Selectors and assessors don't often use IQ tests, but they do use specific ability tests. School marks and university grades are weak indicators of intelligence. Intelligence is a must and it can't be taught or trained. In fact, it predicts speed and retention of learning. Intelligence is fairly easy to measure, and it is not difficult to get a pretty good idea of an individual's capacity. You need to be bright enough to fly high.

2. *Emotional stability.* Neuroticism, or "negative affectivity," is a powerful predictor of job failure. The emotionally unstable are poor at customer relations, become capricious and irascible managers, and are prone to high levels of absenteeism, even accidents. Neuroticism is a powerful warning sign of impending danger. There is a mountain of evidence that suggests both that neuroticism does not change much over the years (even with psychotherapy), and that it is related to long- and short-term career failure. Thus, one selects for its opposite: the stable, the phlegmatic, and the emotionally adjusted. It is in this factor that part of the secret of Icarus lies.

3. *Conscientiousness.* Work ethic is a powerful indicator of success. Often developed in childhood by ambitious, future-orientated, middle-class parents, the conscientious are diligent, responsible, punctilious, and dutiful. They can be counted on, and their conscience is a powerful controller of their work style. Some conscientious individuals may be risk-averse, others too self-deprecating, but they can be relied on. The problem is that they can become driven workaholics who do not have the insight into their drive nor the ability to change. These people may be over-dutiful or over-diligent. We will revisit the important concept of optimality: neither too much nor too little of a trait.

High-fliers interview well: They are polished and have a wonderful reputation. But, as interviewers find retrospectively, the danger signals are ignored. There is a simple principle called "too much of a good thing." For many, it doesn't seem possible that anyone might score too high on integrity or too high on teamwork. However, the former could be rigid zealots and the latter too dependent on others to make decisions or do the job properly. In sum, you don't want employees with too much (or too little) of any one characteristic.

Self-Esteem: Humilility, Hubris, and Narcissism

The self-esteem industry is a big business. Half of the self-help books on the shelves attempt to teach or improve self-esteem. Therapists, counselors, priests, and salespeople affirm that understanding and valuing the self will lead to health, happiness, and success. They are partly right.

The manifestation of too much, as well as too little, self-esteem can be both a cause and a consequence of management failure. Americans have long believed in the power and importance of self-esteem, which partly explains their self-confidence and assertiveness. It is surprising to see young people of average ability look so manifestly confident. They appear to have passed "Assertiveness 101," but failed "Charm 101." They are open and frank about their beliefs, problems, wishes, and values, as if they deserve automatic respect or are fascinating on the topic.

We should clearly distinguish between the genuine and the fake article. There are those who are genuinely humble and meek, believing that their ability and contribution are somehow pretty average, even unworthy. The trouble with humility is that a humble person can easily be abused by those with hubris: when the "yes-man" meets the abominable "no-man," the latter wins. However, deep within Anglo-Saxon culture there is a respect for the amateur, self-effacing person who wins with sheer talent. It's seen in stories such as that of the tortoise and the hare and David and Goliath. It is the story of the victory of the humble and the meek who inherit the earth.

There is a sinister, fake version of this seen in such places as the middle-class dinner party, the academic seminar, and the political debating chamber. It is the false humility that is a sort of attention-getting technique. It is deeply unattractive, difficult to sustain, and therefore easily discovered.

The manager with low self-esteem is not necessarily the manager with humility. You can be confident about yourself, but humble. On the other hand, the person with low self-esteem is probably a handicap to his or her family, self, workgroup, and/or organization. Lacking in confidence and self-respect, this person may be overcautious when required to take a risk, dithering when he really needs to be decisive and pusillanimous when he needs to be brave. Low self-esteem is associated with anxiety, depression, hypochondria, and business failure, hence, the myriad books on self-esteem.

Yet, people with low self-esteem seldom work into positions of power. Low self-esteem prevents risk taking, bold decision making, opportunism, and openness to excitement and challenges, which are the stuff of success in business. We all need enough self-respect for healthy day-to-day functioning. We need to be sufficiently interested in, and confident about, ourselves to function well in the cut and thrust of business life.

It is those with seeming limitless self-esteem and concomitant hubris who are the real problem: Extreme narcissists are a hazard and are not that uncommon among our captains of industry. They are often people who are completely preoccupied with being superior, unique, or special. They shamelessly exaggerate their talents and indulge in addictively boastful and pretentious self-aggrandizement. They are often mildly amusing, even pathetic, but narcissists often possess extremely vindictive characteristics.

The psychological interpretation of unnaturally high levels of narcissism is essentially compensatory. Many business narcissists believe that they have been fundamentally wronged in the past and that they are "owed." Their feelings of internal insecurity can be satisfied by regular adulation, affirmation, and recognition. They yearn for a strong positive self-image to combat their real feeling of helplessness and low self-esteem.

One of the most frequently observed characteristics of the narcissist is *capriciousness:* inconsistent, erratic, unpredictable behavior. Most psychologists believe that the origins of narcissistic behavior can be found in early childhood experiences, such as living with an inconsistent parent (caregiver) who although attentive to outward, public signs of achievement, was blind to and ignorant of (or worse, disapproving of) the child's feelings. Perhaps then, we should blame Daedalus for Icarus' plight!

This inconsistency often leads to a confused young adult who does not develop a clear sense of self nor establish a coherent value system. This can result in a lifelong compensatory quest for full self-regard and self-assertion. The wells of the origin of the problem are both deep and murky, and the passions they engender seem remorseless.

The narcissist is quite plainly dysfunctional. He or she fails to understand or appreciate others, be they colleagues, subordinates, or clients. They often see people as possessions whose major function is as an accessory to their pursuit of fame and glory. Peers, colleagues, and employees are used to reflect their glory.

Personal and work relationships for narcissists are particularly interesting. If the narcissist's "other half" is prepared to offer continual, unconditional, even escalatory admiration, all is well. However, these people must direct all of their efforts to ministering to the needs of their master if they are to overcome the inner emptiness and worthlessness they experience. Naturally, narcissists search these rare, equally dysfunctional, "complementary narcissists" out.

Too Much of a Good Thing

Like Icarus, many high-fliers are narcissists. They find that their narcissism serves them well. They seem confident and give others confidence. However, you can have too much of a good thing: particularly self-love. Selectors make the mistake of assuming that there is a linear, rather than a curvilinear, relationship between a personality characteristic and success. For all traits there is an optimal amount. Thus, for example, courage—moral and interpersonal— is a good business trait. However, those who are too bold can be overbearing and manipulative. Skepticism (not cynicism), that most insightful of traits, can tip over into paranoid suspiciousness. Those who are "cool under stress" or emotionally unflappable can be insensitive and withdrawn. The over-diligent can delegate. The imaginative can be deeply impractical.

What happens to high-fliers is this: Their strengths are noticed and they are fast-streamed. They tend to excel in whichever part of the organization they work. If they work in marketing, they tend to be idea and action people; they are resourceful and imaginative. If they work in finance, they tend to be brilliant not only with figures but also in strategic planning. They love number tumbling and "modeling the future."

They tend to be forgiven their faults. The fact that the high-flying marketing executive is undisciplined, inconsistent, poor at paperwork, and egocentric is ignored and downplayed. They can be unrealistic, impractical, and spend-thrifts. Likewise, the analytic strategists may be prone to analysis paralysis; unable to influence others; and prone to building up large departments of like-minded types almost like a university department.

High-fliers like Icarus zoom ahead with the company's blessing. Their flaws, the wax wings, get noticed too late. That for which they are famous soon becomes that for which they become infamous. Known for their integrity, they can suddenly be seen as rigid, intolerant zealots. Known for their people skills, they can be soft, indecisive, and too tolerant of poor performers.

However, there are two more reasons why high-fliers derail. The first is that of the management culture that models management particularly badly. The second is that they have had no development, in part because it was assumed that they did not need it.

Toxic Models in Management

The results from studies on the origin of delinquency and criminality make for depressing reading. When you observe young children in a clearly toxic family, you feel they really have little possibility of growing up as healthy, responsible, adaptable individuals. The person with an antisocial personality has often had a miserable upbringing, which, alas, he or she often perpetuates, producing a cycle of misfortune, neglect, unhappiness, and crime.

Reading the list of typical characteristics of the dysfunctional parent in the toxic family, it is not difficult to see why children from these families end up as they do. Moody, egocentric, uneducated, immoral "caregivers" give little real care. Instead of providing the loving, stable environment, they do the opposite, which can have a disastrous long-term effect on the child.

The same can happen at work. Dysfunctional managers create toxic offices. Often in a brief period of time, they manage to create mayhem, distrust, and disaffection. This can have long-term consequences even in stable adults. That perfidious issue of "stress at work" and its more serious cousin, the nervous breakdown, are often caused by the dysfunctional manager.

To many, especially young people, a manager is *in loco parentis* (in the position or place of a parent). Managers can have considerable influence over an employee's health, happiness, and future. They can create an environment that allows employees to give their best. They can stretch staff by setting reachable, challenging goals, and they can give them support in doing so. They can be helpful, encouraging, and consistent—or not.

Yet, there are some poor managers who create a working environment at the precise opposite end of the spectrum. Some high-fliers derail in toxic offices; others become toxic managers.

What are the symptoms of the dysfunctional manager?

- *Inconsistency and unpredictability.* This is often the hallmark of the type. They are unpredictable to staff, clients, and customers, even to their family. You can never be sure what they will say or do. They are fickle and capricious. The job of a parent and manager is often to create stability in a world of chaos, a sense of security in an insecure world, not the opposite. A dysfunctional manager is often more than inconsistent in that they give contradictory and mixed messages that are very difficult to interpret.
- *Low tolerance of provocation and emotional sensitivity.* Dysfunctional managers easily fly off the handle. They are known for their moodiness. You quite literally have to tread around them very gently. Jokes backfire, unless they themselves make them. They take offense, harbor grudges, and can show great mood swings, especially when stressed.
- *Hedonism and self-indulgence.* Dysfunctional managers are not puritans; they like pleasure. The golf round on Friday afternoon, expensive meals, and overpriced office furniture are ways dysfunctional managers please themselves. They are often deeply selfish. There can be real problems if their pleasures are addictive, which so often they can be. The hedonistic, addictive personality is a real nightmare not only from a financial point of view.
- *Now-ness and lack of long-term planning.* Dysfunctional parents and dysfunctional managers live each day as it comes, not for religious reasons, but because they can't or won't plan for the future. They don't understand postponement of gratification. Hence, they experience serious setbacks when unexpected things happen. They can't or won't plan for future eventualities for themselves, their staff, or their product.
- *Restlessness and excitement seeking.* Dysfunctional managers are always on the go. They get bored easily and can't seem to pay attention. They seem to have an adult form of Attention Deficit Hyperactivity Disorder (ADHD). They appear to need thrills and variety to keep them going. Inevitably, they find themselves in situations that are commercially, even physically, dangerous. They change often, can't sit still, and rarely pay attention to others.
- *Learning problems.* Dysfunctional managers don't learn from their mistakes. In fact, they don't like learning at all. The skill-based seminar is not for them. Outdoor, physical training perhaps, but not the conference

center. Many have few educational qualifications. They don't value them in their staff or themselves. Hence, they do not encourage learning of any sort, often pooh-poohing the educated staff member.

- *Poor emotional control.* Dysfunctional managers are the opposite of the stereotypical reserved and controlled Englishman. They shout, weep, sulk, and gush with little embarrassment or control. They become well known for their outbursts. This is not the result of therapy: in fact, they just have poor self-control.
- *Placing little value on skill attainment.* The dysfunctional manager does not have an MBA. They despise attempts of the staff to upgrade their skills. They talk about gut feelings, experience or, worse still, luck. They are loath to invest in training on the job.
- *Perpetual low-grade physical illness.* Dysfunctional bosses always seem to be ill. They get coughs, colds, the flu, whatever is going around. They certainly are not health conscious, and they are very liable to absenteeism.

These managers, like delinquent children, may have come from a dysfunctional home or been socialized in a dysfunctional organization. Management consultants often talk about management practices they have come across that are little short of startling. They cause unhappiness and reduce productivity and morale, which, over time, can lead to the breakdown of the staff. Whole organizations can become toxic because of the character of senior managers. Toxic senior managers see the world in a particular way that influences their selection, self-perception, and style.

The workplace can become psychologically as well as physically toxic. Dysfunctional managers spread the disease of stress and incompetence wherever they go. Worse, they model poor behavior to young staff, who may consider their behavior normal. The cure, alas, is often not worth the candle. Dysfunctional managers need more than counseling: They need canceling.

Curiously, some high-fliers will exhibit many of these behaviors in their departments. However, their reputation and halo will often protect them from being discovered until it is too late.

Growing Extraordinary Executives

High-fliers are hybrids. They need careful tendering if they are to be at their best. This is a challenge. Some organizations believe in survival of the fittest. They test and develop high-fliers by putting them through increasingly difficult tasks and tough assignments. However, this frequently leads to derailment.

One grows a manager like a fine orchid, and all successful gardeners know the routine:

- Select good stock or seed.
- Prepare the optimal environment.
- Enrich by weeding, watering, and fertilizing.

- Rotate the crops periodically.
- Occasionally, let good fields fall fallow.
- Look for, and create, hybrids.

The same is true of high-fliers and can help to prevent derailment. Select the best, but beware the concept of optimality. Put people in the environment best suited to their needs, but be aware of their weaknesses and flaws. Resist personal forgiveness and organizational complicity in favor of education and development. Provide them with mentors and fine role models, not toxic incompetence.

Give high-fliers well-planned developmental opportunities and time-out for reflection. Nurture, but don't over-protect. There are enough examples of young prodigies from various branches of the performing arts who never fulfill their potential to be a warning. The spoilt, impetuous, demanding young star is often the product of poor management . . . and will in turn become a poor manager.

Conclusion

There will always be cases of derailed managers. Icarus is a moral about ignoring warnings, hubris, and sensation-seeking. These are warnings to be heeded by organizations in their selection, development, and monitoring of young talent. It's just too expensive and wasteful to find talented people and then paradoxically set up the conditions that ensure they fail. Human resource managers in the new millennium need more than ever to know how to recruit, select, and develop high-fliers. They also need to courageously and self-confidently spot and avoid those with the Icarus Syndrome.

CHAPTER 12

Maximizing the Probability of Success of Newly Recruited Executives

CHARLES G. THARP and BEN E. DOWELL

C OMPANIES SPEND A significant amount of time and money recruiting senior management talent. Alarmingly, newly hired executives have a very high dropout rate and the corresponding impact on both the individual and the organization can be quite disruptive. This chapter explores best practices in the area of executive selection and on-boarding and profiles one company's approach to maximizing the probability of success of newly recruited executives. By adopting a disciplined approach to selection and on-boarding, it is possible to reduce the gap between the success of internally promoted executives and those recruited externally.

BMS: Building a Pipeline to Talent

Bristol-Myers Squibb (BMS) is a global pharmaceutical company with roughly 45,000 employees. Its business is to discover, develop, manufacture, market, and sell pharmaceuticals and related health care products. Like most major corporations, BMS realizes that the key to success and growth is to build both its pipeline of products and its pipeline of talent. To supplement its internal research and development efforts, BMS aggressively pursues product licenses and alliances with other pharmaceutical companies, biotechs, and major research centers. Similarly, in the area of talent, BMS selectively recruits senior talent to supplement its bench of internal successor candidates for key operating and staff positions. Successfully tapping external sources of new products and leadership talent is part of BMS's overall strategy for growth.

BMS is not unique in its focus on external sources of leadership talent. In their study, "The War for Talent," McKinsey & Company notes that many of America's top-performing companies tap external sources for a significant portion of their executive talent. McKinsey notes that even companies known for the high quality of their leadership development programs fill a significant portion of senior positions through external recruiting. General Electric, perhaps the top "academy" company for CEO talent, as evidenced by the number of its alumni who fill the top leadership roles in industry, is reported to fill 20 percent of its senior openings (the top 500) from outside its ranks. At Medtronic, a consistent growth leader and strong performer in the medical devices industry, approximately 25 percent of the top 300 positions are filled through outside hires.[1] BMS has a similar track record; over recent years 25 percent to 30 percent of its new "key executives" (the top 500 positions) have been recruited from outside the company.

Supplementing the internal talent pool with external hires has the potential to benefit the company by:

- Adding technical skills that are not currently present in the organization.
- Increasing the bench of talent in a specific discipline or line of business.
- Bringing in individuals familiar with new business models.
- Increasing the diversity of the existing talent pool.
- Importing experienced leaders from "best practice" companies.
- Providing new ideas and a fresh perspective on key issues.
- Upgrading talent through displacing low-performing talent with more capable individuals.

Unfortunately, these potential benefits are often not fully realized due to the relatively poor track record of many newly hired executives. Manchester Partners International reports that 40 percent of new executives recruited into high-level positions fail within 18 months.[2] At BMS, the historical experience for new hires has also been disappointing and the rate of turnover (both voluntary and involuntary) for externally recruited executives was substantially higher than that for homegrown leaders.

Over recent years, BMS has tracked the success of newly hired executives versus the success of leaders promoted from within the company. This research revealed that the success rates of these two groups of executives as measured by retention rates differed dramatically. For executives hired into the company during the period 1993, 1994, and 1995, only 69 percent were still with the company three years after the year of hire. Of the newly hired executives who left the company, roughly half were involuntarily terminated and the other half left of their own accord. For employees promoted to the executive ranks from within the company during these same years, the retention rate three years postpromotion was 85 percent.

When the time period of analysis was extended beyond three years, an even more striking difference was found between the retention of newly hired executives and those promoted from within. After six years, only 39 percent of the new hires remained with the company, while more than 70 percent of the executives promoted from within were still with the company. Naturally, the company was anxious to discover the reasons for the relatively poor retention experience of new hires and to take corrective actions to reverse this trend.

Executive Turnover: Six Reasons for Termination

An analysis was conducted of each of the cases of executive turnover. From this analysis, the underlying reasons for termination were grouped into six major categories:

1. There was a mismatch between the expectations of the newly hired executives and the reality of the culture and the position into which he or she was recruited. Too much emphasis was placed on recruiting and not enough focus on screening. A common statement made during this period was that "we never lose a candidate we want to hire." In retrospect, this attitude did not allow a proper balance of setting realistic expectations and selling the candidate.

2. Behavior of the newly hired executive did not fit the company culture. The primary focus in the interview process was on results and too little attention was paid to assessing how the candidate worked with others in achieving results.

3. The newly hired executive developed a limited network of support within the company. In a highly team-based environment, such as BMS, establishing relationships with peers beyond the immediate department or function is critical to success.

4. The newly hired executives experienced a change of direct supervisor shortly after joining the company. Given that the average tenure of the key executives in their roles was approximately two-and-a-half years, the new hire would soon be working for a new boss and it was important that a network of support be established beyond the hiring manager.

5. The newly hired executive was brought into the company with the expectation that he or she would be a "change agent." Many executives coming into an organization with this mandate take this as license to do whatever it takes to create change quickly and frequently do not bring others in the organization along. These actions may not endear the new executive to many of the current leaders who helped build the status quo, which ultimately results in the new executive not receiving the support they need to be successful in the long term.

6. The spouse or significant other of the newly hired executive did not relocate or experienced a difficult relocation and adjustment to the new location. With the increasing incidence of dual-career families and the attendant difficulties of geographic relocation, additional strains may be

placed upon the new executive as he or she tries to come up to speed in their new role.

The reasons for the relative lack of success of executives newly hired into the company during this period were very similar to the findings within other companies that experienced similar trends in the turnover of new hires.[3]

Enhancing the Selection Process

Based on these findings, and the desire to increase the rate of retention of new hires, BMS revamped its approach to selection and on-boarding of executive recruits. Specifically, the following changes were introduced to enhance the selection process:

- Detailed position profiles were developed for each executive position. Unlike traditional job descriptions that merely document the duties and scope of a role, the position profile outlines the competencies, behaviors, skills, knowledge, and learning opportunities of each executive position. The position profile is used as the standard against which candidates are screened and selected.
- A more structured and disciplined approach to selection was established that involves the immediate manager, the manager once-removed, the human resources manager, peers, and other key stakeholders in the interview process. Formal consensus meetings were introduced as a mechanism to discuss the input and assessment of each interviewer and to gain commitment and agreement on each candidate. The consensus meetings enhance the quality of decisions and broaden the network of support and ownership for the newly hired executive.
- An external resource is used to provide a psychological assessment and input on the cultural fit of prospective executive hires.[4] The focus of this assessment is to identify development opportunities and to provide an expert, third-party perspective on potential derailment factors.

Additionally, changes were introduced to enhance the on-boarding process:

- Upon hire, the importance of the on-boarding process is discussed with new executives; in addition, they are given an integration plan detailing actions to take during the first six months.
- They are provided a list of the key individuals who will be critical to their success and are asked to meet with them during the first 30 days.
- New executives and their managers receive coaching (from the external consultant who assessed cultural fit) to identify areas that may create issues and actions they can take to mitigate them.
- A new leader integration process was introduced to help accelerate the development of the relationship of the new leader with his or her team. In this process, a facilitator meets with the new leader and he or she direct

reports to discuss concerns, opportunities, and expectations of the new executive. This process, pioneered at General Electric, helps compress the time required for the new leader and the management team to come up to speed in the new reporting relationship.

- If needed, an internal or external coach is identified to help the new executive with development needs identified during the interview process.
- Three- and six-month follow-up sessions are held with human resources to assess how the integration process is proceeding and to make midcourse adjustments.
- To broaden the new executive's exposure to the company, a Key Executive Orientation Program (KEOP) was introduced. KEOP provides an opportunity for new executives to discuss the company's history, values, culture, and strategy with the CEO, senior-operating, and staff executives. KEOP is a highly interactive forum that helps the new executive build relationships with senior company leaders and other new executives. This helps broaden the new executive's network within the company and accelerates the on-boarding process.
- At approximately six months after being hired, the new executive receives a 360° assessment based on the position profile for his or her position. This assessment measures progress and identifies areas of opportunity before derail.

This more disciplined and thoughtful approach to the selection and integration of newly hired executives has produced dramatic changes in the relative success of senior talent imported into the organization. For executives hired in 1996, after many of these changes were introduced, 73 percent of executives were still with the company three years after hire. For the 1997 cohort group, 76 percent of newly hired executives remained with the company after three years. As compared with the earlier experience for the 1993 through 1995 cohort group, where the retention rate of externally hired executives remaining after three years was only 82 percent of the rate of those promoted from within, the retention rate of the 1997 cohort was 93 percent, a dramatic improvement.

Key Learnings

Supplementing the internal pipeline of talent through sourcing talent in the external market is a strategy that has the potential to enhance the capabilities and leadership strength of a company. However, realizing the potential benefits of external recruiting requires that a thoughtful and disciplined approach be applied to the selection and on-boarding of new hires. Properly structuring the selection process, setting realistic expectations of the job and culture, building a network of support, and providing ongoing coaching and feedback are key factors to retaining and developing executive talent imported into a company.

CHAPTER 13

═══◆═══

Learning via Education and Training

D. QUINN MILLS

ONE OF THE single largest opportunities of the human resource function in the 21st century lies in the mobilization of the increasing expenditures that firms are putting into the education and training of their employees for the pursuit of the strategic objectives of the firm. This will be much enhanced by new computerized products for managing individual education and training, but only if human resources leaders aggressively identify and pursue the opportunity.

Learning, generally the responsibility of the human resources function, is of increasing importance for corporations. The significance of learning is reflected in the recent emergence of executive positions such as chief learning officer and vice president for learning, which have a specialized responsibility for learning in a corporation. Generally these executives report to the top human resources executive in the corporation, though in some cases they report directly to the CEO. Also indicative of the increasing importance of learning has been the development and spread of so-called corporate universities, which are a means of gathering and systematizing the education and training provided by a firm. Finally, many companies have begun to work more closely with both universities and training vendors to develop customized learning vehicles for their companies. All of these are certain to progress in the 21st century.

The increasing importance of learning is a reflection of the rapid growth of information and knowledge in our economic society and of the increasing complexity of companies and the business world within which they operate. There is simply much more that needs to be known and many more skills that need to be mastered.

Yet, at the same time that learning is becoming more important, economic incentives are shifting strongly against the provision of more learning that is paid for by the corporation. The key issue of the 21st century is how these conflicting trends will be reconciled to one another.

The Increasing Divergence of Interest about Learning between Corporations and Employees

There is a substantial difference in interest, labor economics tells us, between companies and employees in the arena of learning. *Education* is broad-based and prepares a person for work in many different occupations and industries; education provides a foundation to which particular skills are added. *Training* comes in two forms: general and specific. General training involves skills that are applicable in different companies; specific training involves skills that are applicable only in one firm. Education and general training are attractive to employees because they increase the person's attractiveness to employers generally. In consequence, a firm that provides education and general training opportunities is more attractive to potential employees.

Yet, many cost-conscious managers are prepared to pay for (or provide) only specific training, since general training and education might benefit a competitor. Picture one business manager telling another, "I believe in training and I'll hire every person you pay to train." The point here is that one company gains from avoiding the expense of general training by letting other companies pay for it and then hiring away the people who've been trained. Economists first pointed out this cost calculation a century ago, and it remains the dominant economic incentive in learning today. All serious discussions of education and training in an employment context must consider this cost calculation as a fundamental reality.

The environment in which education and training are provided changes over time, hence, in the employment context, these will be different in many ways in the 21st century. For instance, employees at all levels in companies expect to move more frequently among employers than in the past. This increases their desire for education and general training that will make them more attractive to potential employers. Companies, in contrast, are generally in tightly competitive environments in which they are attempting to minimize costs, especially on education and general training that may end up benefiting not themselves but other firms. At the same time, employees have more control over their careers in companies and are more responsible for their own education and training. The result is a quiet tug-of-war between the employee who seeks more education and general training and the company that seeks to limit costs to specific training. When combined with the lack of corporate-level strategic direction of education and training, these emerge as arenas that have high potential for thorough redirection.

The Special Case of Executive Education

In what appears to be a violation of the cost calculation, corporations have been willing to pay for education and general learning for executives. This is especially surprising since executives (including high-level managers) are among the most potentially mobile of all employees. Until the last quarter of the 20th century, this was not the case. Executives were tied tightly to their companies by several considerations, including the lifetime employment system (by which a person was expected to spend his or her entire career at a single company, and by which a company presumed it would provide employment for key people throughout their careers); the strong culture of loyalty in most large firms, which inhibited an executive seeking a position elsewhere; and the notion that detailed industry and company knowledge, gained via years of experience, was the key to an executive's productivity. An executive who changed companies was like a fish out of water, and therefore was unlikely to be successful. Because of these influences, there was little mobility of executives among firms. Companies could safely presume that the costs they incurred educating and providing general training to high-potential managers would benefit the company, not competitors, in the future.

All this changed in the last quarter of the 20th century. First, the lifetime employment system came to an end; then loyalty eroded; finally, industry-to-executive search firms (headhunters) developed. These factors made senior managers and executives far more mobile than in the past. Companies could no longer count on retaining managers in whom it had made a substantial education and general training investment, so they became much more reluctant to make such investments.

As a result, longer executive education programs, which attempt to educate and not just train managers, are losing popularity compared to shorter, more skill-intensive programs. It's common for business schools and companies, including their HR executives, to attribute this change to the faster pace of business life today and to the unwillingness of companies and individual managers to leave their jobs for a lengthy period (usually three months or so). But this is superficial. The underlying reality is that companies are reluctant to invest large sums of money and lengthy time periods (with the added cost of covering the absent manager's job responsibilities) when the executive may simply take his or her additional learning and move to another company.

A further issue is the mixed track record of multiweek executive education programs. Many of today's chief learning officers are skeptical that this type of instruction makes much real difference to an executive's performance. Also, most such programs have relied only on level one evaluations (I liked this program or I didn't), rather than level two evaluations (I learned something or I didn't), level three (my behavior changed over time), or level four (my company achieved more). Hence, there is little data to refute skepticism.

Lack of Strategic Direction of Training and Education in Today's Corporation

Most major corporations today use two very different mechanisms to provide formal learning (that is, training and education). Training (whether specific or general) is provided via line managers in operating units, with the assistance of training managers who report directly to the business unit manager and have a dotted-line relationship to the human resources function. Education is provided as a benefit via tuition reimbursement programs, which are managed entirely by the human resources function with the business unit manager providing only an administrative input. Companies vary greatly in their use of education and training. It is common, for example, for large firms to provide tuition assistance to employees who are taking college level courses; but Wal-Mart, which is the largest private employer today, provides tuition assistance to its associates (employees) only at the high school or GED level. Statistics are difficult to come by, but it appears that large firms, in general, spend about one-half as much on tuition assistance programs as on training of all sorts.

Generally neither training nor education is managed strategically in U.S. firms today, this despite some rhetoric to the contrary. As much as possible, training is done on an as-needed, just-in-time basis. For instance, one of the supposed greatest advantages of Internet-delivery of training is that it can be provided to the employee at the worksite when the skills involved are needed. That is, training is managed for productivity and cost control. In contrast, education is provided as a benefit, administered rather than managed, and with an emphasis on cost-control rather than on learning. Not even productivity is pursued in providing education.

Yet, there is much to be said for a strategic approach to education and training in corporations. For example, it is well understood today that the most important asset of many firms is the professional expertise of their employees, which is increase by learning. Since this is the case, learning is clearly a strategic element of the business equation. Strategic management allows the corporation to direct its expenditures toward the areas with the greatest potential return, and permits learning to be seen as an investment rather than merely a cost. Thus, over a period of a few years, a company that manages the education and training components of learning in a strategic manner will outperform companies that do not do so. Since HR has a major role in providing learning, it is an opportunity for HR to provide strategic leadership to the firm and to achieve greater business results.

Opportunity for Human Resources to Provide Strategic Direction

In recent years, a gap has developed between the corporation and individual employee development. Prior to the 1980s, employees' careers and development (of which the critical elements were learning, training, and job assignments) were managed centrally by large corporations. A significant shift occurred during the 1980s. Companies began backing away from managing careers, and instead left this function to the individual. This has not been a fully satisfactory shift, neither to individuals nor to the companies. There are many points of stress and oversight in it. In fact, companies must be involved in the individual development process if they are to have an ample pipeline of future leaders, and individuals need to understand how the company will be changing if they are to know which directions of development to pursue. As a consequence, companies have not fully exited the individual development area, and individuals have not been able to completely manage their own development. HR leaders in the 21st century must address this gap and improve the processes by which individuals are developed via education and training.

Fortunately, new technological developments make it easier for a company to manage education and training in a strategic manner. First, computerized learning management systems (LMS), provided by vendors such as THINQ, permit a company to track and manage the learning of individuals; they permit the individual to manage his or her own learning and development in a much more sophisticated way than ever before. For example, within two weeks, DC Metro was able to train every one of its 10,000 employees on matters related to terrorism after mandated to do so on September 12, 2001. The deployed LMS allowed them to react to significant change in an effective, accountable, and measured way.

Boeing and Lockheed are using an LMS to make sure that the right and critical skills are on hand as they evolve in a very difficult market. They are in the process of redefining a number of elements of their businesses. Both companies are leveraging the same system across all their divisions in order to enhance the mobility of people and skills across boundaries with the same benefits that companies got by standardizing on the same accounting system about 20 years ago.

In addition, automation of the administration of tuition assistance by vendors such as MindEdge have provided an opportunity for corporations both to lower costs for this benefit, and by managing it far more directly, to permit tuition assistance to be made a strategic initiative of the firm.

An enhanced or "turbo" LMS adds three things to an ordinary LMS: (1) it integrates both training and tuition assistance into a whole, so that all systematic—that is, excluding learning by experience—learning in the company can be managed strategically; (2) it provides content; and (3) it provides the opportunity to consolidate systematic learning into credentials (degrees and certificates) for people in the firm. For the first time, human resources executives can combine training expenditures with tuition assistance expenditures into a coordinated whole by which the entire education/training expenditures of the firm can be mobilized in support of its learning objectives and business strategy.

Next Steps in Turning Vision into Reality

The key steps in mobilizing training and education expenditures for the strategic advantage of a firm are as follows:

1. Learning must be identified as a separate activity of the organization and staffed with people able to identify, measure, and lead it. Many firms have created the position of chief learning officer for this purpose. This is a separate role from that of knowledge management, although they are related and should be coordinated.

2. A case for learning must be made with top officers of the corporation. The strategic contribution of learning to the business should be identified and its costs and return on investment measured. For example, a firm may want to strongly develop the ability of its managers to lead in rapidly changing times and to do so via innovation. This requires learning that contributes directly to business performance. A further example is to demonstrate the financial return on such an investment.

3. Support of business unit managers for learning should be sought by providing learning as needed (just-in-time), on a cost-effective basis (using online methods to avoid costly in-time and money classroom sessions), and with direct contribution to business performance.

4. Learning should be pressed beyond events (e.g., off-site training sessions) and into the framework of work (as-needed in a cost- and time-friendly manner).

5. Learning should be integrated into the basic human resources framework of the firm (into hiring, retaining, promoting, and performance evaluation processes).

CHAPTER 14

Beam Me Some
Talent, Scotty!

Knowledge, Learning, and Technology
on the Starship Enterprise

ELLIOTT MASIE

I OFTEN IMAGINE what it would be like to be the human resources (HR) manager on Star Trek's Starship Enterprise. Think truly outside the box. Remember, this is the ship that can beam Captain Kirk to a planet's surface, has
elevators that can go vertically and horizontally, and can even create any food
from digital formulas. What tasks would I do and what tools would I have at my
fingertips if I were the HR manager on that futuristic ship? Let's take a hyper-
jump to the future and take a look.

Ubiquitous Collaboration

One of the key tasks of the HR manager will be to maintain ubiquitous and continuous collaboration among the employees, suppliers, visiting aliens, and other
entities throughout the galaxy. The sharing would be ever-present due to its non-
stop, pervasive, and integrated nature. Our employees will leverage communication and cooperation technology tools that are just natural improvements over
today's e-mail, instant messenger, and video-conferencing capabilities. However,
they will have a culture of collaboration efficiency. Teams will come together
knowing a great deal about each member, including past experiences, overt and
hidden talents, thinking styles, and business agendas. Interactions will be automatically recorded, with the easy ability to edit, condense, and republish key
knowledge nuggets. You will not focus on the actual technology . . . it will be

embedded into furniture, worn on our clothing, integrated into the environment, and thus will be a whole lot easier to use.

What is most striking about ubiquitous collaboration is that it will be a measurable indicator. Just as Captain Kirk might ask the engine room for a reading on the fuel cells, he could call the HR cockpit and ask for a reading, which would indicate how internal and external collaboration was functioning. The key to keeping the meter high will be found in the methodology of cooperation more than in keeping digital pipes clean:

- How widely are crew members searching for peers within the organization to assist in new tasks?
- How well are managers facilitating sharing and cooperating through the strategic creation of task teams and via coaching and feedback?
- How efficient is the collaborative process? Are crew members able to participate in meetings and discussions in a fashion that maximizes the value of their time and avoids boredom and distraction?
- How easy is the organization to partner and work with from the perspective of external groups? Is the entry way clearly marked and culturally understandable to new partners?

Context Engines

As the Enterprise zooms through the universe, the crew is exposed to an incredible amount of data and information. The organic hard drives of the ship's computer room have endless storage capacity, and the latest databases can search for any knowledge object in a nanosecond. However, the most provocative aspect of the process is found in the *context library*. The HR manager has responsibility for this collection, which reflects a process and technology that places information into context through the application of other people's experiences with and value ratings of each chunk of information. Here are two examples:

1. A staff member on the procurement deck wants to buy 1,000 melon-like fruits on the next planet that the Enterprise visits. They have searched the galaxy food databases and found five possible melons, their nutritional ratings, safety levels, and current market prices; however, they want context. So, the context library provides ratings from 9,432 previous visits of Federation ships, plus 10 video clips of previous negotiations with that planet's fruit vendors. The context library knows which two ships have crews with similar tastes, so their experiences are given higher ratings. In addition, it knows the Meyers-Briggs negotiation style of the procurement officer, so it can provide usable role models that this specific procurement officer can successfully use.

2. A staff member has been caught stealing aboard the ship. The HR manager prepares to confront this staff member and looks to the context library for assistance prior to the conversation. In addition to the *Employee*

Guidebook and the *HR Manager's e-Manual,* the context library provides access to a select few similar case studies that are tailored to this
particular ship, this particular staff member, and even this particular
HR manager. The ship's computers have an almost unlimited amount of
data, but the context library provides the texture and personalization
that helps the user find the most useful and applicable information. Of
course, the HR manager has been through the "train-the-trainer"
course on context usage, which is designed to teach the manager how to
help the crew leverage this type of information most effectively. By the
way, there is also a context library effectiveness meter on the HR manager's digital dashboard.

Sim It, Scotty!

Throughout the ship, you can hear crew members talking about "Simming It."
This refers to instant simulations that they are conducting as part of everyday
work, as well as an aspect of their training programs. Every piece of equipment
on board has a Sim function, which allows the user to simulate an action; Sim-It
capability is built into organizational and personal computers throughout the
ship. The theory is simple: Try it; make no-cost mistakes; continually improve
your performance; and discuss outcomes with colleagues. Here are just a few of
the simulations that are going on aboard the Enterprise:

- The landing party public relations officer is preparing for the next stop of
  the Enterprise. Rather than just drawing up an action plan, they are about
  to Sim It, which provides the opportunity for them to see how their action
  plan might work out with 73 different reactions. Their Sim-It session
  might be a real-time scenario with other crew members playing the host
  planet's reception party, or it might be an automated simulation with dynamic scenarios programmed into the system. Either way, by the time the
  actual landing session happens, the public relations officer is thoroughly
  prepared for a wide range of outcomes.
- A junior officer is a candidate for promotion to a manager role. Prior to applying for the role, he has spent 30 hours simulating days in the life of a
  manager. This is providing him with a more realistic view of the new job,
  and it is also generating a learning and competency map that he will bring
  to the promotion interview.
- The pilot at the helm of the Enterprise is about to make an important
  route adjustment that requires a hyper-leap. The pilot is one of the most
  experienced officers in the fleet, but she still opts to do three quick, two-
  minute Sim Its of the route change. At the end of each, she and her co-
  pilot discuss the outcomes. When asked if she could make this adjustment
  without a Sim It, she answers, "Of course, but why wouldn't I want to
  practice a key action?"

Compensation Blends

One of the most striking differences we find during our visit to the Enterprise is the compensation blends process. Based on individual compensation blends, we discover that format and style of employee compensation is quite different from crew member to crew member. The HR manager describes compensation blending:

- Compensation blends are an outgrowth of benefit cafeteria plans that were introduced two millennia ago. Employers have found that staff members have different needs and desires for compensation at different stages of their lives.
- Each employee negotiates a compensation blend that contains mixtures of cash salary, deferred salary, invested salary, family benefits, time off, intensity of work, dependent care of children or parents, educational access, sabbatical time, housing and life support, paid vacation experiences, and a dozen other factors.
- The organization evaluates whether the goal is long- or short-term employment and responds to employee requests accordingly.
- Ironically, almost 20 percent of the crew receives no more than a token cash stipend; the balance is paid in other forms of compensation.
- Additionally, staff members are less engaged in comparing each other's compensation blends and are more focused on the overall life quality they can support through their personal blend.
- The HR manager is held to an overall "cost-of-service" target for the staffing load, which is held in context to other factors such as longevity, effectiveness of current staff, and staff/ship morale.

The Enterprise Today

Our fantasy trip to the Enterprise and the future may not be such a fantasy. Almost every technology that I described is currently available. What are missing are the methodologies to leverage the technology for these outcomes. As HR professionals, this is the largest challenge we face in leveraging technology to achieve significant gains in our organizations. It is all about vision and methodology.

There is no reason why we have to wait for the future to leverage today and tomorrow's technologies for these same outcomes:

1. *Ubiquitous collaboration.* HR managers must take responsibility for the use of collaborative technologies to make sure that we get effective and efficient collaboration. We have to blend the technology of e-mail with cultural agreements about how to make it a tool rather than the mass distraction it has become in many of our organizations.
2. *Context, context, context.* As we grow our e-learning and knowledge management capabilities, let's make sure that we grow our context capabilities.

I am not interested in a million pieces of information. I am interested in a few pieces that are just right and that are from sources that I can trust. When I hear about a book, I want to see what 10 people whom I respect have said about that book. The context is critical. Very few HR managers are addressing context. In fact, very little of the e-learning movement is focused on context. Yet, if you look at the heart of effective, tacit, informal learning, it is usually filled with context. As HR executives, we have to be the context advocates.

3. *Simulation.* While most current-day simulation is viewed as very expensive, the price will start to drop quickly. Simulation does not need to be highly animated or contain artificial intelligence in every program. Simulation is a process commitment to provide employees with the ongoing opportunity to practice their skills, even to the point of failure. Pilots will tell you the most important aspects of their training have been in simulators when they accidentally crashed the plane. That type of failure is key to understanding the true impacts of our choices and to find the edge of our competencies. Where technology exists, let's leverage it. When buying new equipment, let's build simulation into it. And, when it is too expensive, let's build simple peer-to-peer simulation games to put ourselves through the paces. HR managers, please start to Sim It!

4. *Compensation blends.* As we live longer, as our work lives are extended, and even as our economies are challenged, the need for creativity and flexibility in compensation packages becomes more and more critical. Linking compensation to the true and changing needs of the workplace will be one of the defining differences between organizations. Talent will flow to organizations that offer packages that match the needs of employees. The definition of compensation will broaden to meet the wider life requirements and desires of the workplace.

The Role of Human Resources

The fifth and less obvious learning on our visit to the Enterprise is the role and status of HR managers. They sit in a cockpit, which displays real time-trending data from the business operations. They understand which "levers" may change key indicators, such as staff readiness and morale. Note where they are sitting: They are just left of the captain. They are part of the management team, and their mission is to provide the talent, the culture, the skills, and the readiness to explore the universe and go where no HR department has gone before!

III

EMERGING
ORGANIZATION
AND CULTURE

———❖———

IN THE STRUGGLE to stay one step ahead of the frenetic pace this new millennium presents, leaders are challenged to build dynamic, entrepreneurial environments. What are some of the factors that will influence this important culture shift? With a more demanding workforce, leaders need to create stronger connections with both their businesses and their employees to convey the importance of loyalty, collaboration, and innovation. Adaptation and flexibility are increasingly recognized as critical for fostering this new culture, and the 21st-century organization should strive to implement these characteristics. The role of HR is transforming, yet again, and its new shape will be better aligned with organizational structure and culture, positioning businesses for continued and improved success.

The chapters in this section closely examine how organizations can build this innovative organization, what the desired corporate culture requires from leaders, how the new global economy affects HR and organizational structures, and what needs to be done to accommodate these changes. The authors provide a road map for organizations to follow as they rise to the demands of these challenges.

CHAPTER 15

Free to Choose

Fostering the Innovative Organization

LYNDA GRATTON

T HE KEY CHALLENGE we face in organizations over the next decade is to create the capacity for adaptation and flexibility. Competitive landscapes
change in complex and often unpredictable ways, consumer aspirations become
increasingly more sophisticated, while "global shocks" rock the foundations of
economic and social institutions. If survival is a characteristic of success, then
only the flexible and agile will succeed. Much of our thinking about flexibility
and agility has focused on those organizational structures that enable agility, for
example, through project team working and horizontal integration.[1] These flexible structures are indeed crucial, and the capacity of members of the HR function to advise on and support the delivery of flexible organizational structures
will be of enormous importance to the senior team.

However, while structures and processes will indeed be critical to adaptability, these are primarily enabling frames. They will not have long-term impact unless the structures and processes of flexibility and agility are aligned
with the mind-set of flexibility. By *mind-set of flexibility* I am referring to the
aspirations and expectations individuals bring to their work: Shorthand would
be to say that the relationship between the organization and the individual employee is adult-to-adult, rather than the past relationship of parent-to-child.
The characteristics of an adult-to-adult relationship is that responsibility is
shared by both, rather than assigned to the parent; that the needs of both are
openly debated and considered; and that there is freedom on the part of both
parties to act. With a mind-set of flexibility, employees are more skilled and
able to make moment-by-moment decisions that are in their interests and the
interests of the organization: to become more flexible in the context of a dem-
ocratic organization.[2]

What might be the foundations for a flexible mind-set, and what are the roles and responsibilities of the HR function to support this mind-set change? I believe that at the core of the flexible mind-set is the notion of choice: that employees are treated as adults, capable of making choices in support of their own development and the organization of which they are a member. With choice, individuals can realign to meet changing circumstances; they can make the moment-by-moment decisions that enable them to be adaptable. Without choice, they are incapable of movement, trapped in a set of parameters and decisions that leave little room for movement, or what has been termed "latitude of discretion."

The foundation of the adult-to-adult relationship is the capacity for autonomous action on the part of both the organization and the individual. Much has been said about the choices organizations can make, but what of the choices of employees? To be flexible and adaptable individuals need the capability to exercise choice in seven dimensions: (1) in the jobs and roles they play, (2) in membership of projects and taskforces, (3) in what and when they learn, (4) in mentors and coaches, (5) in the composition of rewards and benefits, (6) in location, and (7) in time.

A key challenge for the HR function is to create the enabling mechanisms that frame these seven dimensions of choice. In "individualizing the deal," we can learn much from manufacturing and services companies that have been building choice through mass customization for over a decade.

Much of the ethos of the manufacturing and service sectors prior to this period had been the axiom *one-size-fits-all*. Consumers were essentially the same and would be prepared to purchase similar products or services. Technological advances from about 1980 onward fundamentally changed this premise, as it became possible to link the unique needs of every consumer with a customized product or service. Variety and choice became an operating standard in one industry after another as Charles Schwab redefined financial services, the Ritz Carlton redefined hotel service, and Dell redefined financial services. These early adopters inevitably gained competitive advantage from doing so. Charles Schwab, for example, saw their revenues outstrip their competitors from 1989 onward. The ethos was one of consumer choice and mass customization, but the powerhouse behind this was a rapid advance in low-cost, ubiquitous technology. These same technology waves which hit manufacturing and services in the 1980s are lapping at the walls of many organizations in the 2000s. For those who are pioneering employee choice, at the core is inevitably Web-based technology. The analytic and decision trees behind British Petroleum's (BP) MyJobMarket, for example, may be invisible to employees, but are supported by recently developed enabling technologies.[3]

The lessons from mass customization are clear: Build deep and intimate knowledge of your consumer, leverage technologies as fast as possible, and create broad variety from which consumers can choose.

The senior team at Tesco, a giant food retailer with more than 260,000 employees in Europe and Asia, has leveraged its consumer insight capabilities to build employee insight since early 2001. By interviewing thousands of employees and by using focus groups and direct observation, they have built a descriptive landscape that has segmented current and future employees by aspirations, working patterns, and life events. This research has enabled them to really understand what is important to their employees . . . be they "work-life-balance" types, who want choices around time; "work-to-live" types, who want choices around remuneration and benefits, or "live-to-work" types who value being able to influence the work they do, their learning opportunities, and their mentoring choices. Other pioneering companies are building variety across one or more of these dimensions of choice.

The Pioneers of Choice

Here are examples of these pioneers:[4]

- *Choice of job.* Central to enabling individuals to build their knowledge and relationships and essential to the flexible organization. Oil giant BP's MyJobMarket enables current jobs and projects vacancies to be accessed by all employees, worldwide. Employees are also able to post their résumés and receive weekly job and project matches.[5]
- *Choice of project.* As organizations become more agile, so the primary unit of work will migrate from full-time jobs to a portfolio of projects. At the Danish hearing-aid company Oticon, this has been the organizing principle for over a decade. Employees are free to nominate and create projects they believe are crucial and choose projects that will build their own skill base.[6]
- *Choice of learning activity.* This is a primary capability, as employees must continually build new skill profiles. At the computer services company Unisys, employees have unlimited access to choose from a wide range of learning opportunities, with an automatic sign-off. Any training can be taken, if the employee has the time. The match between employee learning style, development needs, and the learning portfolio is supported with a Web-based agent.[7]
- *Choice of mentor and coach.* As the support for learning increasingly focuses on mentors and coaches, smart organizations are enabling mentors and coaches to support talented people from across the company. At McKinsey and Company, all client assignments are communicated via VOX, the company's intranet. Client managers also post their experience and interest so that associates can make informed choices of which projects to be considered for.[8]
- *Choice of rewards and benefits.* At the pharmaceutical company Astra-Zeneca, information about the total cost of remuneration is shared with

each employee who is then free to create any personalized combination. This includes cash, health care, increased holidays, childcare vouchers, cars and bicycles, discounted retail vouchers, and pensions. Since its launch, over 85 percent of employees have chosen to create a package that is unique to them at that time. Employees access online advice, workshops, and expert advice to ensure that they make a wise choice.[9]

- *Choice of location.* Following the launch of "Achieving Balance," 5,600 British Telephone (BT) employees now work permanently from home, and 60,000 employees have the technology to work from outside the office if they so choose. This has released 220 million pounds in real estate costs and the productivity of home workers is among the highest in the BT workforce.[10]

- *Choice of time.* Flexible working patterns are crucial for any company operating in the 24/7 global marketplace. From an early pilot in the 1990s, BT has been developing a portfolio of work-life choices accompanied by Web-site and phone-line support. Over 60,000 employees now work in a time-flexible manner. By 2001, 9,600 people were either working part-time or job sharing. BT research on these groups suggests that they are more productive and committed to the organization.

Building choice makes sense: Choice communicates clearly that the old parent-to-child relationship has been firmly replaced by an adult-to-adult relationship. The benefits of the shift in this relationship are three-fold. With this change comes renewed self-assurance and flexibility. Employees who are able to craft a working life that they find fulfilling and stimulating are more likely to stay with a company. As BT found with its home workers, providing the freedom to choose makes sense cost-wise.

Yet, there is resistance to enabling choice in organizations. The mechanics are seen to be too costly, although Web-based technologies are making variety almost cost free. Power is a more important source of resistance; much of the power that resides with managers is based on the assumption that it is they who are most able to make decisions on behalf of their teams. Employee choice shifts the axis of this power from manager to employee. Finally, schooled in the paternalistic ethos, perhaps executives now doubt the aptitude and competence of their employees to make wise choices.

The Value of Choice

These companies have faced real challenges: in creating the technological infrastructure that underpins choice, in supporting managers to move away from the concerns they have about fairness and equity, and in creating sufficiently rich and meaningful information for employees to exercise choice and make wise decisions. Yet, each continues to invest in and support employee choice because the value of choice is tangible to them. They have built employee engagement and choice; they have used employee choice as a lever to integrate mergers and joint ventures; and, through choice, they have created a stronger foundation for justice and fairness.

First, these pioneers of choice are learning that employees who are given a choice are more engaged and more likely to stay. At BT, for example, people who choose to work from home are on average 20 percent more productive, 7 percent more satisfied, and deliver greater customer satisfaction.

Next, for some of these pioneering companies, building choice has created a shared platform of variety for employees whatever their heritage. When BP CEO John Browne supported the creation of a global platform for employees to access job and project opportunities, his aspirations were clear, "Everyone in BP, regardless of their company legacy, could plug-in and be part of the global operating systems." Integration was also the key driver for choice at AstraZeneca following the merger in 1999. Calculating the cash equivalent of every individual package and making the same 18 options available to all brought a level of transparency that established a shared baseline.[11]

Finally, by building choice, creating transparency, and making the rules clear, these companies are eliminating many of the side deals and the injustice and unfairness that can be associated with them.[12]

Lessons from the Pioneers of Choice

Each of these pioneers has created enormous choice for employees on one or more of the dimensions. There are three fundamental lessons that those executives, who are unclear or apprehensive about employee choice, can learn from these pioneers.

First, as in any functioning democracy, freedom of choice has responsibilities and duties associated with it. There is no such thing as a right without a responsibility. In these companies, the making of individual choice occurs within a context of responsibility and duty. At BT, for example, employees prepare a detailed business case that shows the benefits of their working flexibly or from home. This describes the way in which they will modify their working routines, the impact on colleagues and customers, and the support they need from the organization. This business case becomes the explicit contract between the employee and the organization. Further, well-honed performance measurement processes ensure that the performance responsibilities of the individual are adhered to.

Next, these organizations have kept rules to a minimum. Perhaps they have learned from the natural sciences, that in those "self-organizing systems" found in biology or quantum physics, order emerges from chaos under conditions of a few, simple, unifying rules or principles.[13] This simplicity is found throughout these pioneers. At AstraZeneca, for example, there are no rules about the composition of the package that an employee can build. A young mother may build a total package that has a small cash element, the bulk of which may be made up of subsidized childcare vouchers and discounted retail vouchers. Another young person may choose to put the bulk of his or her annual entitlement into the car of his or her dreams. The rules are simple and transparent: Everyone knows the base from which they can work, and everyone has equal access to the same transparent choices. This simplicity of rules is also apparent at BP.

Like most multinational companies, BP had an internal market for jobs with many rules, such as how long a person could stay in a job, what type and grade of job they could apply for, the protocols of line manager involvement in working with an individual's career plan, and inline managers' powers of veto. In the initial stages of the Web-based job market, these rules remained. However, they were quickly eroded. As e-HR team leader Greg Grimshaw remarks, "We quickly realized that the internal market for jobs had to work the same way as the external market. As long as you give people enough information about how careers can develop in BP, and increase their knowledge of the possibilities, then they will make wise choices."[14]

Greg's words lead naturally to the third lesson from the pioneers, that the freedom to choose can only be effective if rich and meaningful information is shared across the company. Scientists in the natural world have observed that the capacity of self-organizing systems for rapid adaptation and change is determined by the richness of information that is shared within the system. The same is true of choice in organizations. For employees to make choices that are mutually beneficial to themselves and the organization, they need to understand the choices available to them and the consequences of these choices.

Conclusion

A framework of choice is central to any organization in which the senior team is striving to become agile and adaptable. As we can see from these pioneers, the technology that underpins choice and customization is already in place. What is needed now is a fundamental change in mind-set, and members of the HR function have a key role to play. The first part of this role is to work with line managers to put in place performance measures capable of accurately measuring individual and team output. This clear line of sight between individual endeavor and corporate success is crucial. Next, to identify which of the seven dimensions of choice would be the most appropriate lever to begin this process. Finally, HR must work with the senior teams to articulate the values around individual choice and the benefits of diversity.

CHAPTER 16

<small>⟹⬥⟸</small>

Building a New Partnership

ALLAN R. COHEN AND
DAVID L. BRADFORD

IT IS HARDLY news that leadership is getting tougher and will continue to do so. In turn, the role of human resources must change. This requires a new form of partnership, one in which both leaders and HR managers understand the business, understand the employees, and take appropriate action that deals with both sets of needs.

Why Is Leadership Getting Tougher?

There are a number of forces at work making leadership more challenging:

- *Unpredictable crises.* Terrorism is only the worst of these; in an increasingly interdependent world, oil shocks, war, government overthrows, and natural disasters all demand a difficult combination of courage and openness.
- *Acceleration of technology.* Whether it is the rapid product cycles, disruptive or totally new technologies, product lines with incompatible characteristics to manage, new availability of information at all levels of organizations, or new ways of doing business, as with the Internet, leaders can no longer expect to have all the answers. Instead, the way that leaders will add value is by releasing and focusing the competencies that exist throughout the organization.
- *Industry boundaries crumbling.* Because of technology changes and new regulations, deregulation, or re-regulation, new competition arises from unexpected sources. No longer does work have to be done face-to-face, so airlines, for instance, now compete with phones, video conferencing, groupware, virtual teams, e-learning, and instant messaging.

- *Increasing pace of change.* In general, everything is moving faster. Long-term strategy is now measured in months, not years. This acceleration arises not only from the factors previously mentioned, but also from Wall Street with its unforgiving demands to meet quarterly predictions. The frequency of mergers and acquisitions, consolidation, technology shifts, and educated consumers with far greater access to information, all contribute to the increased pace of change and the expectations for rapid results. Even new CEOs are given less time to prove their worth.
- *Greater uncertainty.* Large bets required without all data in. It isn't only the chip business that requires $2 to $5 billion plants to expand to meet uncertain future demands. As soon as any business becomes commoditized, which happens faster than ever, it is the innovative products and ventures that make profitability possible. These require larger bets about unknowable demand, technical feasibility, first-mover advantage, or scarce talent.

All these changes demand that the leader not only *manage* change, but *produce* it if the organization is to stay ahead of the curve. This can feel increasingly difficult given the nature of the workforce:

- *Increased professionalization of the workforce.* With more education and higher job demands for reasoning, analysis, and judgment, employees at all levels have greater expectations for meaningful work. They seek opportunities for development and expect greater autonomy.
- *War for talent.* There are simply not enough skilled professionals to go around, and this won't change in the foreseeable future.
- *Change in the employment contract.* There are few companies left that will not have to reduce their numbers to respond to frequent drops in customer demand. The implicit contract, therefore, has gone from "permanent employment" to (at best) "employability." Even when that is honored, employees are increasingly cynical, suspicious, and unwilling to invest themselves wholeheartedly in needed organizational change efforts. General Electric, for example, now celebrates its annual process of getting rid of "C" players who have not improved from their forced curve rankings. Although some imitating companies have had to back off, the shock has spread everywhere, and it is harder to generate the kind of employee commitment and initiative needed to transcend competitive pressure and the fast pace of change.
- *Difficulty in building a common culture.* When the dot-coms were thriving, employees were in constant motion, leaving their employers for the next great set of benefits and the chance to get rich on stock options. The current halt in availability of jobs to move to is unlikely to last, making it a challenge to build a common culture with agreed-on values—characteristics that supposedly are necessary to build excellent companies.

Implications for Leadership

As a result of the combination of these forces, leaders will be required to develop skills that go beyond what they have been used to. They have to:

- Accept that they can't have all the answers.
- Live with, even embrace, more uncertainty and ambiguity.
- Handle (and produce) continuous change.
- Combine head and heart, demonstrating full toughness of analytical skills and business acumen while also being caring, open, and vulnerable.
- Use power on behalf of organizational goals, both directly *and* collaboratively as needed.[1]
- Create effective teams quickly, even when composed of dramatically more diverse people (including differing nationalities as well as other differences) or members who are not co-located.
- Tap talent throughout the organization—finding, recruiting, retaining, and growing people at all levels—discovering how to compensate managers for successful initiative will become critical in order not to ossify into bureaucracy, and understanding individual needs and coaching for effectiveness and personal growth will be mandatory.
- Rapidly build and integrate cultures, as mergers and acquisitions, new product teams, and other recombinations of people come together and move apart.
- Articulate and build commitment to vision at the company, unit, and personal leadership style levels, showing people the meaning behind their work and the leader's expectations.

Implications for the Roles of the Leader and Human Resources

"Division of Labor" between Line Managers and HR No Longer Works (If It Ever Did)

Many of these skills and attitudes are those that in the past have either been assumed to be unimportant or have been handed off to human resource departments. Too often, leaders have believed that toughness was the most important part of the job and that there shouldn't be time wasted on soft stuff, or they called in HR whenever some "sensitivity" was needed. Leaders did the task work and HR the people work. In times of labor shortages (usually stimulated by rapid economic growth), HR got to the table as people issues moved to the forefront, but as soon as top managers felt they had the upper hand over employees, things settled back to the (heavily lopsided) split. Everyone knew that profits, numbers, products, and markets were what really counted. As a result, human resources managers were frequently marginalized.

The Leader Must Integrate People Development with Task Performance

It is not enough that leaders pay more attention to human resource issues; people concerns have to be fully integrated with task issues. No longer can "soft" and "hard" be seen as separate domains. Leadership is not practiced on alternate Tuesdays at 9 A.M.; it is inherent in everything that managers do—or do not do. Making a bold investment decision in the face of opposition, for example, is about finance, market demand, and technology, and about getting people to invest themselves. By "invest themselves," we mean speak up to provide information even when it is in conflict with the leader's predispositions, collaborate with one another, and willingly accept the leader's judgment and good faith when their views are overridden. Managing people and managing tasks are inexorably intertwined.

The increased rate of change requires that *people issues* can't be so easily delegated to HR, since leaders will have to be able to respond in real time as they interact with others in the organization. Leaders will have to respond rapidly and appropriately to numerous challenges: to subordinate concerns and anxieties, to conflicts over direction and work style, to critical decisions that cannot be resolved by waiting for more data, and to the need for rapid teamwork across many boundaries. If they avoid all these problematic territories, organizational members will think them to be too cowardly, too conflict-avoidant, or too detached to be respected and followed.

Organizations spend over $60 billion a year in training and development, but the best developments occur in real time on the job. Organizational, interpersonal, and team goals are best accomplished through actually doing the organization's work. It isn't as effective to have separate team-building sessions, for example, where the team completes exercises to teach lessons about teams, and then goes "back to work." The kinds of lessons learned that way seldom stick as well as those learned in the process of doing significant tasks. As an example, consider the experiences of Pharmco (name disguised), which desperately needed to create effective teamwork among the top executive team, improve relations between the CEO and COO, end blaming and finger-pointing—and accomplished all that during meetings where as a team they made strategic decisions about shedding business units, reorganized to consolidate sales and research and development among units, reduced numbers of key players, and cut expenses by 10 percent. By looking at the way they worked and related in the process of wrestling with these tough decisions, they were able to both improve the business and improve the workings of the executive team.[2]

Furthermore, in the whirling and changing world we have described, going off to make human relationship changes and then being done for an extended period just isn't likely. Change will be rapid and frequent, so the leader must act in the moment, seizing on everyday incidents to "teach" the individuals and the organization how to function. In short, leadership is not divisible into task work and people work. They are interpenetrated.

If human resources cannot contribute as either a totally marginal functionary or a substitute player for leaders, how can it provide what is needed in the challenging world of the future?

Human Resources Needs to Be as Concerned with Tasks as with People

Just as leaders will see that the human issues are best handled and developed through work tasks, HR professionals must follow this integration as well. They can't and shouldn't push people issues for their own sake, but in the service of performance.

HR needs to understand and accept leader business goals and concerns, and make their arguments in terms of these goals and concerns. First, the partnership with business leaders must be a special partnership in which there is both specialization and joint ownership of all the problems of the business. While it isn't reasonable to expect HR experts to know as much about capital asset pricing models, return on net assets, market segmentation, global tax rates, economic lot size, or the DuPont model as the business people responsible for various functions and business units, they at least have to know what the leaders are talking about, the main assumptions behind their models and decisions, how they are measured and rewarded, what they are struggling with, and how the possible tradeoffs in critical decisions are considered. Why would a leader be confident about partnering with someone who has a special set of glasses on that block most of what the leader sees?

HR Needs to Speak the Language of the Leader (When in Rome, Speak Italian!)

At the most basic level, HR professionals need to understand and use the language of the business partners. (This is the advice the HR person would give the leader going abroad!) When they don't, they are dismissed: Recently a group of internal and external HR consultants was working on how they could better partner with line managers. In a role-play, in which one team member attacks another, the first HR person playing their manager said, "I think this is an issue of values. Ann, what are your values and are you acting on them? And Ted, what are your values?" This didn't seem to work so a second person tried it and said, "You aren't communicating well; Ann, what is your point? Be quiet, Ted, and let her finish. Now Ted, it's your turn." After another two similar approaches, the facilitator asked, "Is this how line managers talk?" An embarrassed participant exploded, "No, this is what they call "nursemaid" talk, and they laugh at us and don't listen to what we have to say."

HR initiatives and proposals need to have business/bottom-line rationale, not "I stand for caring for people and you should too, because people should be happy." If any action can't be shown to help reduce costs (including long-run ones like turnover and lack of creative problem-solving), win business, or build capacity for future business, it isn't likely to make headway, except with line managers who are currently enchanted with some soft fad, or where the manager is desperate. This does not preclude advising line managers on the likely consequences of their actions, including the impact on others in the organization, but the consequences need to ultimately be business-related.

HR Must Move from Being a "Deliverer of Services" to "Delivering HR Competencies"

Too often in the past, HR people claim, "We possess these very esoteric skills (in team building, conflict resolution, third-party negotiation, etc.) that only we, with our training, can do well." This attempt to gain importance lessens HR's centrality. It means that HR is called only at the problem stage, after the important decisions are made.

If line managers are to blend people and task domains, they need to have many of the skills held by competent HR staff. While line managers will never be as proficient in the HR area as the HR specialist (nor will the HR person be as competent as the line manager in business issues), there are many HR skills that line managers must have. They will have to be able to deal better with conflict, build teamwork, coach poor performers, and so on. They won't be able to wait to put out all people fires only when the HR fire trucks arrive.

This moves the HR specialist from just being a "deliverer of services" to passing on those skills. HR people need to learn to be credible coaches and teachers, not just in formal classes, but in their everyday interactions. Every time the HR specialist comes in to facilitate a teambuilding session or help untangle an interpersonal problem, the leader (and members) should become more competent to do it the next time. The HR person shouldn't just solve the problem, deliver the Silver Bullet, and ride off into the sunset, but should also explicitly pass on the knowledge that made this intervention successful. As power (and money!) is increased by passing it around rather than hoarding it, so is the value of human resources increased if managers acquire those competencies and experience their value. This doesn't mean that HR will ever work itself out of a job. Given the complexities of organizational life, the new problems (and opportunities) that constantly arise make it impossible for HR professionals to render themselves obsolete. By looking for ways to get the line managers to incorporate more good human practice into their daily interactions, the HR person keeps learning and growing and increasing in value to the organization.

Strengthening HR for True Partnership

If HR people can walk the delicate line between providing the most sophisticated human interaction and organizational expertise that only they can provide and being an observant coach and advisor to the line manager, they can achieve the kind of partnership effectiveness that will be organizationally useful and personally fulfilling. If HR is too important to leave to HR people, as one of our colleagues put it, it is also too important to leave solely to line managers. The world is too complex and too difficult for managers always to be on their own trying to perfectly combine task expertise with interactive skills. HR leaders can be valuable partners, providing coaching at times, a sounding board at others, expert advice on how to deal with difficult human situations when they have the expertise needed, and sometimes, acting as a business problem solver helping engaged and overwhelmed line managers to do the work of the organization.

The "soft stuff" is critical in the world we have described, and those who can do it without acting as if the rest of the business tasks don't matter will be central contributors. They will help conserve scarce resources and get employees to invent how to do more with less. They must generate the willingness for employees to take responsibility, even when that is risky; for employees to speak out when they know what the manager needs to know; and to seek new and better ways of doing everything.

The objective is to be included in the front end of problem solving (or problem finding), when the ideas are being explored and there is no obvious solution. Too often, however, HR has been brought in after the important business decisions are made—expansion, reorganization, cutbacks, and investments—to make sure that no (unanticipated) blood is going to be on the floor. HR needs to move from mop-up to cleanup hitter, or at least become part of the starting lineup. The more HR understands and contributes to business decisions, the more they will be invited to play—as leaders in their own right.

Contributing employees are those who do not just offer opinions based on their functional backgrounds or assignments; they use their general knowledge of how the parts of the business interrelate and their thinking skills to contribute in areas that might overlap with their specific domain. HR people should offer no less; by fulfilling this expanded role they will get the respect and centrality that they deserve.

CHAPTER 17

———⊰◆⊱———

Get Down to Business

KATE DCAMP

HR Leaders as Business Leaders

TO ACHIEVE THE highest return on human capital in a significantly more complex business world, a new type of leadership is required from human resources. We have a critical role as business leaders responsible for maximizing the return on the investment in human capital.

Management "Theory X" and the classic organization relied on highly defined structures, hierarchy, and policies that made the relative authority of each manager clear. Goals were set top down in the organization, and managers were responsible for ensuring that each individual on the team met the goals set for them.

Business Today Requires Different Kinds of Leaders

While the workforce and rules of business have changed, in this age of widely available information through technology, the training and development of managers has not made the shift required to build leaders. Then, add to the mix: (1) the globalization of business (see the section on globalization in this book); (2) generational changes from the post-World War II generation to today, which has given us a workforce with different starting points on Maslow's hierarchy (see Beverly Kaye, Devon Scheef, and Diane Thielfoldt's chapter in this book); and (3) the competitive advantage gained by operating without the hierarchy that once defined a well-managed company.

What management does today is different than what the workforce has been prepared for. Just in the past few years, business has become much more difficult. Just five years ago, few U.S. companies had to be concerned about emerging businesses in China or Brazil and their potential impact within the next few years. Besides changes in the global nature of business, talent management is also much more complex. Moving from Theory X management to what is required to motivate and inspire the new workforce is a critical change, which will define who gets the talent and who keeps it.

This new management paradigm is highly dependent on human resources functioning at a different level, as business leaders, responsible for developing leaders who can operate using influence and inspiration to manage today's workforce. In the digital age, leaders drive results by gaining agreement and a common understanding of the principles, values, and goals of the organization.

Knowledge workers, who possess an expertise of their own, are a greater percentage of the workforce than ever. The automation, outsourcing, and off-shoring of transactional work have boiled the professional worker's job down to the unique skills and ideas that he or she brings to the organization. The ability to follow established procedures is not as important, and very few people are hired without professional expertise. They no longer learn "all they know" from the employer. A new way of managing is required to retain the highly creative talent that is most likely to develop a next generation of products, to think beyond the current distribution channels, and to envision future customer needs.

Today's managers must unleash the creative potential of the workforce, while teaching employees how to work in teams and design scalable processes with sustainable results tied to corporate goals. This is different for most managers and stretches their skills and capabilities. Through information filtering, managers have controlled established procedures and defined decision-making structures. Understanding the people who work in the organization as individuals is a fundamental of management. Assessing the skills and passions of each individual and matching these to the right company goals maximizes the return on the individual's capabilities. This is the new art of management.

HR Leaders Must Understand the Business

Managing the new way requires those in HR to understand the business well enough to provide leaders with real-time information and to counsel them about the quality of the matches they are considering. Is the team working cohesively? Who are the influential leaders? Do they have a clear picture of the business goals? Do they agree that these are the right goals and that they are achievable? It is only the people in an organization who stand between a great goal and an outstanding achievement. Managing through influence and inspiration will produce the breakthrough results that differentiate a company from its competitors. Separating the work into small, measurable tasks to ensure that it can be monitored will never produce innovation or competitive advantage, and that model attracts and retains the wrong people.

Like many small, young companies, Cisco was resource-light and opportunity-rich in its early days. Employees had a chance to work on a variety of projects that made a difference to the company, and they had a tremendous opportunity to learn. Today, Cisco is revisiting that idea and moving people to the strongest business need while nurturing our talent. We find something that people love to do. We find their passion, rather than wasting time trying to motivate people who are not passionate about their roles.

Today, HR must provide more context and be a sounding board for managers who are leading teams with specialized talent beyond the manager's expertise. Yet, leaders are often selected because they demonstrated functional excellence rather than leadership finesse. Human resources must be the two-way communications and the "new way of management experts" in this age of greater dependence on fewer people. An effective human resources function can connect the dots between the business goals and what the workforce thinks it needs to do to contribute to the goals. To understand and see the disconnects between the business goals and the actions of people within the organization is a more complex and higher art than what has traditionally been required of the human resource function.

In the old model of HR as business partner, business leaders decided what to do, and HR (was the "partner" who) implemented the decisions. At the high end of this model, HR influenced the implementation plan and may have helped reverse some decisions based on legal risk or new information the business leader did not have.

Business Leaders Bring Something to the Table

What does HR as a business leader look like? HR should be "at the table" as issues are discussed and debated—before decisions are made. This does not mean that the CEO must tell everyone to listen to HR or that an invitation will arrive in the mail. This is the age of managing through influence and inspiration, and this applies to HR as well. To be seen as a business leader first, it is critical that HR leaders find the right insertion point.

HR can move an organization toward using real data to manage, reward, and promote their human capital rather than through sound bytes and anecdotes, which characterize people assessment in many companies. To begin, HR can change the way talent is viewed: from a single, manager point of view to multiple points of view. This can be done through organized observation and neutral rater assessments, employee pulsing, 360° reviews, and skip-level meetings, to name a few. Companies can use multiple instruments, approaches, and points of views to know and understand the organization's best performers and highest potential talent.

Next, changing what managers are valued for and measured on is important. If managers can succeed simply by adding up what their teams complete, without demonstrating any influence or value added, it will be difficult to upgrade to the quality of leadership needed to succeed in the future.

Data, such as pulse surveys and 360° feedback reviews, create a barometer of the effectiveness of managers. Such data help to redirect the efforts of managers toward excellence by giving them a "needle to move." Pulsing surveys should focus on the business-relevant information rather than the traditional "attitudes." The relevant question is not, "Do you like it here?" but rather "Are you empowered to fix a problem for customers quickly enough to retain their business?"

At Cisco, we survey our employees yearly, as a management index. Questions might include, "Do you have the information you need to serve the customer?" Because we do focus on regions and workgroups, we have created peer pressure to get high participation. HR builds the survey and works as a business leader in this active-listening process. We are developing data that is focused and actionable by individual managers. We are diagnosing trends (and looking for variation in scores) to find the strongest leaders, so that we can help others who are not. We believe we can continue to make an even stronger company one leader at a time.

Business Leaders Bring Answers and Ask Questions

Moving people in and out of HR to get a wider perspective is also valuable. An engineering manager brings important insight into the real problems of managers in the organization. Providing competitive intelligence about the people and structure of business competitors and other best-in-class companies is also important. You can help to answer (and provide questions about) why competitors may have better margins or growth than your company, and how they are doing it. Is it product excellence, salesforce effectiveness, service quality, a superior distribution model, a leaner organizational structure, or better hiring and development practices? HR can bring data to the table regarding performance measures used in competitor compensation plans, especially the sales plans. Is it even possible for a competitor to do a less effective job with people and still outperform your company financially? In today's people-dependent business model, it seems absurd not to look at competitor management structure and practices routinely.

When designing HR policies and programs, it's important to get managers outside of HR involved. We can share the problem we are trying to solve while painting the bigger picture and exposing managers to the art of HR. When managers come to HR seeking approval for a solution they are ready to implement, we can take them back to the business problem they're trying to solve. We can ask them if there is a prima facie case for change and how, or if, the current situation causes the business problem and for whom. We can ask the following questions: Does the manager have multiple data points on what the problem is and what caused it? Has anyone asked the customer if this is really a problem? Does the solution solve the problem identified? Does it cause new problems that are potentially worse than the problem it's solving? We can brainstorm with the manager to help them to the whole solution.

Human Resources at the Table

When HR gets to the table, we must exhibit business leader behavior: an interest in and point of view on all aspects of the business, not just the ones with HR implications. Today, virtually every business issue has HR implications, but they are rarely the whole story or even the best place to start in looking at a problem. HR needs to show we can measure what we do: We can draw a line from practices and actions to business results. We need to be able to measure increased productivity, increased agility, and the state and direction of the culture from top to bottom.

HR leaders, like all business leaders, must get out of the office and be involved with field operations and customers, including those in other countries. If HR is to be more than a back-office function, we must go beyond phoning or e-mailing HR out to the company. HR must spend time with the managers and employees, shoulder-to-shoulder, sleeves rolled up, tackling real business problems. We have to use a variety of communication vehicles to support a personal and involved approach.

For example, at Cisco, we have regular and frequent face-to-face meetings with employees, but we leverage our technology of Internet protocol television (IPTV) and videos-on-demand (VODs) to send a more personal message when others might just send an e-mail. HR leaders, like all business leaders, must be visible and consistently "on-message." Technology helps us meet some of these new challenges more quickly and in a global manner.

Not every business leader or CEO will gravitate naturally to having HR as business leaders. It may be a new idea for them. Yet, when a CEO views HR this way, it changes the insertion point. A solution can be to build relationships with the people who report to the CEO and his or her staff. We can find out what is going well and what isn't. As a co-champion for change, we can pilot a new program in those areas. It's smart to start that change with a stakeholder who will benefit the most from the change: In other words, go where the need is.

Finally, focus your time as an investment, too. Consider whether what you are working on now has a high return to the company. If not, find at least one thing that will have more impact. Find an insertion point: something that you can bring to the table. Start working on it now!

CHAPTER 18

━━━◆◆◆◆━━━

Accommodating Change in the 21st Century

YVONNE R. JACKSON

"PEOPLE CHANGE WHAT they do less because they are given analysis that shifts their thinking than because they are shown a truth that influences their feelings."[1]

Never before in the history of business has trusted leadership been a more important requirement. The leadership agenda for the 21st century must be compelling enough to reignite the questioning chaos of today's business environment. Now, more than ever, leadership and change require disciplined action. Leaders need to be passionate and willing to courageously "stand up" to the tough business, ethical, and moral issues and, to be successful, need to surround themselves with people who do the same.

The role of human resources leadership in the 21st century carries with it the complexity of our changing times. The roles of business partner; champion of change; employee advocate; functional leader, with accountabilities for large organizations, huge budgets, and corporate resources; employee communicator with corporate responsibility; and confidant to the CEO and other business leaders have more strategic value than ever before. At the same time, HR leadership carries more emotional weight, as those in HR find themselves accountable for advising and guiding leaders and the organization relative to the fiber of human capital.

Most often, business leaders are managing multiple constituents with their communication plan: the customers, the street, the national and local governments, and, finally, the workforce. On the other hand, the purpose of HR leaders is not only to develop the plan for action but also to lead, stimulate, and challenge the discussions at the management table; to test new theories or best practices; and to define the change tools that connect the workforce to the management system. As we look at leadership for the future, the need for an engaged work-force is the key to the future of sustainable change. Leaders create organiza-tional culture by setting an example, which is based on those things that they believe privately and recognize publicly through the reward system. Although the entire organization will not know the details of every decision, they will feel their rigor modeled throughout the company.

In this chapter, I describe two examples of leadership. Both examples have some flaws, but each can provide a basis of potential sustainable change. As I outlined the leadership strategies described in the remainder of this chapter, I discovered that both, for the most part, used the McKinsey 7-S model, yet the critical difference of change had to do with the leadership itself. While neither leader could be characterized as charismatic, both were passionate about their quest for change and would not settle for the simple answers. In addition, the assembled leadership teams, although in neither case high performing, collabo-rated and agreed on the ultimate goals and sacrifices to be made. After the business strategy was developed, both leaders took time to personally engage the workforce.

Restaurant Chain Story

This story begins with a multibillion-dollar, system-wide food company that was not retaining its customers. The problem, it seemed, stemmed from a con-fusing, mixed-fare menu. As a result, out of every ten customers, six did not re-turn. This was a wake-up call for the leadership team and ultimately became the burning platform for change. For several years, poor customer experience had been severe, and previous leadership regimes had hired three different marketing heads and two new ad agencies in the space of five years in attempts to solve the problem. Their solutions were new marketing themes and new ad-vertising campaigns, which attracted new customers but not repeat customers.

After an exhausting review of the previous five years, the new CEO hired an external consulting firm to review its operations and to work with the leadership team to develop solutions and a plan of action. Senior management appointed a team of content experts, ultimately termed the *reengineering team,* to work with the outside consultants and to present a proposal to the executive committee. Two essential problems in the business strategy were quickly uncovered:

1. From a product standpoint, the customers were confused about what a good eating experience was.
2. The customer experience was dissatisfying.

The bottom line was that the operational complexities in each restaurant were too cumbersome and difficult to manage. Additionally, it was not clear to cus-tomers what type of food the restaurant was offering because, in an attempt to increase sales, the number of items on the menu had been expanded to such an extent that it became confusing. Preparations of each of these food items also created operational complexities with each restaurant, thereby decreasing speed and accuracy of the order.

The CEO led the charge to systematically reengineer the company. First, the executive committee and the CEO had to define the company's vision and then convince their constituents of the action plan. It started with a clear mission statement: "To be the best hamburger business in the world in terms of customer satisfaction and restaurant profitability." This unambiguous statement cleared the way for a marketing strategy involving two components: hamburgers and customer service. The company reduced the number of operationally inefficient food products and reengineered the organization to focus the entire business on its restaurant operations. It was a clear rallying cry for the company: It fit with the 50-year heritage of the business, and it was something that all associates in the company could understand and endorse.

Taking the message out to the organization was a tough job: The business consisted of nearly 11,000 units, making communication a challenge. It had multilevels of a franchised ownership structure, which also required information and ultimate buy-in; and the new flatter and leaner organizational structure did not allow for command-and-control decision making. A different style of communication was needed. With clarity of vision, the CEO began with his leadership structure and that of the franchise community. He personally took on the challenge of meeting all of his constituencies in the organization, visiting regions, countries, and restaurants and, in doing so, modeled his passion, commitment, and the burning platform. As Jim Collins wrote in his bestseller *Good to Great*, leadership often starts with "getting people to confront the brutal facts and to act on the implications."[2]

Douglass Company

"Traditional management teaches us that leaders ought to be cool, aloof, and analytical—separating emotion from work. Yet when leaders discuss the things they are the proudest of in their own careers, they describe feelings of inspiration, passion, elation, intensity, challenge, caring, kindness, even love."[3]

In my practice, I have never experienced a more energized can-do attitude than that of the Douglass Company (name changed by author). The road to its success, while strategically imperfect, is a story of passionate leadership and culture change.

This is a tale of a leader and the path of change that came with his leadership. It depicts a dramatic culture change driven by fundamental competitive and business issues and leadership that had the passion to make a difference.

The company—a large, multibillion-dollar, high-talent organization—had four key product-services businesses that sold and provided services for small, commodity-driven computers to large-scale, highly profitable IT services. Each had a regional sales structure that was autonomous and independent in its thinking. The previous leadership team had acquired and attempted to integrate two of the four businesses with mixed success. Midstream in these efforts, the team became distracted from the business environment and organizational needs of the businesses. Instead of focusing on the highly competitive environment, it was bogged down with huge losses because of poor results and internal issues of integration, as well as with outsider questions about some business practices. The team members were completely disenfranchised from the leadership opportunity and the employee base. After an exhaustive external search to find a new CEO, the board appointed new internal leadership to combat these challenges.

At first, the new CEO focused on the challenging business issues and on setting goals to stem the profit hemorrhaging that was taking place in one of the company's key revenue-generating businesses. At the same time, he worked to develop strategies that focused on building the revenue capability of the other three businesses. The competitive landscape, which was changing dramatically from being hardware dependent to becoming more solutions oriented, would ultimately require the services and hardware product groups to work more closely together to maximize the sales proposition.

The CEO then focused on the best way to organize the business. The goals were to: (1) generate maximum synergy around core functions, such as procurement and supply chains; and (2) to create relatively loosely autonomous business entities that would help these product-services business leaders understand and be responsive to the competitive environment worldwide. Finally, the biggest challenges for the CEO were to improve employee morale, which was at an all-time low, and to integrate the several organizational cultures that existed because of the recent acquisitions.

You could argue that driving a significant change in a company's culture while maintaining the *best* of the existing culture requires a planned, systematic, well-designed road map. In fact, because the CEO had a passionate, intuitive, emotional, and nonbureaucratic leadership style, this wasn't possible.

The drama begins with the strategy. The leadership team defined both the competitive landscape and the strategy it would ultimately employ. Although the strategy would evolve and change over the course of the next three years, the team began with the development and model of the organization and the need to reengage and build some organizational trust by reconnecting senior management with the workforce. Second, the organizational structure was designed to mirror the competitive product-services segments. Third, because several key functional areas were without leadership, key positions were filled externally. This also served to balance the largely internal business leadership. Then, a critical set of management tools and actions was put in place to drive a value structure that focused on three areas: (1) clear business and organizational results, (2) customer satisfaction, and (3) employee engagement. The critical tools were leadership communication, both external and internal; a performance management tool called the *balanced scorecard*, which tied leadership to clear objectives and bonus payout; weekly business-results staff meetings; and finally, an internal workforce feedback tool, which was given annually to all associates in the worldwide workforce.

Each of these factors alone would not have driven the desired culture change results. However, all of these together contributed to a significant increase in employee morale, an engaged workforce, and a newly defined culture as measured by the annual workforce survey.

Leadership Communication

The internal communication structure was built around three themes:

1. Large, organizational meetings hosted by the executive leader as he traveled around the world and the executive roundtable-centered model.
2. Monthly management calls with the top 300 to 500 people in the company.
3. Small employee roundtables made up of 12 to 15 associates from a particular business, department, or facility.

Organizational Meetings

The senior management team took on the role of traveling and holding these large-scale meetings, which gave associates the opportunity to hear and get perspective on the new business strategy and to get a sense of the magnitude of change required to compete. The CEO was masterful with large organizational meetings. In his first year, he met with nearly 10,000 associates.

Monthly Management Calls

Monthly management calls with the company's top 300 to 500 people were hosted by the CEO. Each call featured a business update from the CEO, as well as one or two leaders in the organization who shared information about their business or area. In most cases, the head of customer satisfaction reported on how the company was doing concerning its focused customer satisfaction measures. (This was a focus of the change strategy and a heavily weighted item of the balanced scorecard.)

Small Employee Roundtables

The third model used was termed *small employee roundtables*. Each roundtable was composed of 12 to 15 associates from a particular business, department, or facility. These roundtables allowed for more informal, focused discussion by the associates, especially in response to three questions:

1. What did they do at the company?
2. What kept them up at night, or what was the single biggest obstacle to getting their jobs done every day?
3. What did they like about the company?

These discussions helped the executives understand what was happening in each group, department, or facility; and they showed employees that the senior leadership team was interested in and willing to work on their issues and challenges.

Balanced Scorecard

The Douglass Company used the balanced scorecard process, originally created by Robert S. Kaplan and David P. Norton, to set clearly defined goals in four key areas of importance as defined by the board of directors and the CEO:

1. Financial and market goals for the business unit.
2. Customer satisfaction (for the company and each business, measured quarterly by independent survey).
3. Operational improvements (dependent on the CEO's direction and/or the business/departmental needs for business operational improvements).
4. People—two corporate presets were developed each year to ensure that the organization was focused on critical areas. This measure was developed by the CEO and chief people officer in concert with the executive committee (see Figure 18.1).

Weekly Business Reviews

While business strategy meetings were held quarterly, the weekly business reviews were imperatives for the leadership team. In this weekly meeting, the CEO reviewed the progress of the business, including supply chain issues and

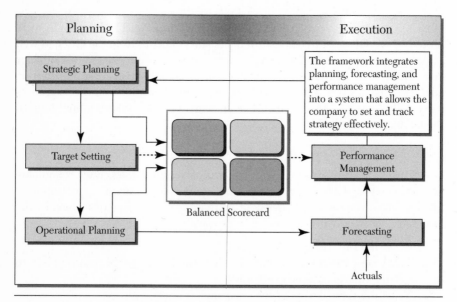

Figure 18.1   Integrated Planning Framework. This integrated planning framework depicts the linkage between strategic planning through to performance management. It ties together the planning processes (reflected on the left side of the frame) with actual performance (reflected on the right side of the frame).

other critical business issues. Important decisions were often made during these meetings, and it was in these meetings that the CEO gave his critical review of the business.

Voice of the Workforce

The *voice of the workforce* was an associate feedback mechanism designed to give management feedback from associates around the world. It measured both the associates' understanding of the business strategy and the multitude of vehicles used to communicate those strategies. The survey instrument was designed for more than once-a-year attitude measurement. In a customer-driven organization such as this one, the voice of the customer is usually integrated into the change strategies; however, this management team felt that the employee voice should also be integrated into the company strategies as customer feedback. Managers got behind the survey process, and they wanted to see their results improve. Many of the management communication products referred to the survey results, demonstrating that the leadership team was taking action. In short, the survey was not an HR initiative, but rather a part of the leadership agenda, and it reflected the belief system of the leadership team. Along with the HR management tools, which served in many cases as feedback loops, the aggressive and passionate leadership transformed the company culture. When these two things come together, a company has the ingredients to create change.

Human Resources Role in Change

The significant and telling ingredients in both cases of change leadership described here are bold, decisive action; yet, more important are the passion and trust that the CEO and senior leadership teams established with their workforces. Both leaders and leadership teams understood that their workforces were major business drivers, and in both companies, significant change had to occur if the businesses were to continue.

In my experiences with these companies, I have found that when a turnaround is required or frame-breaking change must occur, human resources leadership is critical. HR teams must have the skills to be business partners, confidants, and professional change agents to handle the tough business decisions that often affect large segments of the workforce, its development, and its engagement. In the case of the restaurant company, the performance management system had to be redesigned to support a flatter, leaner, team-based organization in which the span of control was sometimes 100 people to one vice president. Because most of the work took place in these teams, the performance management tool was designed to have a team-evaluation process versus having the manager complete performance appraisals each year. The manager in this case reviewed the team evaluation and followed up with a career discussion. In the case of the computer company, the balanced scorecard was the basis for the senior management team's incentive system.

The communication vehicles and workforce feedback tools at times were partnered with public relations and/or communication organizations. This ensured that communication to the workforce supported the business strategy and methods of the leadership agenda. In many cases, I have seen workforce feedback tools that are designed around employee satisfaction. However, during a change process, it is also important that the company's leadership receive feedback as to employees' understanding of the change strategies to ensure that the strategies are being communicated well.

Finally, while the leadership practice agenda is often overlooked, it is probably the most important. In both companies discussed in this chapter, these leadership programs were forums for the middle and senior managers to meet and dialogue about what they felt was happening in the company. These programs should be designed to provide information about the company, and the information should be used by middle managers to own and develop a personal leadership agenda in other settings.

Recently, I have noticed that the HR executive, as a new member of the executive or operating committee table, has forgotten what brought him or her to the business table: the workforce. Recognizing their responsibilities and capabilities, HR leaders must not only understand how to involve the workforce in an ongoing dialogue but also stand up for this constituency if there is to be sustainable change in any organization. Associates in organizations usually have the answers, and if treated with trust and respect, they will give management workable solutions to problematic business issues. With the right management and feedback tools, the passionate and trusted leader brings out the best qualities of each individual, thus not only accommodating change in the 21st century, but also sustaining and engaging a high-quality workforce that is capable of leading the organization to success.

What is needed to accommodate change in the 21st century? A passionate, trustworthy, modeled leadership; disciplined and defined action; and a mechanism for systematically listening to the workforce, so that employees feel engaged and thus supply the energy to the organization that ensures sustainable change.

CHAPTER 19

Managing Global Total Rewards

RICHARD KANTOR

Shift from Total Compensation to Total Rewards

A S WE ENTERED the 21st century, *total compensation* (and *total remuneration*) began giving way to the concept of *total rewards*. This shift is more than just a change in nomenclature; it reflects a broadening view of how companies can attract talented people, influence and recognize desired behavior, and reward positive results. The movement to a *total rewards* approach represents an important mind-set shift involving an expanded view of what the employer provides to the employee and what the employee wants from the employer. Differences in national (and organizational) culture play a big role in how employers and employees define the total *package.*

The precise definition of *total rewards* varies from company to company, but it normally comprises the following five elements (see Figure 19.1):

1. *Indirect financial rewards* typically includes health and welfare benefits, paid time off, retirement plans, perquisites, and recognition. Together

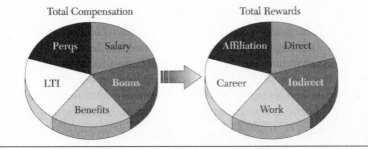

FIGURE 19.1   The Shift from Total Compensation to Total Rewards

with direct financial rewards, this represents what is typically referred to as *total compensation*.

2. *Work content* relates to the quality of the work itself (e.g., variety, challenge, autonomy, and meaning), and this, by extension, includes the quality and impact of performance feedback.
3. *Career value* is the opportunity for personal growth, capability improvements, organizational advancement, and employment security.
4. *Affiliation* refers to the rewards that accrue from association with the company. This can be a sense of status that comes from working for a reputable organization, or it might relate to access that the organization provides to colleagues or other groups of people.
5. *Direct financial rewards* refers to pay components including base salary, cash allowances, incentives, and company ownership. This is the foundation of the total reward package.

In the past, the focus was mainly on pay and benefits. However, today's broader notion of total rewards centers the focus on *everything an employee gets* as a result of working for a company.

Globalization has played a key role in this shift to the broader view. As companies have worked to manage their total compensation programs on a global basis, many have realized that the most important elements of the package (those that help to attract and retain the best talent) often are not "pay and benefits." In fact, frequently what differentiates the multinational employer in a local marketplace is precisely the *other* elements of the total reward package (i.e., work content, career value, and affiliation). This observation has helped employers to see that these other elements also play an important role "back home" and, as a result, there is a new focus on managing the complete package.

The eye-opening role that globalization played in terms of the "discovery" of the total rewards concept has led to the word *global* more often than not preceding the term *total rewards*. Accordingly, it is in the global sense that these concepts are explored throughout this chapter.

Given the number of organizations that have worked to improve their approach to global total rewards, and given the impact that this subject has on business results, it makes sense to take a step back to ask two key questions:

1. Why are so many companies focusing attention on this now?
2. What can be learned from the work that the pioneers have already done?

Why Such Interest in Global Total Rewards?

The increased focus on the development of a global total reward strategy is easy to explain: It helps organizations address many of the key issues that they face, such as:

- *Managing costs.* Total rewards represent a major cost element and, for most companies, a cost item that is under increasing pressure. A sound global total reward strategy redirects money away from ineffective programs and toward more effective reward elements. It can also be used to identify cost-saving opportunities.
- *Driving strategy.* As the economic and competitive environment intensifies, organizations are concerned about sending clear messages and eliminating conflicting messages. The global total rewards program is a key message sender—companies need to make sure they are sending the right messages and aligning all the components of the employee experience.
- *Generating results.* Organizations are focused on increasing performance and accountability of the workforce: utilization, productivity, controlling people costs, employee revenue generation, and customer satisfaction. All of these aims can be better met with a sound global total reward strategy that focuses attention on the right areas and rewards desired results.
- *Achieving more with less.* Organizations are struggling to manage engagement with fewer goodies to hand out. Redefining rewards as "everything an employee gets as a result of working for the company" is a good place to begin. More than this, developing a global total reward strategy is a way to define the most engaging mix of these elements for different employee groups around the world.
- *Moving with increased speed.* The global total rewards strategy helps to define what is "in bounds" and what is "out of bounds" in terms of acceptable and desirable reward practices. Clearly articulating the desired state helps local managers around the world to respond more rapidly to shifting competitive landscapes. In addition, acquisitions can be integrated more quickly.
- *Making HR accountable.* Organizations are looking to make HR accountable and more effective in the 21st century. This involves managing costs and enhancing productivity by eliminating inefficient HR processes and cluttered communication channels. A global total reward strategy provides a real, tangible place to begin that effort. It also represents an area of tremendous potential in terms of generating quick wins and meaningful results.

What Can We Learn from the Pioneers?

Five main categories describe the key observations gathered from previous work done in this area:

1. Identifying the elements of a global total reward strategy.
2. Implications of thinking globally (about total compensation).
3. Striking the right balance (between desire for consistency and desire for cultural adaptation).

4. Getting from here to there (managing change globally).
5. Managing the global employer brand (and the importance of reward).

Each of these categories is discussed in more detail throughout the remainder of this chapter.

Observation 1: Identifying the Elements of a Global Total Reward Strategy

Sometimes, organizations have asked for help developing a global total reward strategy without having a clear idea of what a strategy would encompass. The typical global total reward strategy addresses the following elements:

- *Strategic perspective.* A total reward strategy begins with an articulation of the organization's values and business strategies. Well-crafted reward strategies are clearly linked to the aims of the business. The written statement of total reward strategy is the place to be clear about where, when, and how these links between business goals and rewards should and should not be made.
- *Statement of overall objectives.* The reward strategy should include statements that describe how the reward system will support the needs of the business and the company's customers, employees, shareholders, and other key stakeholders. This typically includes a delineation of the role of each reward element.
- *Prominence.* The statement of total reward philosophy describes the overall importance of rewards relative to other tools that can focus and affect actions and decisions (e.g., shared values, job design, promotions, clear strategies, feedback). In addition, a well-crafted reward strategy describes the degree to which rewards are expected to drive employee actions and decisions through variability, influence over outcomes (controllability), and the explicitness of the pay-performance link. One way to think about prominence is to imagine your employee talking to a friend about working for your company. Prominence involves two key questions:

  1. How early in the conversation would you like the employee to stress how attractive the total reward package is (as opposed to other things such as the culture, the quality of leadership, the focus on customers, etc.)?
  2. When the employee does eventually talk about the reward package, which *elements* of the package would you like to hear mentioned first, and which should be mentioned last (or not at all)?

- *Performance measures.* A total reward strategy should clearly identify the performance criteria to be rewarded, the appropriate level of measurement (e.g., corporate, business unit, geographic region, workgroup, individual) for each, and which reward elements will be linked to which measures.

- *Competitive market reference points.* The total reward strategy should describe the types of companies, industries, or other reference points that will be used as the basis for determining the competitiveness of the reward package.
- *Competitive positioning.* The strategy should also clearly describe the desired competitive position relative to the competitive reference points in the labor market. Ideally, it should also define how the competitive positioning is expected to vary with performance or other criteria.
- *Degree of internal equity and consistency.* The statement should address the extent to which the total reward strategy will be applied uniformly throughout the company, both horizontally and vertically. Companies often take a view that both internal and external relativities are important, which is true. However, defining a strategy is about making choices. A good global total reward strategy clearly defines which is more important when the two are in conflict.
- *Communication and involvement.* The strategy should define how much information about the reward programs will be disclosed and explained to employees. It also should outline the degree of participation that employees will have in the design and ongoing administration of the reward programs. This should include a clear delineation of where HR's responsibility for designing and managing rewards ends and management's accountability begins. In addition, the strategy should define the organization's policy toward employee unions, work councils, and other representative or collective bargaining units.
- *Governance.* While core principles governing the reward program should remain fairly constant, the underlying programs need to be revised and refreshed periodically to ensure that they are competitive and compelling. The reward strategy should delineate how frequently such reviews will occur and who will play which roles in carrying out the review and in any redesign that is deemed necessary.

Observation 2: Shifting from Common Platforms to Common Principles

Experience tells us that when organizations begin to think globally about their approach to total reward strategy, it is best if they can shift their conceptual approach to the topic to achieve success and avoid frustration. This shift involves thinking about common *principles* rather than common *platforms*.

Many organizations manage the rewards for their business units in a single country by establishing programs with similar (or identical) design parameters. For example, companies might implement a bonus program with a maximum payout equal to 200 percent of target or a savings plan with a 50 percent match. These design criteria might then vary slightly for different employee groups or business units. But, by starting from the same platform, these organizations effectively ensure that programs are designed to support the same underlying goals.

A quick comparison of the programs can be used to highlight different underlying principles. For example, when salespeople have a higher proportion of their cash compensation delivered through variable pay, certain conclusions can be made about the different assumptions concerning the most appropriate way to motivate and reward salespeople as opposed to other employees.

As businesses or employee groups in the organization become more diverse, the applicability of common platforms often becomes strained. This is one reason that we usually see significantly different total compensation programs for business units engaged in noncore activities or for unique employee groups (e.g., top executives, salespeople).

When total compensation programs are extended to other countries where competitive, cultural, and legal environments differ dramatically, applying a common platform typically is no longer feasible. The context is simply too different. As a result, most organizations we have worked with shift their thinking (or aim) from common platforms (i.e., program design) to common principles. In other words, they seek to ensure that the programs are designed to achieve the same ends while recognizing that the means may well need to vary from country to country. They realize that doing the same thing in different context often yields a different result. In addition, most organizations want the same (or at least predictable) results. This is best achieved with clear principles.

Establishing clear principles and then allowing the means to the ends to vary from country to country also helps to empower local line and HR managers to design appropriate programs. Usually, these are the people in the organization who understand how best to achieve the desired results while respecting the proper principles. This leads to the third observation.

Observation 3: Striking the Right Balance

Making the two shifts described previously often forces organizations to confront the crucial issue of how best to balance the desire for global consistency and control with the desire for local effectiveness and efficiency. The possible approaches are illustrated in Figure 19.2.

In resolving this issue, it is important to note that there is not a single correct approach. Much of the literature on globalization might lead us to suspect that the top right quadrant is "the place to be." However, rather than focusing on which approach is theoretically most appealing, we have observed that well-managed global organizations do not pursue some theoretical ideal. Rather, they identify the approach that makes the most sense for their business, and then they rigorously review, redesign, measure, and readjust to make sure that the chosen approach is being faithfully applied. They manage to it *consistently*.

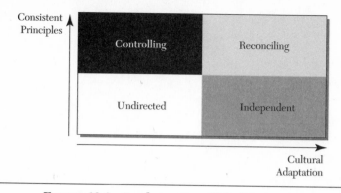

FIGURE 19.2   Implementing Global Programs

Alignment Is Key

Successful organizations around the world start with a clear set of business goals that are well understood and embraced throughout the organization. These goals serve to dictate a strategy for achieving the results. The strategy includes a description of the kinds of people and the number of people the organization needs to produce the results. Successfully managing HR in a global setting requires the same basic focus that is applied in successful organizations domestically: a focus on alignment. A critical role for the HR function in a global organization is to ensure that the people programs are properly aligned with the aims of the business and helping to produce desirable results. This concept is illustrated in Figure 19.3.

Observation 4: Managing Change Globally

After the direction is established, there remains the issue of how to move the organization from where it is to where it needs to be. The aim is not simply to modify programs and policies to bring them into alignment with a statement of global principles. The aim is to drive change in the organization so that business results improve. Successfully managing change in a global business requires integrating the key principles of change management with an understanding of national cultural differences.

Change management techniques are often well understood and well applied by HR and business leaders. When working globally, the additional nuance of national culture sometimes leads to changes that do not "stick" or, even worse, change initiatives that backfire. On the other hand, knowing how to work through the cultural differences helps to make sure that aligned programs produce transformational changes in the organization. A great deal has been learned about making change stick. Much of what it takes has to do with understanding culture and how it affects people's expectations during times of change.

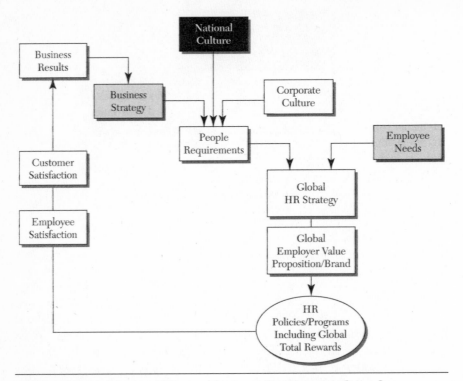

FIGURE 19.3   Achieving Alignment between Business Results and
HR Programs

Understanding National Culture

Culture has been defined as the "collective programming of the mind which distinguishes one group of people from another."[1] Essentially, it is the way in which a group of people solves problems and reconciles dilemmas. Culture needs to be distinguished from *human nature,* which is inherent and genetic, and *individual personality,* which is not about groups.

Looking at different cultures does not imply a *normalcy* for you or your group. It does call for suspending judgments when dealing with groups that are different from your own. Culture exists at national, gender, generational, social, and corporate levels.

Reward programs are designed to motivate people to do certain things or behave in certain ways. Reward and culture are inextricably linked because culture directs our actions by providing people with a meaningful context in which to meet, think about themselves, and face the outer world. It is the filter through which the reward system's messages are received and interpreted. Understanding culture is critical when managing change and designing reward programs.

How Culture Affects Change Management

The impact of culture on transitions is vast. Table 19.1 shows some examples of how one dimension of culture (environment) affects change management. Similar analysis can be prepared for other dimensions of culture.

Applying This Information to the Establishment of a Global Total Reward Philosophy

While this information is vitally important when implementing changes in a global context, it is also important to have in the back of our minds when we consider establishing a global framework for total rewards. We do not want to create a set of guiding principles for our reward programs that are virtually unrealizable, given cultural constraints. At the same time, though, we do not want to be a slave to national culture. By explicitly defining what we stand for (i.e., our organizational culture) and then carefully selecting employees from the culture in which we are operating who are predisposed toward "our way of thinking" and properly managing and rewarding those employees, an organization can create the organizational culture it needs to deliver desired business results.

In fact, an important question for an organization to consider as it expands internationally is: "Are we small enough to go counter to the local culture?"

TABLE 19.1 Impact of Cultural View of Environment on Change Management

Environment	Determinist	Fatalist
Description.	People can and should seek to control the environment by imposing their will on it.	People must go along with laws, directions, and forces in the environment.
Impact on transition.	People are likely to view change as something to respond to or even resist; discomfort when environment seems out of control.	People are likely to view change as an external force from which we should accept guidance; comfort with shifts and cycles as long as they are "natural."
	Reaction to change: How can we take hold of chaos and master it? How can we shape it?	Reaction to change: How will we use the force of change to create a more effective combination and harmony? How should we be shaped by it?
	Management's role is to devise and communicate a strategy—a plan designed in advance to wrest competitive advantage from other companies; the employee's job is to implement the strategy.	Employees are expected to devise strategies for coping with day-to-day problems; the job of top management is to take these emergent strategies and give recognition, status, and formal sanction to those proved most valuable.
	Focus is on self, function, own group, and own organization.	Focus is on "other," customer, colleague, and so on.

Source: ©1998. A. Trompenaars and C. Hampden-Turner, *Riding the Waves of Culture.* (New York: McGraw-Hill, 1998). Reproduced with the permission of The McGraw-Hill Companies.

When organizations need to recruit limited numbers of people, it is easier to select from a narrow slice of the distribution of cultural norms.

Observation 5: Managing the Global Employer Brand

Finally, global total reward strategies play a crucial role in helping employers define their global employer brand.

Reward systems affect organizational performance and individual behavior largely through the impact they have on people's beliefs and expectations about how they are rewarded and will be rewarded. Expectations are particularly important in influencing motivation. They also have an important influence on organizational culture and the organization's ability to attract and retain talented employees. To be effective, a reward system must impact perceptions and beliefs in ways that produce desired organizational behaviors.

The perceptions and beliefs that individuals develop are partly a product of the practices and behaviors of the organization, but they are also influenced by statements that the organization makes—or fails to make—about its values and intentions. Regardless of what an organization says or does not say about its reward practices, individuals form beliefs about how rewards are administered. These beliefs represent a key element of the employer's "brand" in the market for talent.

Employees and prospective employees develop their beliefs after considering their experiences with the organization, what they are told by others, and what they are told by the organization. Personal experience and cultural orientation become the filters through which individuals interpret this information to make plans for developing a satisfying and rewarding situation for themselves.

The key issue for the organization is how to influence the beliefs that individuals develop. If the organization is silent in terms of what it is doing, it may cause individuals to develop a lower impression of the brand than they would have if the organization had stated principles that effectively guided individual beliefs. Drafting a written statement of total reward philosophy can help to achieve appropriate brand positioning.

Accordingly, a global total reward strategy generally is crafted to meet two primary aims:

1. To articulate a distinctive value proposition for current and prospective employees that attracts and retains people with the capabilities and values that the employer needs to succeed.
2. To provide a framework from which the employer designs, administers, and evaluates effective reward programs with the maximum motivational impact to drive desired behaviors and results.

In essence, the total reward philosophy helps to establish the employer's brand.

After the statement of total reward philosophy is developed, it should drive and guide the organization's reward system practices and be a relatively permanent piece of the organization's culture, history, and policies. The core principles should not change, except in those extraordinary circumstances when major strategic changes need to occur in the way the organization is managed and run. After the reward strategy has been established, it should be communicated frequently and reinforced publicly by the organization's leadership and through employee communication material.

Looking Ahead

This notion of managing the employer's brand is putting a sort of evolutionary pressure on the relatively young notion of global total rewards. While some employers are making the shift from *total compensation* to *total rewards*, others are already shifting from *total rewards* to *total employment experience*—in other words, going beyond "everything an employee gets as a result of working here" and thinking even more broadly about "everything that touches an employee and prospective or former employees." The pace of change in the 21st century certainly is fast!

CHAPTER 20

Globalization of HR

21st Century Challenges

ROBERT J. JOY AND PAUL HOWES

THE PAST TWO decades of the 20th century have seen enormous changes in how businesses operate geographically, driven by twin revolutions in transportation and telecommunications. They have both made operating across borders easier and, to an increasing degree, essential. Add to that the advance of free trade as a political driving force more strongly than at any time in the past century, and we have had powerful forces for change.

However, with change comes the increasing complexity of working across multiple time zones, with multiple cultures, economic and political situations, and business environments. Human resources grew up as a purely national discipline and, to this day, remains subject to largely national legislation on all aspects of employment. In other words, few HR professionals and few line managers are truly prepared for the new global world. In addition, operating globally requires you to rethink how you view HR and operate in a global environment. Consequently, we contend that globalization will be *the* biggest single challenge facing HR professionals over the next century.

Three Strategic Themes

In this chapter, we attempt to prove our contention with three strategic themes:

1. HR must think of itself and operate as a business globally.
2. For maximum effectiveness, HR leaders must understand cultures around the world.
3. Thinking globally is a major change for most people.

HR Must Think of Itself and Operate as a Business Globally

The principal role of human resources is to build the capability of its people to deliver business results. To accomplish this, it must have the best talent in the right place, at the right cost, and at the right time. While we can stretch analogies, this role closely parallels that of a global business—that is, having the right product in the right place at the right cost and time. The alignment of these two processes, considered separate in many organizations, is really the key to HR's operating as a business partner on a global basis.

Look at how the delivery of products and services has changed globally over the past several years, and observe some meaningful parallels with what HR needs to do:

- Organizations have become more geographically spread around the world. A random selection of large U.S. companies revealed that every one of them had an increasing proportion of revenues from overseas, compared to ten years ago: They have become more global. Many companies have centralized manufacturing operations in particular countries to obtain economies of scale, which can overcome transportation costs.
- Branding has become global. Sony, Coca-Cola, Marlboro, IBM, McDonald's, and Colgate are universally recognized symbols of what they represent.
- The bar has gone up on speed, new ideas, and customer service. Customer expectations have risen because they can.
- Margins have shrunk as competition has intensified, and technology has put more power in the hands of the consumer and the major buying groups. Products are *mass customized;* that is, the underlying system is geared to mass production but allows the customer to design his or her own product or service.
- Some work, even customer-facing work, has begun to move geographically away from the customer. Advances in telephony now allow people in India, for example, to make outbound calls to the United States at a much cheaper cost than Americans can call one another.

What Are the Parallels Facing HR in Global Firms?

- HR's job is to manage talent delivery as a brand manager manages the delivery of the particular brand he or she is responsible for. As with consumer branding, you can control some elements in the short term and others you cannot. The growth of global brands has affected HR, too. Many people around the world join Colgate precisely because it is Colgate. It provides potential global opportunity and a promise of an employment experience that is noticeably different from that of a local company. Just as branding causes a consumer to purchase a product because of an expected experience, employees have expectations of us as employers; it has a side effect of extending the employment promise. Done right, global branding provides global companies with a real competitive advantage in the employment marketplace.

- As a truly global company, Colgate has realized that the bar has been raised on the expectations needed to provide a workplace that attracts the best talent. Consistent with its branding efforts, it realizes that it must also provide the *best place to work* for its people and define the key parameters consistently on a global basis.

- For HR, the parallel with shrinking margins is increasing pressure to do more with less. Just as every global business has eliminated complexity in its operation by focusing on global advertising, global packaging, and global formulations, HR must also relook at its global processes to eliminate, streamline, and standardize where necessary. The Corporate Leadership Council reveals that in the United States between 1992 and 1998, the average number of employees per HR person increased from 84 to 111.[1] This trend will certainly continue, and the pressure on HR to reduce costs, streamline processes, use technology, and be more efficient will intensify. This will be a key component of managing globally. Just as the bar has significantly risen on any global business to improve its speed and its customer service, HR has a parallel challenge.

All this is stretching current HR capabilities in many organizations, but there is a further point in our "HR needs to be run as a business" analogy. HR has a top-line role: The activities it needs to perform to meet the needs of its customers. However, it also has a bottom-line role: It must minimize the cost of running itself. This is the difference between running an HR function globally and running a global HR function.

We are not yet seeing much evidence of this in the marketplace beyond regional shared service centers, but the consequences of moving to this next stage can be profound. For example, it may well be that, to minimize cost associated with particular processes, HR may want to establish operations in a country in which the company has little to no other presence.

At the extreme, even companies with no current international presence (e.g., local or regional hospital groups) may find that they need to open back-room operations in another country to keep their own costs down. Such a prospect is daunting indeed. It may be simpler to outsource to another company that does have such operations.

For Maximum Effectiveness, HR Leaders Need to Understand Cultures around the World

Operating globally increases corporate revenues, but it also creates complexity beyond what would be present if a company stayed in one market. Some of the complexities are discussed in the following sections.

Understanding How to Motivate People in Different Markets around the World

In North America, we are primarily driven by monetary rewards. Other cultures value recognition, titles, personal connections, and status more. Most people value all of these factors, but to different degrees. Knowing and understanding this variation help avoid projecting our own cultural values onto others and help us to be more effective in every market, rather than just the English-speaking world.

For example, knowing the talent shortage for managers in China, company XYZ decided to put its managers there on a long-term incentive program with a four-year pay-out period. One manager actually left because of the program, saying that "the Americans" did not understand that money was not as important for him and that he resented the idea that his loyalty could be bought.

Moving People from One Place to Another

In a global company, moving people from one place to another is not dominated by moves to and from the headquarters country. Instead, talent is moved around the world for development purposes or to meet short-term needs in a particular place. Consideration needs to be given not only to the needs of the company, but also to the skills and aptitudes of individuals and to how likely they will be to succeed in the culture of the host country.

Talent Management and Nurturing Global Leaders

Colgate emphasizes talent management through a few main processes:

1. Identification of its best talent on a global, regional, and local basis.
2. Consistent feedback to let people know how they are doing and what's coming next.
3. Focus on retention using cash and stock.

Colgate does all of these things through a "high-touch," highly personalized environment (which would have helped the company with the Chinese employee mentioned previously). Monthly senior-management people reviews ensure that Colgate leaders get to know the talent around the world. These reviews give them the opportunity to get acquainted with key people, obtain an overall view of performance and potential, and discuss candidates for key positions. After a person is identified as a global, regional, or local high potential, his or her compensation and reward mechanisms are reviewed and often enhanced.

Building on Colgate's long history of a strong global network, a group of these high potentials are invited to headquarters each month to participate in a customized *visibility* trip. During this visit, they meet individually with senior leaders who talk about the business and candidly share their own personal leadership lessons. They get the opportunity to sit face to face with division management from five international regions to network and build their own personal connections.

Creating and Managing Teams from Multiple Countries

Working within multinational, multicultural teams is a difficult skill to learn, and not everyone can do it successfully. As companies operate more globally, the number of times this skill is needed increases dramatically.

In a truly global company, multicultural teams are a way of life. To proactively build this capability early in its future leaders, Colgate routinely has multifunctional, multicultural teams work on business-based projects in its leadership development programs. Each year, "early in-career talent" and director-level high potentials are responsible for completing a project aligned with one of Colgate's key business objectives. Sometimes, this work is face to face, and sometimes it is completely virtual. The one certain aspect is that it is *global*.

What Is Different about Global Companies?

Most of the items discussed in this chapter are already known, but:

1. Many will become new to increasing numbers of companies over the years to come, as companies expand overseas.
2. Intensity increases with the move to running a global HR function.
3. Consequences of not doing them well intensify with the importance of global operations.

Even beyond these items, as companies begin to run their HR functions globally, there are additional areas in which they can add value to their business beyond what most currently do; for example, with strategic planning, siting of operations, and process management, all of which can be impacted by national cultures.

To harness the terrific potential of a globally diverse workforce, there must be alignment between the workforce and the company's goals. The creation of alignment is a process that depends for its success on effective communication with the company's managers and the entire workforce. Consequently, there must be a global process to communicate effectively across cultural, language, and geographical boundaries to ensure alignment against the key priorities that define business success. HR must be a key partner in this process. It cannot effectively be delegated to other functions such as public relations or marketing, precisely because of the need for alignment with other HR initiatives.

Thinking Globally Is a Major Change for Most People

Thinking globally does not come naturally to many people. It is more difficult for people who have grown up in large countries, who have had less exposure to foreigners or foreign news. The smaller the society in which a person grows up, the more outward he or she has to look for business and/or world news and the more familiar he or she is likely to be with people from other cultures. This may explain the success of Singapore, for example.

However, global thinking can be learned, and it is noticeably different from thinking nationally. Two examples should prove this point:

1. You are the head of a European business making automotive components and need a plant manager for a new joint venture in China. Many candidates are possible from your plants in Europe or the United States, but they are expensive, at the wrong stage of their careers, or not people-oriented enough to succeed well there. You could hire from the outside, but that carries a risk that the newcomer will not represent the company well to its Chinese partner, with whom you want to do much more work in the future. The solution actually adopted: Pick an Indian manager from one of your Brazilian plants.

2. A United States company has a need for a 24-hour call center to provide customer support for a major application being implemented around the world. Three possible solutions, the first of which was the one originally under consideration, are:

—Run three shifts from Arkansas.
—Run three shifts in another location outside the United States.
—Run one shift in each of three locations around the world and have the call center follow the sun.

Each of these works best in different situations. The point is that thinking globally widens the range of possible outcomes and allows for better decisions.

Thinking globally is not always beneficial, however. If the concept is not understood, being global can easily degenerate into centralization and/or a desire to manage details. Colgate has operated successfully on a global basis for some years and has arrived at what it believes is the right answer, at least for today's times: Stay out of the detail and manage to high-level principles and to as few as possible.

By managing to a few key principles, Colgate keeps its people involved around the world. They're not stretched too far or wasting time developing their own principles, but they do get to think about how to apply the principles consistently. Also, by having the same set of principles around the world, it is easier to interact across borders and move talent around.

Many of us, especially in North America, are more uncomfortable with ambiguity than we admit. It requires a leap in the dark and a lot of faith in employees around the company to say: "Take these principles and apply them as best you can in your context." Sometimes we don't like the outcome, but the price is worth paying in much greater passion and commitment from employees around the world.

Conclusion

Operating an HR function globally aligns with the business models that will be required in the future. If HR is to take its role as a contributor to improving the capability of its company and maintain its role as a business partner, it must move to operate globally. If it has not happened to you yet, maybe it is time to reflect on the global Boy Scout motto: "Be Prepared!"

CHAPTER 21

―――⬥―――

Challenges of a Global Marketplace

HOWARD MORGAN

THE CONCEPT OF organizations that operate and do business internationally is certainly not a new one. For over half a century, many of the world's largest companies have had global presence. Consequently, you would expect that the procedures and methods for recruiting and managing employees in a global context would be well defined. That would be true if today's definition of the term *global* were the same as its definition 50 years ago. However, like most things in our lives, *global* just isn't what it used to be.

Fifty years ago, global operations meant that a company did business in a number of countries and markets around the world. Many of the truly world-wide players were based in the United States and had operations in every major international market. The staffing of leadership roles consisted of senior employees from the United States, as expatriates and middle-management positions and below held by employees from the country of operation. While many of the basic operating principles have remained constant, the underlying philosophies have dramatically changed.

In part, the reason for these changes stems from the fact that we are truly becoming an international economy. Technological and communications advances in the past 50 years have had a profound effect on the way consumers act and companies operate. In the past, consumers, businesses, and their employees primarily lived and made decisions on either a local or regional basis. Today and into the future, the world will have fewer and fewer boundaries to constrain businesses, cultures, or consumer demands.

. Because of these advances, broadening consumer sophistication, and increased competition, companies have had to fundamentally change the way they conduct business. It is no longer acceptable for suppliers to ship pieces or parts to head office locations to be distributed internally. Manufacturing operators now demand that parts arrive *just in time* at the location of the plant. The cost and logistics of warehousing are increasingly being assumed by the supplier. Moreover, the rapidity of technological advances has allowed competitors to have quicker response times than ever before. It is also interesting that, whereas 50 years ago most multinationals were based in the United States, today many of the world's largest organizations are based offshore. Similarly, in the past, large acquisitions typically originated from U.S. businesses. Today, many of the largest global acquisitions have involved internationally based organizations acquiring companies based in the United States or internationally, and this trend appears to be growing.

Customers' purchasing patterns and demands have also gone through a transition. The introduction of catalogue, online, discount houses, and home shopping networks has caused a shift in buying patterns. Consumers want more choices and greater convenience. An example of these changing patterns is evidenced by an international organization that sold more of its product in three hours on the Home Shopping Network than it did through one of its retail outlets during an entire month. Customers have greater access to goods and services than ever before.

If these changes have affected business-to-business and consumer patterns, it is not surprising that they have also affected how companies manage their human resources and organizational structures. Some of the major operational considerations that organizations are facing in this new global economy are discussed in the following sections.

Outsourcing

Worldwide access to technology has affected us in a number of different ways, but it has had a profound effect on the use of external human resources to both augment and replace internal resources. The lower labor cost in overseas companies has made the outsourcing alternative a highly attractive one. It is not that resources in other countries have not been used previously; it is the fact that these people are no longer employees—they are under contract. Not having them as part of their organizations results in savings in both supervisory time and money for companies.

The human cost of outsourcing is a challenging one. Often, committed employees are faced with the realization that their jobs may be taken by companies that specialize in using the talents of people halfway around the globe. Many of the tasks that these employees perform can easily be done remotely. As well, the upgrading of educational systems globally has opened up a new talent pool of gifted, inexpensive resources. The savings are hard to ignore for businesses faced with increased competition, declining markets, and changes in consumer loyalty. Companies are forced to look for other methods to remain competitive in the marketplace.

Outsourcing is not limited to offshore service providers. For the past ten years, U.S.-based organizations have looked at a variety of options to minimize costs to stay competitive with their international counterparts. Many of the support functions of companies have been outsourced to companies specializing in these services. This has allowed organizations to focus capital and resources on areas where they have a strategic advantage.

Most organizations struggle with the values and moral dilemmas that come with removing jobs and careers from existing resources. When assessing organizational restructuring, the key consideration for businesses is to determine which options are consistent with their stated value system. Having a set of values does not preclude an organization from taking advantage of outsourcing, but it does have a direct effect on how the restructuring should be considered and how the affected employees are treated.

Organizational Restructuring

Formerly, global businesses had independent organizations in each country or region in which they operated. These structures most often mirrored that of the parent company. The head of the country or region would report into corporate headquarters, but he or she had the autonomy to run the business. In recent years, however, there has been a growing trend toward global reporting lines based on specialty or function. As business lines grow in complexity and specialization and as markets become more demanding, it is becoming more difficult for regional managers to have the knowledge and expertise to effectively lead the leaders of these products and/or services.

This shift has led to many companies' becoming truly global for the first time. The expertise of an organization is no longer confined to the headquarters; rather, expertise could be located in any country or region in which the company operates. The general thrust is to put the talent where it can have the greatest impact on the success of the business. Key roles in all parts of the world report directly into a headquarters location. They may have a matrix reporting relationship to a local site leader, but their primary relationship is to an expertise head. This may result in employees having a boss-subordinate relationship with a leader whom they may see only once or twice a year.

To make this "virtual" reporting relationship work, it is important that role expectations and structured communication be clearly defined at the outset. These parameters are critical because the normal relationship-building process is not possible. Parameters should include not only alignment around goals but, more importantly, a sharing of expectations around issues such as frequency and types of information to be shared. In addition, there should be a dialogue about how the individual's performance will be assessed and the means of gathering the data to perform the assessment.

Communication Challenges

While advances in technology have made it easier to keep in touch with people globally, an entirely new set of challenges has surfaced. The major one is the complications that arise from dealing with individuals working in multiple time zones. Meetings, teleconferences, and one-on-one updates are no longer as simple as wandering down the hall or picking up the telephone. Trying to coordinate meetings with people around the globe has tended to favor the time zone where the corporate headquarters is located. The result is an increasing lack of respect for people's time and personal lives. While the average hours worked has been increasing for everyone over the past ten years, the coordination of worldwide resources has meant late nights for many in locations in Europe and Asia. Little or no thought has been given to ensuring that the burden of off-hour meetings is shared equally with team members. To combat this typically North American bias, the meeting times should be rotated and arranged based on team membership, not geographic location.

Another respect issue concerns location and frequency of meetings. Many senior leaders in organizations are finding that they are spending more and more time traveling to attend corporate meetings. Increasingly, the requirement for timely decision making and quicker solutions has meant spending more time on strategy and planning. Global organizations then must deal with the best way to overcome this dichotomy. While videoconferencing technology has advanced, as have net-meeting capabilities, the difference between personal attendance and virtual participation is noticeable. It is very hard to feel truly involved when the majority of participants are in one room and several team members are participating from remote locations. Without a truly focused effort to include distance participants, they may not be involved at levels that ensure quality solutions. In fact, teleconferencing has encouraged multitasking more than true participation. Many times, group members that are connected through telecommunication are working on e-mail or other projects while "attending" the meeting.

The answer to this challenge is to recognize that these communication channels are more complicated than the traditional "walk down the hall" or "setting up a personal meeting" methods of the past. It is important to treat the communication obstacles as business issues and to come to an understanding with individuals or groups on how to minimize the downsides of the challenge. Like most difficulties, this can be solved with discussion and thought. The problem is manifested when we rely on technology to solve the entire problem rather than recognizing that it is only part of the solution.

Assessment and Development

Having global experience has always been considered valuable. However, for many years, middle managers and senior leaders who took global assignments found themselves moving from one international post to another. It was not uncommon for leaders to relocate to an international post, only to find them spending the rest of their careers offshore.

The trend toward a truly global economy has changed that. Having global experience has moved from desirable to a critical component of a senior leader's development. It is unlikely that a senior leader can rise to the executive level of a global company without a significant assignment in at least one of the world's economic regions. It is now being factored into the development of "high-potential" performers earlier than ever before. Customers are requiring that companies demonstrate a knowledge and sensitivity to the cultural characteristics of their markets. It is no longer good enough to simply be located in the geographic arena; you must have a true understanding of cultural implications to be successful.

Having an organization's best performers located around the globe presents its own unique challenges. It is very difficult to assess a leader's total performance when the assessor sees him or her infrequently. You can, of course, assess his or her business results, but the trend for the past ten years has been to find a balance between results and the manner in which you obtain them—both the *what* and the *how*. The disastrous results of companies such as Enron and WorldCom have placed more focus on ensuring that organizations are conducting themselves both ethically and in the best interest of the shareholders. While global operations have not seen the same level of scrutiny, it is likely that they will have an increased level of review in the future. Systems need to be developed that both assess and capture the true impact/value that global executives are having on their businesses. The development of global leaders also requires some thought and planning. The resources for completing their developmental goals may not be available where they are located. It may also be logistically difficult for the developmental plan to be formalized and acted on.

The key issue is that these leaders should not suffer from being located away from the headquarters. They have the same right to a thoughtful and accurate assessment of their potential as do those in closer locations. It is important to increase structured communication with these managers to ensure that their development needs are not ignored. In days past, there was a tendency for expatriate resources to be forgotten. Fortunately, that is now less likely to occur because of the importance of the world's economy. As well, these leaders have been placed around the globe in recognition of their "high-potential" status. As such, a considerable investment has been made to ensure that they are given every opportunity to be successful. However, it does take time and effort to ensure that the company's international talent pool is developed as much as possible.

Cultural Sensitivities

In the past, a global organization's idea of cultural sensitivity was to make sure that all relocating leaders received a two- to five-day orientation on the countries to which they were relocating. Because many of the opportunities and problems were solved locally, this system worked and usually met the needs of the market in which the executive operated. Now that we have moved toward a truly global economy, the quick sensitivity training of the past does not suffice. Leaders who operate any portion of a business with international dealings must truly get to know the market in which they are operating. Customers and consumers are demanding that companies really understand the uniqueness of their culture.

This cultural impact is also felt in the way employees view international companies. We have a tendency/bias to view a distant organization as neither understanding nor appreciating the unique realities that we face on a daily basis. Many times, this is indeed true. However, often it is just a way to justify our differences in substance and approach.

The solution for organizations is to understand that each culture has its unique identity. As with all people, we have greater affinity for some cultures while others are more difficult to understand. The question is not whether these unique qualities are good or bad; it is how we learn to better understand them and acquaint ourselves with their differentiating characteristics.

In a global company, it is important to understand the unique needs of employees in each location and find ways to capitalize on their traits. Many times, we find ways to use cultural differences to explain away our relationships with others rather than finding the benefits that a diverse employee base brings. In an organization, there is a need to treat cultural "violations" as a learning opportunity rather than a chance to reinforce the insensitivity that a lack of knowledge can bring.

Team Effectiveness

A true global team has its own set of rewards and opportunities. It is presented with the cultural, geographic, and reporting relationship challenges discussed earlier. The difficulty is getting the team through the various stages of team development with ease and efficiency. Because the forming stage is based on arriving at a clear set of goals, objectives, and roles, it is especially critical for the leader to put in as much structure as possible. A global team should not be considered the same as nongeographically diverse teams. The composition of the global team must be carefully selected to focus on distant collaboration and contain credible members who can go to the resources in their regions and drive solutions.

The benefits of an international group of team members can truly help organizations be more responsive to the global marketplace. This international group allows for global solutions rather than regional solutions. It does, however, require that team members have a better understanding of the cultural expectations and beliefs of each culture represented on the team.

A global marketplace provides significantly more opportunity to both individuals and to the organizations in which they work. It provides access that previously was not possible. Moreover, technology has enabled smaller companies to operate on a more equal footing with their larger counterparts. However, the true value comes when the human capital is developed in a way that allows for the maximum benefit to both the person and the organization. To make that happen, we need to look at the systems and processes that employees work with and ensure that they are modified to reflect the realities of the new marketplace in which we operate.

LEADING CHANGE: THE ENDURING TASK

D URING THIS PERIOD of random and unpredictable turbulence, no organization is immune to the overwhelming effects of change. The companies that survive will be those that evoke our greatest human capacities through the organizational culture: the need to be involved in respectful relationships and the desire to contribute to a higher purpose. Now more than ever, the credibility of leaders is being questioned, and corporations are under intense pressure and scrutiny to change their organizational cultures.

In this section, the authors share their thought-provoking insights on the skills organizations can call on to successfully maneuver and survive these turbulent and uncertain times, and they unveil insight about organizational change and how it is managed. These authors impart knowledge gained through practical experience, reveal the missing links between business and leadership strategy, and describe the essential components to leading change that every HR and business leader needs while riding the rough tides ahead.

CHAPTER 22

*When Change Is
Out of Our Control*

MARGARET WHEATLEY

Uncertain Times

IN JUNE 2002, Jeff Henley, chief financial officer of Oracle Corporation, spoke about prospects for the second half of the year. His comments were startlingly different from the upbeat statements typical of one in his position: "We are hoping for a revenue recovery in the second half of the year. But I said that same thing six months ago, and I have lost confidence in my ability to predict the future."[1] In his humility, Henley is describing the new world of the 21st century and this interconnected planet of increased uncertainty and volatility. Organizations are now confronted with two sources of change: the traditional type that is initiated and managed and external changes over which no one has control. We are just beginning to experience what it is like to operate in a global environment of increasing chaos, through events that are beyond our control and have a devastating impact on our internal operations and culture.

The business news is filled with stories of the perils of interconnectedness. One country suffers economic problems, and analysts are quick to say that its problems will not affect other countries. Then, we watch as an entire continent and those beyond are pulled into economic recession by the web of interdependence. Or, we read how the actions of a few corrupt executives bring down an entire company (and industry), even though tens of thousands of people with integrity work there.

Interconnected systems are always this sensitive. Activities occurring in one part of the system always affect many other parts of the system. The nature of the global business environment guarantees that no matter how hard we work to create a stable and healthy organization, our organization will continue to experience dramatic changes far beyond our control. For example, Continental Airlines had spent years developing a strong culture. "Our employees believe in this company and will do anything for our president."[2] Then came the events of September 11, 2001, and Continental, like all airlines, suddenly found its entire industry and business model at risk.

There is no company, industry, or nation immune to these potentially devastating system effects. One executive in a large corporation commented: "It was always dysfunctional, but it was working. Now it's not. It's a different feeling than years ago. Now we can't influence outcomes. We're 'at the top,' but feeling that things are being 'done to' us." Another executive said simply: "What used to work doesn't: The old strategies don't work."

When so much is beyond our control, when senior leaders reveal their feelings of powerlessness, what skills can we call on to successfully maneuver and survive the turbulence?

New Organizational Dynamics

In an era of increasing uncertainty, new organizational dynamics appear and old ones intensify at all levels of the organization. It is important to notice how these new dynamics affect employees, leaders, and core operating functions.

Employee Behaviors

Uncertainty leads to increased fear. As fear levels rise, it is normal for people to focus on personal security and safety. We tend to withdraw and become more self-serving and defensive. We focus on smaller and smaller details—those things we *can* control. It becomes more difficult to work together and nearly impossible to focus on the bigger picture. There are physiological impacts as well. Stress deprives the human brain of its ability to see patterns. People become reactive and lose the capacity to understand their work as part of a larger system. We also have difficulty with memory and become forgetful. Then there are the physical manifestations of sleeplessness, restlessness, sudden anger, and unpredictable tears.

Obviously, each of these has negative consequences on work behaviors for individuals and teams. As people experience their growing incapacity to get work done well, they often blame themselves for failing to produce. One woman executive expressed: "So many good people are failing at the changes they're committed to."

Pressure on Leaders

Because of increased fear, many people turn with unreasonable demands to leaders. We want someone to rescue us, to save us, to provide answers, and to give us firm ground or strong life rafts. We push for a strong leader to get us out of this mess, even if it means surrendering individual freedom to gain security. However, the causes of insecurity are complex and systemic. There is not one simple answer, and not even the strongest of leaders can deliver on the promise of stability and security. We seldom acknowledge that; instead, we fire him or her and continue searching for the perfect leader. A troubled male executive described it this way: "We still charge the leader to provide solutions. When he doesn't, we then sacrifice the king/priest to atone for the sins of the system."

It is critical that leaders resist assuming the role of savior, even as people beg for it. This can be extremely difficult as people grow more fearful and fragile. Sophisticated emotional skills are required, especially if people have been directly affected by external events. In these cases, the leader must simultaneously struggle to provide emotional support while also working to maintain decent levels of productivity. If the leader has also been personally affected by recent organizational challenges, it becomes very difficult to inspire confidence. For instance, one woman leader asked: "How do you maintain credibility when you (as the leader) are not sure you want to be there?"

Core Functions

It wasn't long ago that companies engaged in five-year strategic planning. Those sweet, slow days seem very distant now. Many of the primary functions of business and of human resources—planning, forecasting, budgeting, staffing, and individual development plans—worked only because we could bring the future into focus. The future felt within our control. Shortly after September 11, the CEO of a major technology company reported that it was impossible to complete a reliable budget for the coming year, even though they had a very good record at forecasting in the past. His proposed solution for dealing with so much uncertainty was to submit five alternative budget scenarios to his board.

It is important to note how many people in organizations have honed their skills at predicting or anticipating the future. Businesses have depended on and rewarded their expertise, but now these skills can be a liability. They may lull the organization into a false sense of security about a predictable future and thereby keep people from staying alert to what is going on around them in the present. Yet, ironically, these experts are often charged with bringing stability back to the organization. The organization may clamor for new planning tools and processes and push planning staff to find new modes of prediction. Staff members often suffer severe burnout as they work zealously on the impossible task of stabilizing an inherently temperamental world. A wise planning executive commented on how he has changed expectations of his function: "I tell people we're not going to get any more clarity. This is as good as it gets."

The Great Paradox

I have painted a fairly grim picture of these new organizational dynamics spawned by tumultuous times. However, a great paradox points to the hopeful path ahead. It is possible to prepare for the future without knowing what it will be. The primary aspect of preparing for the unknown is attending to the quality of our relationships—in how well we know and trust one another. For instance, people in New York City and Oklahoma City had engaged in emergency preparedness drills before confronting the real thing. By working together on these simulations, they developed cohesive, trusting relationships and interagency cooperation. They had prepared only for simpler disasters, but when terror struck, they knew they could rely on one another. Elizabeth Dole, when president of the American Red Cross, said that she didn't wait until two in the morning when the river was flooding to pick up the phone and establish a relationship.

When people know that they can rely on one another, when there is a true sense of community, it is amazing how well we perform. This was the experience of the community of Halifax, Nova Scotia, on September 11. Forty-two planes were grounded at their small airport, and 8,000 distressed and stranded passengers suddenly appeared on their doorstep.

The community's openhearted response transformed the city, and it led to relationships with strangers that will last a lifetime. "It was one of those times when nothing was planned, but everything went so smoothly. Everybody just kind of pulled together," said one community member.

New Organizational Capabilities

To counter the negative organizational dynamics stimulated by stress and uncertainty, we must give full attention to the quality of our relationships. Nothing else works—not new tools or technical applications and not a redesigned organizational chart. The solution is *one another.* If we can rely on one another, we can cope with almost anything. Without one another, we retreat into fear.

There is one underlying principle for developing these relationships: People who are engaged together in meaningful work transcend their individual concerns and discover new capacities. Several ways to work with this principle are discussed in the following sections.

Nourish a Clear Organizational Identity

As confusion and fear swirl about the organization, people can find stability and security in purpose, not in plans. Organizational identity describes who we are, the enduring values we work from, and the shared aspirations of who we want to be in and for the world. When chaos wipes the ground from beneath us, the organization's identity gives us some place to stand. When the situation grows confusing, our values provide the means to make clear and good decisions. A clear sense of organizational (and personal) identity gives people the capacity to respond intelligently in the moment and to choose congruent actions. Times of crises always display the coherence or incoherence at the heart of our organizations. Are we pulling together or rushing off in many different directions? Do people's actions and choices accord with the stated values, or are they basing their decisions on different values and thereby displaying the real rules of the game?

It is crucial to keep organizational purpose and values in the spotlight. The values come to life not through speeches and plaques, but as we hear the stories of employees who embody those values. It is important to use all existing communication tools and invent new ones to highlight these personal experiences. United Airlines now communicates these stories twice weekly as one means to support employees during very difficult times.

Focus People on the Bigger Picture

People who are stressed lose the ability to recognize patterns and to see the bigger picture. As people become overloaded and overwhelmed with their tasks, they have no time or interest to look beyond the demands of the moment. Therefore, it is essential that the organization sponsor those processes that bring people together, so that they become aware of one another's perspectives and challenges. If the organization does not attend to making these processes happen, people will continue to spiral inward. This inward spiraling has a devastating impact on performance. People become overwhelmed by the volume of tasks, they lose all sense of meaning for their work, and they feel increasingly isolated and alone. Everybody is busier and more frantic, but the major thing produced is more stress. The other serious consequence is that both individual and organizational intelligence decline dramatically as people lose the larger context for their work.

It is important that the processes used for bringing people together are not formal. People need less formality and more conviviality. They need time to decompress and relax if they are to be able to listen to one another. Processes, such as conversation and storytelling, help us connect at a depth not available through charts and PowerPoint presentations. However, people do not recognize how much they need this time and often resist such informal gatherings; when they attend such a gathering, they suddenly notice what they've been missing.

Demand Honest, Forthright Communication

In a true disaster or crisis, the continuous flow of information gives people the capacity to respond intelligently as they seek to rescue or save people and property. They are hungry for information so that they can respond to urgent human needs. They take in the information, make fast judgment calls, try something, quickly reject it if it doesn't work, and then try something else. They call to one another, provide information freely, and contribute what they can so that everyone is more effective in the rescue effort.

Even though most organizations do not deal with this level of crisis, the lessons are important. People deal far better with uncertainty and stress when they know what is going on, even if the information is incomplete and only temporarily correct. Freely circulating information helps create trust, and it turns us into rapid learners and more effective workers. Often, it is not the actual situation that induces stress as much as it is that people are not told what is going on or feel deceived. The greater the crisis, the more we need to know. The more affected we are by the situation, the more information we need. After every commercial air crash, families who have lost loves ones complain about not being adequately informed by the airlines. They want to know the details of how their loved ones died: This disclosure often brings relief to those grieving. Yet, the airlines are constrained by potential legal liability from sharing the details that would ease grief. The families end up suing the airline to get the information and add emotional damages to their suits.

Prepare for the Unknown

The U.S. military has invested large sums of money in the development and use of complex simulations that prepare troops for different battle scenarios. Similar simulations are used by most civil defense and community agencies. Yet, it is surprising how few companies engage in any type of simulation or scenario work. The evidence is dramatically clear that this type of preparation allows people to move into the unknown with greater skill and capacity. While traditional planning processes no longer work, it is dangerous to abandon thinking about the future. We need to explore these newer methods that project us into alternative futures. As people engage in processes, such as scenario building or disaster simulations, they feel more capable of dealing with uncertainty. Individual and collective intelligence increases dramatically, as people become better informed systems thinkers. In addition, trusting relationships develop that make it possible to call on one another when chaos strikes.

Keep Meaning at the Forefront

Often, in organizations we forget that meaning is the most powerful motivator of human behavior. People gain energy and resolve if they understand how their work contributes to something beyond themselves. When we are frightened, we may focus first on our own survival, but we are capable of more generous and altruistic responses if we discover a greater purpose to our troubles. Why is my work worth doing? Who will be helped if I respond well? Am I contributing to some greater good?

Of course, the work truly does have to contribute to something meaningful. People do not step forward to support greed or egotists or to benefit faceless entities such as shareholders. We need to know that our work contributes to helping other human beings. My favorite example of this desire to contribute was expressed in the mission statement created by employees at a facility that manufactures dog food. They expressed how their work was serving a greater good when they wrote: "Pets contribute to human health."

Use Rituals and Symbols

As shrines appear on streets mourning the dead and other demonstrations of grief flare on TV screens throughout this sorrowing world, we are becoming aware of the deep human need for shared symbolic expression when we experience something tragic. We also have the need for celebration when we have experienced something wonderful.

The use of ritual and symbols is common in all cultures; although it almost disappeared in the United States until our lives became so stressful and isolated. Now, we are rediscovering this basic human behavior. Because they are so basic to humans, symbols and rituals appear spontaneously, even in organizations. No one department has to create them (a scary thought), but the organization does need to notice them when they appear and honor them by offering support and resources.

Pay Attention to Individuals

There is no substitute for direct, personal contact with employees. Even though managers are more stressed and have less time, it is crucial to pick up the phone and connect with those employees whom you want to retain. Have personal conversations with key people, experienced workers, innovators, those just joining the organization, and younger workers new to the workforce. All of these people and more need to know that their leader is thinking about them. When people feel cared for, their stress is reduced and they contribute more to the organization. One of the key findings in the field of knowledge management is that people share their knowledge only when they feel cared for and when they care for the organization. It is not new technology that makes for knowledge exchanges, but human relationships.

The Difficulty in Investing in Relationships

None of these suggested behaviors are new to organizational advice. Most of us have had enough experience in organizations to know the importance of relationships. So why, as the storm clouds thicken, do we not focus on investing in those processes that would create healthy, trusting relationships? One answer to this is that many organizations deliberately stay distant from their employees because they hold a dangerous assumption. The assumption is that organizational flexibility is best achieved by letting employees go when times get hard. The ability to remain efficient is primarily found in the organization's ability to downsize staff. If you need to downsize, so the assumption goes, you do not want to know your employees or get personally involved with them.

What is most dangerous about this belief is that it is partly true. Organizations do need to be able to shrink and grow as times demand. Yet, it is absolutely possible to achieve this workforce flexibility without sacrificing loyal, dedicated, and smart workers. Years ago, Harley-Davidson had to let go nearly 40 percent of its workforce. This was a wrenching, but crucial, decision for its survival as a company. However, Harley management took the time to pay attention to those individuals who were leaving and those who were staying. Every employee had a personal conversation with the CEO and received complete information about the company's circumstances. People understood why they were being let go, appreciated the personal conversation, and expressed their love and support for the company. Over the years, many of those employees stayed in contact and were rehired as Harley prospered.

One Prediction about the Future

There is only one prediction about the future that I feel confident to make. During this period of random and unpredictable change, any organization that distances itself from its employees and refuses to cultivate meaningful relationships with them is destined to fail. Organizations that succeed are those that evoke our greatest human capacities: our need to be in good relationships and our desire to contribute to something beyond ourselves. These qualities cannot be evoked through procedures and policies; they are available only in organizations in which people feel trusted and welcome and in which people know that their work matters. The evidence is all around us, and here's one powerful story.

On September 11, the Federal Aviation Authority (FAA) cleared the skies of nearly 4,500 planes carrying 350,000 passengers in just a few hours. (Seventy-five percent landed within the first hour, which was more than one landing per second.) It was an unprecedented feat for the agency—one that had not been simulated since the end of the Cold War. And it was the first day on the job for the top FAA official who gave the initial order to clear the skies. Controllers had to land these planes, while also staying vigilant for signs that any other planes had been hijacked. They succeeded through intense cooperation, absolute focus, and dedication, and because they made decisions locally, including some that were outside of policies. In the months following, officials tried to capture this astonishing feat in new procedures, but then they scrapped the idea. "A lot of things were done intuitively, things that you can't write down in a textbook or you can't train somebody to do." What is the FAA's policy and plan for preparing for another crisis of unknown dimensions? It will ultimately rely on the judgment, intuition, and commitment of its controllers and managers.

CHAPTER 23

———≫·◊·≪———

Mother's Work Is Never Done

Myths and Facts about Organizational Change

JAMES O'TOOLE

Human resource executives often have responsibility for managing organizational change efforts. Since 1969, I have observed several dozen such programs and, alas, I must conclude that few have been as successful as their initiators had desired. There were many reasons that the results of those efforts were disappointing—ranging from cases of cold feet among those who needed to be leading them, to a reluctance to link financial rewards to new behaviors necessary to make a desired change successful. But, in too many instances, the shortfall in performance resulted from HR managers' misperceptions about what organizational change is all about.

In general, HR people are enamored with formal "change management processes," which often causes them to succumb to an assortment of myths concerning how change occurs, who leads it, and what determines its effectiveness, such as:

- *Myth:* Change management is a structured and discrete program.
  Fact: There are many forms of organizational change, the most effective of which are not based on structured models.
- *Myth:* Change is a finite, singular program managed by HR or organizational development experts.
  Fact: Change is an ongoing process and a task of operating leaders.
- *Myth:* Leading change is the most important CEO skill.
  Fact: It is second in importance to the ability to identify and execute an effective strategy.

These countervailing "facts" are derived from neither academic theories nor the many models of change proffered by consultants. Instead, the lessons are drawn from three decades of well-documented information about how change actually occurred at one large business, the Corning Corporation.

Eras of Change

If nothing else, Corning's long and highly transparent experience can serve as a reality test against which HR managers can measure the validity of their assumptions about organizational change. In each of the four eras of change described in the following sections, Corning's leaders did "the right thing" in terms of employing state-of-the-art strategic responses to meet each of the various crises the company was facing. Significantly, the net effect of each of those change efforts was to set the stage for a subsequent round of change.

Change 1: Meeting the Challenge of Globalization

In the mid-1970s, Corning was headed by Amory Houghton, great-great grandson of the founder of the glassworks company started in 1851. In 1975, the company faced a competitive crisis. The glass industry was becoming a global business, yet Corning was decidedly domestic in its strategic outlook. Corning needed to learn how to compete internationally, which meant it had to organize itself to succeed overseas and to successfully meet foreign competition at home. Like most large corporations at the time, Corning adopted a matrix structure of dual managerial reporting to balance the needs for simultaneous centralization of policy and decentralization of marketing. One result of the global restructuring was a boost to the company's capacity for coordination and cohesion in the process of technology transfer. However, the matrix structure was not a panacea. To meet the challenges of quickly developing technologies and entering new markets, the company found it practical and efficient to form strategic alliances with some 40 companies, sharing expertise, risk, and opportunities. For example, they formed joint ventures with Dow Chemical, PPG, Genentech, and Ciba-Geigy to enter dynamic new fields such as fiber optics and laboratory testing. In terms of now-common approaches, such as globalization, joint ventures, and matrix management, Corning was a trendsetter.

Change 2: Vertical Alignment

James Houghton became CEO of Corning in the same old-fashioned way his brother Amory had: He inherited the job. When he took over in 1983, Corning's domestic operations were suffering from poor labor relations, outmoded plants and technology, and declining market share. Less than a decade later, the company was producing new, high-quality products and was well positioned to be a profitable player in the emerging global economy. Here are some things Jamie Houghton did to create that transformation.

He formed a team. One of Houghton's first acts was to assemble a six-person leadership team (dubbed *the six-pack*) of managers who shared his belief that Corning needed to change if it were to survive.

The team created a vision. The six-pack identified a new strategic direction for Corning. Then, they affirmed a set of values consistent with, and instrumental to, the achievement of that vision. They also identified *quality* as the unifying theme for a companywide process designed to change the culture, behavior, and practices of everyone in the firm.

The team changed its behavior. Because they were inexperienced, the six-pack began by making all the classical errors associated with failed change efforts: They announced a "program" and then sat back expecting it to be implemented; they failed to fully engage workers, the union, and middle management; they delegated the leadership of change while devoting their own efforts to their usual managerial tasks; and they continued Corning's tradition of command-and-control management. Not surprisingly, the quality program went nowhere until, in the midst of considerable frustration, Jamie Houghton finally understood what change required. He realized that he and his team would have to lead the change, that he and his team would have to involve others in the effort, and that they would have to win over skeptics and resisters by giving them a real stake in the process. Jamie, who had been spending about a third of his time on the quality initiative, then put aside all the nonessential activities that unproductively devour the day of an executive and devoted 100 percent of his time to leading change at Corning.

The team created an architecture for change. Houghton and the six-pack concluded that their role was to create the conditions under which others could effectively identify and implement the needed changes. This was easier said than done. Resistance to change was rampant in light of Corning's history of adversarial labor relations. Why should its unionized workforce accept responsibility to help management achieve its goals? Why should workers trust a management that had been repeatedly untrustworthy in the past?

Jamie patiently hung in during the fray. He kept delivering the same thoughtful message, building his credibility through consistency, and demonstrating that he wasn't going away. Finally, the workers started to hear his message: The best way to ensure their jobs in the future was for *them* to improve product quality and the overall efficiency of Corning's operations. Top management would provide the workers with objectives, resources, training, and support; in exchange, the workers would find the most efficient ways to provide the highest-quality products in the industry. To sweeten the pot, the company agreed to share financial gains with all employees.

They established boundaries. In essence, Jamie and the six-pack told the workers that they had authority to make whatever changes were necessary to achieve their quality goals. Still, the workers balked. Based on experience, they doubted Jamie meant it when he talked about empowering them. "Come on," they said, "tell us the truth: How much authority do we really have?" It was at this point Jamie earned his spurs as a leader. He told the workers they had full authority within the confines of each plant to make whatever changes in organization, technology, and governance *they* felt were necessary. For instance, they could set their own staffing levels, even reduce the authority and number of managers and supervisors in a plant. Yet, he made it clear he was not writing them a blank check. They were *not* empowered to act in ways that violated the basic values of Corning, to move outside the scope of the overall corporate strategy and objectives (e.g., they could not choose to drop the glass business and make surfboards), to engage in top-management concerns (e.g., they could not issue their own financial paper), or to make decisions that affected other Corning operations without their full concurrence.

He redefined leadership. Because the transformation of Corning required the active involvement of everyone down the line, it became clear to Houghton that the major obstacle in the way of that happening was the prevalent philosophy of leadership in the company. "We have traditionally viewed leaders as heroes who come forward at a time of crisis to resolve a problem," he wrote in 1992. "But this view stresses the short term and assures the powerlessness of those being led."[1] Because his goal was to put the burden of change on the followers, he resolved that he and the six-pack would have to abandon the traditional view of a single leader as font of all wisdom and adopt, instead, a philosophy of shared, transforming leadership. As he explained:

The true spirit of leadership is the spirit that is not sure it is always right. Leaders who are not too sure they are right are leaders who listen. Leadership is about performance over time, not charisma—about responsibility, not privilege. It is about personal integrity and a strong belief in team play . . .

Which points to one more element of leadership: developing strong subordinates and potential successors and staying out of their way. Companies can no longer afford leadership by the few. If organizations are to move ahead and not just play catch-up, every employee must become a responsible leader . . .

Employees must have responsibility and the power that goes with it; anything less leads to cynicism and skepticism—and nothing is more demoralizing for employees than to find their skepticism justified.[2]

He persisted. For nearly a decade, Houghton practiced what he preached. He said the same things repeatedly until everyone finally got the message. His was a simple story about quality (basically the philosophy espoused by the late management guru W. Edwards Deming), about values (integrity, performance, technological leadership, and respect for the individual), and about the responsibility of everyone to contribute to making the company competitive in world markets. There was nothing particularly original or sexy about Houghton's ideas. There wasn't anything many other CEOs had not said except they said it once or twice, and they said a lot of other things, too—sometimes contradictory, but most of the time just confusing followers about what the message, the focus, the basic purpose, and the goal of the organizations were.

Jamie Houghton predictably, reliably, relentlessly, and boringly spouted the same simple message until everyone believed he meant it and until everyone could repeat it verbatim if he was hoarse on any given day. Informants tell me that when employees saw Jamie striding down the corridor, they rolled their eyes and said, "Uh-oh, here he comes again!"

Why is repetition of "the message" one of the most important things leaders do? Because people *forget*; because people get *distracted*; because people get so caught up in the intricacies of their work that they *lose sight of the purpose of what they are doing*. Yet, people in positions of authority believe, because they have imposing titles, that they can say something once (or twice) and safely assume that their people will have heard, understood, believed, and then committed themselves to act on it. Such would-be leaders do not understand human nature or the limits of their own power.

Houghton and other true leaders understand that it takes about 20 repetitions just to get from stage A to stage B, and even then, only their direct reports will have gotten the message. If they are to have half a prayer of changing the behavior of everyone down the line, they must devote some 70 percent of their time to repeating the message. Leading change is repetitious work. It requires commitment: Whenever there was pressure from Corning's board or Wall Street to cut back on the company's expensive quality training program, Houghton drew a line in the sand and said that training was integral to the long-term change effort. In so doing, he reinforced his commitment to his principles in the eyes of Corning's workforce. Through thick and thin, he repeated his message, reaffirmed his commitment to change, and behaved consistently with his redefinition of leadership.

With each passing year, he was able to report to Corning employees and shareholders that the company's quality, productivity, competitiveness, and profitability were improving. However, in his last report to shareholders in 1993, he noted that Corning's competitors had enhanced greatly their ability to move quickly and to change their own practices. He warned that those new challenges would require renewed effort . . . and then disaster struck. Houghton stepped off a curb and was hit by a careless taxi driver.

Change 3: Horizontal Adaptability

About that time, Houghton's quality orientation had begun to show signs that it would be an insufficient response to the emerging challenges of the fast-growing markets Corning was entering: optical fibers, life sciences, and other high-tech businesses that were taking the company far afield from the housewares that had been its primary business. Worse, in 1993, Corning was hit with an enormous one-time charge to cover legal settlements related to the (separately managed) Dow Corning's ill-fated silicon breast implants. As luck would have it, all of this conspired to come together in the same year, leaving the company unable to meet its earnings target for the first time under Houghton's leadership.

Jamie's response was to kick himself upstairs to the chairman's post and to name a member of the six-pack, Roger Ackerman, as Corning's CEO. Houghton charged Ackerman with not only turning around the immediate financial situation, but also comprehensively changing Corning's culture to meet the realities of its new markets and energizing the company to create the ongoing capabilities necessary to drive profitable growth in the future.

Houghton did *not* require Ackerman to either preserve or justify his ten-year quality emphasis. Instead, where Houghton's change effort had focused *vertically* on quality improvement in each of the company's discrete business units, Ackerman's would be a comprehensive, integrated approach that encouraged the *horizontal* flow of information and cooperation across organizational boundaries. In other words, Houghton's efforts focused on gaining organizational alignment, whereas Ackerman's were directed more toward building adaptability.

That does not mean Ackerman threw out the past or ignored all Jamie had accomplished. Rather, he built on that sound foundation. In his "Corning Competes" initiative, Ackerman preserved the basic values of the company. For example, in setting a numerical target of reducing operational costs by $450 million over three years, he stipulated that this must occur without radical downsizing, which would have a negative impact on the employment and economy in Corning, New York (the company town).

Although Houghton's health would force him to retire before Corning Competes was far along, he supported Ackerman's efforts to change key aspects of the Corning culture—to speed up decision making, to create greater cost consciousness, and to share best practices. Ackerman's approach to change was somewhat different from his predecessor's. To create the necessary cross-functional mind-set for horizontal change, Ackerman co-located Corning Competes team members in what would become known as the Donut Factory. (It was housed next to a Dunkin' Donuts outlet on Corning's Main Street.) The mission of the teams was "to engage the organization and challenge it to seek new ways of conducting business." In the absence of a real crisis (the breast-implant tragedy was not of Corning Inc.'s making), Ackerman's challenge was to get people to not only act but, first, see the need for action.

Ackerman believed that rigorous analytical content was a prerequisite for effective action, so in Phase 1 of Corning Competes, several teams were assigned to work full time to create an objective, unassailable case for change. Ackerman describes Corning Competes' four phases:

Using an analytical, hypothesis-driven approach, the Phase 1 teams scanned the entire enterprise to find opportunities for improvement that would have the highest impact. . . . After the opportunities were identified, follow-up teams were established to drive the process forward. Moving from Phase 2 to Phase 3 involved the development of specific and quantifiable improvement opportunities and the preparation of implementation plans. Phase 4, the final step, was to implement and track results.[3]

During all four phases, Ackerman's top management team played the central role of communicating the effort to all levels of the company: Going after the hearts and minds of Corning's vital constituencies—employees, suppliers, and customers—involved everything from town meetings and monthly Corning Competes bulletins to focus groups, surveys, and the establishment of a 1-800 line. The goal of this communication process was to reach every employee on a regular basis with a consistent message. There was a focus on building in a feedback loop so that employees could express anxieties about the process. This resulted in "Headlines in a Hurry," an electronic message center that responded to employee questions, typically within 72 hours. Senior management was heavily involved throughout the process, clearly demonstrating that change started at the top of the organization.

In addition to communication, top management's role included setting stretch goals and then holding people accountable for results. *But the actual work of change was done by the teams.* In all, some 300 Corning people, from the shop floor to the boardroom, spent time at the Donut Factory. This level of participation was necessary to ensure that the recommendations of the Corning Competes teams were sufficiently owned by the line organizations that were responsible for implementing them. The most successful of such initiatives, according to Ackerman, were those in which a product champion emerged who assumed responsibility for seeing that recommendations were implemented: "The ability to drive change often comes down to a simple yet resolutely abstract concept—leadership."[4]

In fact, phalanxes of leaders were needed "to ask questions, follow up, measure, and reward new behaviors," according to Norm Garrity, president of Corning Technologies.[5] Such leaders let it be known to line managers that "they wouldn't go away" until the operational people implemented the necessary changes. Such persistence paid off: Corning Competes exceeded its cost-reduction targets in each of its first three years. Moreover, the effort institutionalized new behaviors across the organization.

Change 4: Leading in Adversity

By 1996, Corning's stock was flying high on Wall Street, and Jamie was able to retire from the board. Ackerman retired as CEO five years later, just after disaster again struck the company, this time in the form of a complete collapse of the telecommunications industry that was the prime customer for its fiber optics. Corning's share price fell from a high of $113 in 2000 to less than $3 in 2002. At age 66, Jamie Houghton was called out of retirement by Corning's board and given the task of putting the company back on the right strategic track. This time, the challenge was fixing Corning's product portfolio by balancing its recent overdependence on fiber optics. Equally important, Houghton pledged to develop the leadership potential of his 42-year-old heir apparent and to step down as soon as he and his own youthful six-pack were ready to assume full control.

Lessons of Experience

If 30 years of experience at Corning demonstrates anything, it is that change cannot be managed. Yet, HR executives routinely advocate change management processes that partake of the characteristics of cookbook recipes: step-by-step guidelines and procedures that outline in minute detail who does what, when, and how down the line. This is attractive because it gives the illusion of executive control. Change efforts can be assessed in measurable terms of completing tasks on time and on budget. Such programs can be managed by HR and organizational development people, and they have clear beginnings and endings.

Unfortunately, as the Corning experience shows, even when change is headed by the leader of the organization, and even when the effort is correctly conceived as a highly participative, messy, unpredictable endeavor involving trial, error, learning, and innovation, there is no end to it. In fact, effective change requires strategic leadership, not change management. What organizational change is really about is leaders who create the need and context for continual change and who provide a strategic vision and an environment in which all of their people can pursue it—along with incentives for them to find the best ways to get there. Strategic leaders thus institutionalize change, recognizing that even if they momentarily get things right, the world will soon change and make their once-brilliant strategies wrong. Strategic leaders, thus, focus their efforts on meeting external challenges and on creating the internal capacity and incentives for all their people to be constantly renewing the organization. They do so because they understand that the leadership lesson to be learned from companies such as Corning is that "mother's work is never done."

CHAPTER 24

Unilever's Path to Growth

Reflections on a Journey in Progress

ARJAN OVERWATER AND THOMAS W. MALNIGHT

UNILEVER, THE ANGLO-DUTCH consumer products company, has a long history and a vast array of businesses focused on selling food, personal, and homecare products to consumers around the world. Formed by the 1930 merger of Dutch margarine company Margarine Unie and British soap maker Lever Brothers, Unilever is the world's largest tea, ice cream, margarine, soup, deodorant, and shampoo company. It is also a leader in many other categories and businesses. Revenues in 2001 totaled 52.2 billion euros. The company's focus is reflected in its statement of purpose: "Our purpose in Unilever is to meet the everyday needs of people everywhere—to anticipate the aspirations of our consumers and customers, and to respond creatively and competitively with branded products and services which raise the quality of life. The company has long been renowned for its depth in developing markets, its homegrown talent development, and its emphasis on being 'local' and relevant to consumers wherever they are."[1]

Unilever's strengths also portray its challenges. Given its diversity—in terms of both businesses and geography—strategy making had been focused within individual local markets and businesses, with relatively weak integration across borders. There had been a long history of people being strongly networked with informality driving career development. There had been a strong tradition of local entrepreneurship, often involving getting things done by "working around the system." The company had a wealth of highly talented and creative people and a strong internally focused, polite, and often forgiving culture. With frequent movement of executives, there had been a tendency to worry more about one's next career step, as opposed to winning in markets.

In the late 1990s, Unilever's chairmen, Niall FitzGerald and Antony Burgmans, faced the challenge of how to accelerate top-line growth. Some of the company's leading competitors were growing faster and operating with higher margins. They realized that without attacking the heart of the problem—how the company operated—Unilever's ability to successfully achieve its growth ambitions would be difficult.

In many regards, the challenges facing Unilever were typical of those facing the leadership of many large and successful companies. The company's strategy, as articulated in its well-publicized "Path to Growth," outlined important directions and challenges and was widely communicated both within and outside the company. Path to Growth focused on six key priorities: (1) reconnecting with consumers, (2) focusing the company's brand portfolio, (3) pioneering new channels to reach consumers, (4) ensuring a world-class supply chain, (5) simplifying the organization, and (6) building an enterprise culture. *Enterprise culture* was defined as a more daring, risk-taking, externally focused culture, in which employees would be encouraged to explore and identify new sources of revenue and growth against which their performance would be assessed. The company completed several major acquisitions providing important new growth platforms.

Unilever's acquisitions of Best Foods®, Ben & Jerry's©, and Slim•Fast® provided additional brand platforms, management bench strength, and best practice in a number of areas, and positioned Unilever in new and growing categories.

Following the acquisitions, a new organization was implemented to structure the company's diverse worldwide businesses, providing accountability and ownership for the company's complex worldwide operations. Supporting the new organization, the company had made significant changes in its top management positions, with new executives appointed to key positions throughout the organization.

Unilever had a long history of initiatives and other actions in supporting these advancements and had developed (multiple) elaborate frameworks and models across the organization to address both the strategic and organizational challenges of growth. The company made extensive use of leading consultants and academics to provide guidance and direction. However, despite these efforts—putting in place the growth strategy, growth platforms, structure, and key executive team—top management was concerned about the pace of change in actions and behaviors within the organization in owning and driving growth in markets. The challenge facing Unilever top management involved moving beyond growth frameworks and models to simultaneously build intellectual and emotional commitment for the Path to Growth strategy and its implications at all levels of the Unilever organization.

In addressing the challenges of accelerating growth, Unilever top management embarked on a journey that would extend beyond the scope and focus of its past efforts. The description of the journey provided in this chapter is the culmination of the effort of many: business leaders who were eager to change their business and motivate people for a different level of results; the chairmen in initiating and leading a number of change interventions, and thereby role-modeling through their own actions the change they wished to see in the company; and company human resources staff who with the help of a team from IMD, the Hay Group, Multi-Level Travel, and others, helped design and drive the overall journey across the business. The process that ensued is not the story of a single event or even a single series of events. It is rather a persistent change journey focused on altering the company's core culture and way of working, providing the context for creating a different type of company. It is a journey that is not complete, but that is clearly a work in progress.

Genesis of the Journey

During the Christmas break of 1999, a number of HR vice presidents worked with the board and selected other executives in a workshop held in Noordwijk, the Netherlands. The workshop focused on how to define the desired culture the company wanted to move toward, and specifically those areas that needed immediate attention to make the shift happen. Targeting top management with specific development actions and moving out people who were not going to make the shift happen was already clearly on the radar screen. Activating and energizing our total leadership community for change and moving people in the desired direction was the next big issue on our agenda. In preparing for the journey that would follow, more than 75 executives from across the company were interviewed, providing important guidance to the ensuing process. Five major insights emerged from these interviews:

1. Move beyond more intellectual discussions and focus on actions to win in markets. As one participant noted, "Focus on implementation—we have done enough general thinking—now what. Establish priorities and get on with it. We need to establish some clear priorities and build and focus our passion around them."
2. Provide a forum for open discussions, including discussions with top management, with mutual commitments for follow-up. In the words of one executive, "It will be essential to take top management out of their roles as judges and have them involved as participants jointly addressing the challenges ahead. We need to ensure the commitment and involvement of the entire senior-unit management as committed sponsors."
3. Bring together management teams that can own and take responsibility for winning in the markets. "Take a team of executives and work out what is limiting growth and how to move forward," said one manager. "Focus on surfacing and tackling the real problems. Focus on real and open dialogs within the team and with the top. Focus on how to build worldwide leadership in an area, coming up with concrete choices and proposals."
4. Break the comfort zone, internal focus, and limitations of current thinking. In the words of one manager, "We need to move outside our typical

internal focus and look at the market realities. We need to start with where we want to be in the future, not where we are today. We spend too much time discussing what we can and cannot do, not what we have to do."

5. Integrate the process with prior initiatives, with limited use of new frameworks. Said one executive, "Our executives are well educated and progressive. We have had seminars on almost any topic that we can imagine. We have elaborate frameworks for any challenge. We don't need new ones. Rather, we need to integrate and act on what we already know."

What followed was a series of interrelated "events" that represent a launching of important components of the overall growth journey. The series of events focused around two major theses: (1) building strong and committed leadership communities with a passion for and ownership of the future of each business, and (2) building specific and focused growth action agendas owned by each leadership team. Each event contributed to one or both of these objectives.

Leadership Journeys

Costa Rica: Rebuilding the Top Leadership Community

Starting the journey, the chairmen invited the top 100 executives to come to the beach in Miami one Sunday morning early in January 2001. No more information was given. At the beach, everyone was given the opportunity to leave everything they had brought behind and collect a new set of clothing and luggage clearly aimed at a prolonged stay in a hot climate. The jackets came off and the jungle shirts went on! The group traveled in planes to Costa Rica where the next day a visit was made to the INBio Institute, which is a magnificent initiative to log every living tree and plant and insect in the rain forest in Costa Rica. It supports a huge conservation effort. From there the group took off in Jeeps to the Pacific, slept in a small plantation village, hiked to the coast, and went by boat south to the jungle where the rest of the journey took place.

The dialogs that took place both facilitated and "unfacilitated" were very powerful. During the initial dialog, all participants were asked to share a symbol of their personal leadership. This launched the reflection, "Which leader do I want to be?" The overall trip was geared at assessing personal life priorities against the background of the collective challenge to change Unilever and its culture. The energy that had developed for personal and collective change was palatable. During the trek, people moved geographically as well as psychologically. The group started as a well-intended group of individuals and came back as a team committed to collective action.

Iceland and Croatia: Connecting with Emerging Leaders

Two subsequent journeys have taken place with the "next generation" of top leaders: one to Iceland the same year and one to Croatia in the summer of 2002.

Again, both were highly successful and provided a base for individual reflection and change and collective action. Chairmen Niall FitzGerald and Antony Burgmans led these journeys. A joint theme that emerged is that where the top talent puts their time, talent, and energy is critical. Most participants came to the journey with a very specific question in mind: "Do I want to stay with this company for the long run?" In other words, "Is there alignment between my company's values—embodied by the chairmen—and my personal values?" They came back with an answer. Related questions revolved around balancing personal and business life more effectively, personal growth in the context of a changing and challenging business, and values and inspiration. These journeys also provided a unique context for the chairmen to connect with young leaders, listen to their aspirations, and shape a long-term vision for the company together. Because of the natural settings in which these journeys took place and the depth of discussions, a strong sense of community emerged. Beyond the journey, participants often referred to the group as a strong support network. Before the Croatia trip, each manager spent two to three days with another organization, "getting into the skin" of another person. These organizations were very different from Unilever. They ranged from an orphanage, an AIDS support group, and the local police division to local household and hotel maid services companies. Again, people's perspectives were affected. Common responses were "I had no idea I knew so little on this subject" and "I thought I understood this cause, yet I absolutely didn't." People were forced to adapt to the perspective of others, and it helped them to evaluate again who they are and what is important to them.

These "outside-in" experiences are proving to be of great value. The chairmen participated themselves, as did another board member. The participants were deeply affected by the commitment of the people they met and by the realization of their own biases and limited knowledge of others' realities. Listening to the experiences of others and creating dialog broadened their sensitivities. Again, sitting in the rain in a tent (or under a tent roof) somewhere in Croatia, a community got strengthened: "Let's understand our own passions better, re-prioritize them, and become better leaders for this business challenge that faces us." One of the key words coming back throughout these journeys was trust and "accountability." "We are all accountable for turning this total business into a growth business; we are responsible for our own personal balance and for the context we create for others. Understanding each other personally, therefore, creates trust. It supports a collective journey of 'meaning making.'"

Starting a "firelighters" community of talented future top leaders proved a tactic that linked the very top of the concern and their priorities and passions to those that in future years will need to accelerate the company and need to "make it happen on the ground." The connection between the chairmen and talented "middle management" was made. Another program is strengthening the same effort: "leaders in action," which for the past two years has been the management development program for high-potential managers. Its starting point is that strong leadership requires a high degree of self-awareness and that strong personal change leads to business change. The program is now being put into action with management teams, and it produces high levels of individual change linked to high levels of business commitment and change. One of the components of the program is a collective "community serving" program. The group is responsible for choosing and carrying out a day of entertainment and fun for those who are less fortunate than themselves. By involving a high level of fundraising and execution, such projects create a strong collective sense of purpose and of achievement: "Together we can have an impact on the world."

Enterprise for Growth Workshops

Between January 2001 and February 2002, a total of 16 "Enterprise for Growth" workshops were held in a chateau outside of Paris, which involved more than 500 company executives. These workshops brought together between 15 and 60 executives who represented the leadership teams of various businesses across the company. The workshops started from the top of the organization, with early sessions involving the global divisional directors with their divisional executive teams, followed by each business group. Each workshop had three objectives: (1) building the collective leadership team for each business (beyond the board), (2) developing a shared strategic agenda, and (3) aligning team behaviors and individual action commitments to support the agenda in action.

Unilever HR staff, IMD, and The Hay Group jointly developed the process for the workshops. The workshops followed four important guiding principles. First, there was extensive top-management involvement and ownership. For each workshop, a Unilever chairman and global division director participated in the event. Importantly this participation was not in the form of a presentation or talk, but rather it occurred in an informal environment focused on setting the tone, context, and expectations for the event. A key focus of these dialogs was sharing where Unilever was in its overall growth journey and what top-management expectations were for the entire leadership team and for each participant as senior leaders at Unilever. The dialogs also provided an opportunity for raising any issue in an open-forum setting.

Second, the business group leader owned the workshop process for their unit and largely ran discussions and sessions supported by the facilitators throughout the process. In preparing the events, we worked hard with leaders on how to lead the event. Our simple principle was that from the beginning to the end it was to be an event between the leader and his or her group. At no point did we want and allow professional facilitators to engage the teams. The reason for this is fairly simple: The facilitators were there to challenge and coach the leaders and prepare the intervention with them. If, however, at the event they are seen as the ones driving and facilitating, it reduced the interaction and leadership that a president developed with his or her team. Ultimately, the power of action will rest on the quality of interaction that they are able to build with one another.

Finally, there were no presentations or new frameworks in any session. There was extensive use of prior work, but all prior analysis and "intellectual materials" and data were posted on the walls for people to read as a basis for discussions. Each workshop focused on dialogs among the leadership team members to build common agendas and actions. Consequently, the final schedule was constantly modified throughout the program, with an overriding philosophy of working around dialog outcomes and not schedules.

Leadership Team: Deepening the Dialogues

Each workshop initially focused on deepening the dialogs among the leadership teams through a series of discussions initially conducted in small groups (three or four individuals), with common themes collected from across the groups. These discussions took place in locations outside of the meeting rooms, usually in natural settings, to create an environment outside the normal experience.

The discussions addressed topics such as "hopes and fears for our business and our leadership team," "myths and taboos that affect how we interact with each other on a daily basis," and "addressing and managing conflict as a leadership team."

The goal of these discussions was to surface reality, to bring to the forefront issues that the team often suppressed but which had a significant impact on how the group worked and interacted. The goal was not to resolve each issue, but rather to use the honesty of the discussion to create a sense of openness and ownership to the process, thus strengthening the bond between team members. The importance of the discussions was apparent when looking at examples of topics that were raised in the discussions. For example, in discussions of *taboo* topics (issues that we do not openly talk about and address), some examples of issues that were raised included:

- Conflict.
- Direct honesty.
- Addressing underperformance.
- Openly disagreeing with plans and targets.
- Holding senior managers accountable.
- Using intuition and feelings as "data."
- Stopping projects or initiatives.
- Talking about personal failure.

Not openly addressing these topics limited the power of interactions within teams. Similarly in terms of *myths* (stories or legends that we do not question but accept as truths), some examples included:

- Doing a good job if THEY allowed it.
- Solving problems, if THEY would let us.

In terms of the way we work:

- All good plans are complex.
- All problems can be solved with a process.

- Our processes are not bureaucratic.
- Everything needs to be reinvented.
- All our decisions are based on value-add.

Here the issue of accepting ownership and accountability for the power of the team, as well as the widely spread complexity, suggested important barriers to address. Finally, in terms of directly addressing how conflict was handled with teams, in our team, conflict is:

- Dealt with outside the room.
- Delegated upward.
- Delegated downward.
- Dealt with by spending money (e.g., consultants).
- Driven toward the lowest common denominator.
- Ignored, avoided, or resolved slowly.
- Managed as part of annual plan discussion.
- Resolved by individual lobbies, vested interests, compromise.
- Avoided by debating endlessly.
- Bad for your career.

The surfacing of reality, addressing these issues within the team and considering the impact on the rest of the organization, provided an important input for the discussions that followed and focused on strengthening the personal bonds among leadership team members. Each team was given the opportunity to talk together about what kind of environment and legacy they wanted to create, to take an assessment of where they were as a team, and to make decisions on how they would work together going forward.

From Strategy to Agenda: Owning Our Future

The second area of focus in the workshops involved building on and moving beyond existing definitions of strategy, and the associated rigorous analysis and insights, to a more direct question: "What are the three to five things that we have to get right to win in our markets?" These discussions focused on building a collective basis for action for each leadership team, a process that entailed first defining each team's collective ambition ("What do we want to achieve as a leadership team?"), and then creating an agenda to achieve this ambition.

Rather than immediately addressing the agenda of the business unit, it was again important to first surface reality in these discussions, this time by starting outside the company and looking at its major markets and competitors. Initial discussions centered on, for example, taking the perspective of the top management of a leading competitor to understand their ambition and agenda to recognize the frequent similarities not only in ambition but also in strategy. These discussions openly addressed the similarities and differences across leading competitors in an attempt to understand what factors would determine success in the markets.

These outside-in discussions laid a further foundation for discussions on each unit's "Must-Win Battles"—those strategic thrusts identified as key to achieving the defined vision. First in small groups and then with the entire leadership team, the dialogues focused on identifying the few items that each unit would have to get *right* to achieve the collective ambition. This agenda reflected the topics that would be discussed at executive meetings and used as the basis for resource allocation and prioritization decisions. Given the importance and impact of the outcome of these dialogues, discussions were passionate and raised many critical issues of debate within the team. Here, the length of the discussion process and coming to consensus was difficult to determine in advance and varied widely across the sessions. In many instances, the unit leaders could have predicted the outcome of the discussions. However, an important challenge in the process was to not have the "leader" predetermine or control the discussions. Participation in the debate and decision making were important criteria for ownership of the resulting decisions.

To avoid having these discussions result in just another "meeting agreement" to be ignored later, a second phase of these agenda-setting discussions involved creating a charter, defining responsibility, and agreeing on a specific schedule for follow-up. The charter represented a more detailed treatment of each must-win battle, including a definition and measurement of success (overall and one year forward), the major gaps to address, and a list of "must-do" and "must-stop" activities to achieve success. These discussions again raised the passion of team members, as they reflected on the detailed implications of the decisions being made by the group.

Team and Individual Behavior and Action Commitments

The third phase of each "Enterprise for Growth" workshop involved focusing on action and behavior commitments to support the growth agenda, as well as to strengthen the bonds among the leadership team. The discussions that took place in this phase addressed two major topics: (1) what are acceptable and unacceptable behaviors for leadership team members, and (2) what individuals should commit to (in terms of their actions and behaviors) to contribute to the growth agenda. An important focus of these discussions involved accountability and feedback. As such, the discussions addressed not just defining behaviors, but also committing team members to hold each other accountable for them. The power of these discussions came through the openness and trust between team members, which the process had contributed to creating throughout the event.

At the end of each workshop, the process had the leader review all of the decisions and commitments made throughout the program and make their personal commitment to own and follow up on the agenda, thus holding themselves and the team accountable for the follow-up actions. This phase of putting it all together was frequently an important point in building a new bond between the leader and the team. The workshop process was often difficult and contentious, with frequent conflict and passionate discussions and debate. Often the leader was visibly exhausted physically and mentally. The leader was challenged to facilitate and guide the difficult discussions, often taking a new leadership style and role. This final phase of the process was aimed at sealing their leadership through their commitments to the group.

Some of the Truths We Found

When looking back at what worked and what did not, some of these *simple truths* (as we called them) emerged:

1. *Separating strategy-making from action and behavioral commitment is a waste of time.* One of our key early realizations was that Unilever did not suffer from a lack of strategy; it suffered from too much of it and too little consequence management was applied in ensuring that things got done as agreed. A strong feeling persisted in Unilever that coordination across units produced often more hassle than help. By a change of words (from "strategic thrusts" to "must-win battles"), we changed how "strategy work" was perceived: urgency and drive entered the discussions. An emotional connection to an intellectual agenda started to occur in each of these sessions. Questions such as, "What hinders us from achieving this?" and "What got in the way in the past?" entered into the fray. Instead of reasons not to, people changed the debate to "Why not?" and "Can we go faster and drive our ambition higher?" This change of focus raised aspirations and created positive energy around the strategic agenda.

2. *The leader leads.* The success of this approach, explained above, is very simple: The more the leader challenges, supports, and coaches his or her people through the event (in other words, role modeling real-life business), the more results can be expected. One of our strongest learnings, therefore, is that building business literally goes through building leadership.

3. *Developing individual commitment embedded in group action.* Corporate change occurs when people change. People change when they are committed and willing to. Change without a context of group support is extremely difficult to sustain and develop. Our key learning here is that change clearly needs to be embedded strategically; it then needs a strong leadership community to drive the individual change and actions that will take place. People saw others committing and together they often were at the same place of commitment or resistance. You have to use the group strongly to move individuals, and clearly strong leadership of the group by key executives is what moves—and inspires—the group.

Continuing the Journey

Unilever's growth journey is far from complete and numerous activities are still occurring throughout the organization. "Enterprise for Growth" workshops

have been cascaded down into the organization. Business units are taking ownership of, and being held accountable for, *must-win* battle agendas. Leadership
teams are measuring and reviewing their progress in maintaining behavior and
action commitments. A whole new phase of activity is emerging to accelerate
growth and change the way in which the company works. The results of the
journey to date are positive. Follow-up surveys indicate significant progress has
been made, while indicating the need for reaffirming commitments and actions
in other areas. There is a clear recognition that the growth journey is making
progress, but it is also a work in progress.

Many successful companies around the world share the challenges faced by
Unilever top management. What can management do when, despite having the
strategy and organization "right," sufficient changes in behavior and action do
not follow? How can a company move from intellectual frameworks and models
to becoming part of the fabric of the organization?

Unilever's growth journey involved readdressing important components of
its past efforts—strategy, organization, teams, and individuals—and integrating
each of these components as part of a single voyage. While this journey gener-
ates deep change in the corporate culture, it is also important to stress that it
builds on the deep-rooted strengths that Unilever has developed throughout its
rich history: the strong emotional bond with the employees; their strong loyalty
to Unilever; the powerful and informally built networks; and ultimately their
genuine care for the company's future.

CHAPTER 25

—═➤◆◄═—

Finding the Missing Link

Connecting Your Business Strategy and Leadership Strategy

MARC EFFRON

DEVELOPING LEADERS IS a popular topic at most *Fortune* 500 companies today, and leadership development groups are ubiquitous at most good-sized companies. While this is a welcome and long-overdue trend, it is undermined by the lack of any clear strategy, in most cases, regarding how leaders should be developed. All too frequently, leadership programs are a jumbled collection of tactics with no foundation and few tangible results rather than actual leadership strategies.

If we, as HR leaders, truly want the envied "seat at the table," we need to dramatically increase our capability to deliver great leadership talent to the organization. We can start by translating business strategy into a leadership strategy—detailing the competencies critical for business success and better defining how to select, develop, align, and reward our leadership talent with the needs of the business.

This chapter presents directions for building the business case for a leadership strategy, illustrates how leadership capabilities differ with various strategies, and suggests which leadership systems should be aligned to support your strategy.

Tactical Successes, Strategic Failures

It is not difficult to understand why much of the leadership work done by HR leaders in corporations today is tactically focused:

- *Tactics are rewarded.* The metrics for evaluating the success of developing leaders are not in place in most corporations. As a result, the next

215

closest metric for success—tactical execution of programs—is what gets rewarded and reinforces the view that any action is better than no action.

- *Functions are king.* Each HR function pursues the tactics that will deliver on its individual or departmental goals. These independent actions lead to tactics that are rarely tied together into a comprehensive strategy for developing leaders and are almost never linked to the business strategy.
- *There is no "right way."* It has been said that leadership is the most researched and least understood management topic. There is not yet one clear model of leadership behavior that directs us to the "right" answers. Without this guidance, we are frequently seduced by the latest leadership trend, the idea heard at the recent conference, or the current leadership bestseller.

However, building leaders in your organization can be more than just a hopscotch path from tactic to tactic. With relatively little effort, you can develop a leadership strategy that provides a clear road map for building leader quality and depth.

So, what is a leadership strategy, what are the implications of various strategies, and how can you build the strategy that is right for your company?

Creating a Business Strategy—Leadership Strategy Link

At its core, a leadership strategy should describe how you would support the business strategy by selecting, developing, assessing, and compensating your leaders. Companies with strong leadership strategies carefully plan each of those areas so they both support the business strategy and integrate with the other leadership tactics. This focus on strategy doesn't mean HR should ignore tactical execution—in fact, tactical execution is the area where we in HR still fail most often. But, before executing, make sure that you execute on the right tactic, in the right way, and at the appropriate time for your business.

Fit: The Foundation of Leadership Strategy

The first step in developing your leadership strategy should be identifying the types of leaders who best fit with your business strategy.

It is a well-researched fact and rather intuitive that leaders perform best if they fit with their work environment. *Fit* is the extent to which a leader's values, personality, experience, and philosophy on running a business align with the culture and strategy of the firm. The closer your leaders fit with the firm, the more effective and engaged they will be.

To assess fit, you can look at two key dimensions of the organization—its business strategy and the degree of change it faces.

We use the *Strategic Leadership Matrix* with our clients, which looks at each of these dimensions to help identify what type of leaders and leadership systems "fit" with our strategy.

Strategic Leadership Matrix

The *Strategic Leadership Matrix* combines these two critical business dimensions—the extent of change facing the business and the degree of growth or return intended by a company's strategy—to understand the type of leaders and leadership systems needed in a business. (See Figure 25.1.) Before we discuss how to use this tool, a few definitions are provided:

- *Return strategy versus growth strategy.* Any business strategy can be simplified so that it is represented on a continuum from primarily seeking growth to primarily seeking financial return.
- *Growth strategy.* A growth strategy is primarily focused on revenue growth—it is likely that marketing, sales, new products, and innovation are all hallmarks of your company. While you may also strive to have efficient manufacturing processes, Six Sigma, and so on, these are not your bases for competition (see the box at the top of p. 218).

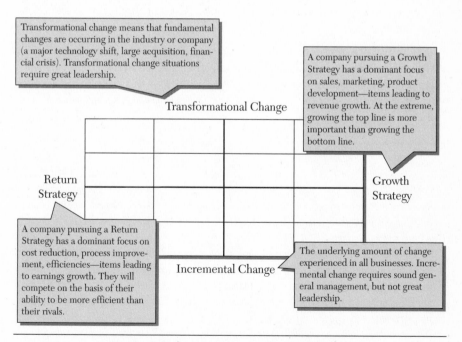

FIGURE 25.1   Strategic Leadership Matrix

GROWTH STRATEGY

One example of a strong growth strategy was Amazon.com in the 1990s. One of the earliest entrants to online retailing, Amazon focused on aggressively growing the top line (revenues) of the business. This allowed them to realize the cash flow growth necessary to continue building the business to the size necessary for efficiency.

During that period, Amazon valued a dollar of top-line growth over a dollar of bottom-line growth because even if a company loses $.30 on every $1 of product sold, $500 million of cash flow can fund much more expansion than $50 million in cash flow. That additional investment can later pay off any debt built during that period (or deliver earnings that appeal to the stock market so shareholders benefit). Amazon's leader then and today, Jeff Bezos, can be described as the ultimate growth leader.

- *Return strategy.* A return strategy says that cost reduction, efficiencies, and process improvements are the heart of your competitive strategy. While you may intend to grow while executing the strategy, you will compete on the basis of having a more efficient organization than your competitors.

It is unlikely that a successful leader at Amazon would be a successful leader at Wal-Mart, even in a similar role. As described earlier, the tendency of leaders to stay in similar business environments means that the go-go growth leader would likely not fit well in the low-cost Wal-Mart culture. Research has shown

RETURN STRATEGY

One of the most successful firms of the late 1990s and early 2000s is Wal-Mart, whose legendary focus on cost control secured ownership of a marketplace formerly dominated by K-Mart, Woolworth, and a few other firms who compete primarily on price.

While Wal-Mart was one of the fastest growing companies of the 1990s, its strategic choice for competition was to be the low-cost provider of products and services. Wal-Mart made significant investments in novel logistics arrangements, including direct electronic links between individual store inventories and their major suppliers to facilitate reordering. This type of improvement was grounded in reducing inventory costs and product shortages. Wal-Mart's strategy clearly falls into the *return* category.

that leaders tend to prefer working in specific strategic situations—the successful turnaround artist probably isn't interested in working in a fast-growing startup, and a growth leader would likely not choose to work in a company on corporate life support. A good leadership strategy acknowledges this and tries to closely match leaders with company environment.

- *Transformational versus incremental change.* The other key dimension of leadership fit involves the degree of change in an organization.
- *Incremental change.* While most companies today face a challenging business environment, this new pace of change has become expected, in contrast to the greater predictability of years past. We call this underlying level of change experienced by all businesses *incremental change,* and most leaders are able to manage this level of challenge.
- *Transformational change.* Other firms are undergoing more dramatic change (large acquisitions, industry transformations, financial crises), which is called *transformational change.* These companies need leaders who can guide the company through turbulent times. Others may need what leadership scholar Jim O'Toole calls *yellow light leaders*[1]—individuals who are effective midway between the incremental and transformational view. In either case, these leaders are capable of, and interested in, steering a company through more turbulence than many of their peers.

Similar to leaders' fit with business strategy, these leaders need to be comfortable with and capable of dealing with degrees of change. Those who thrive on new situations, enjoy uncertainty, and tend to be charismatic are closer to the transformational end of the spectrum. Those who prefer less drama in their work likely fit best at the incremental end. The effective leadership strategy defines the change needs and ideas for leaders who fit with that environment.

These two continuums capture the key issues of *fit* between leaders and company environments. By combining them, you see how very different leaders are needed to support different business environments.

Applying the Tools

Map your company on the *Strategic Leadership Matrix* (see Table 25.1). To see where your organization might fall on the *Change* axis, ask the following questions, answering both about today and about the next three to five years in your business.

To understand where you are on the *Strategy* axis, choose the statement from either column 1 or 2 that best describes your business strategy today and over the next two to four years (see Table 25.2).

Now, graph the results, starting with the *Today* state. For *Change,* count the tick marks and move up one notch from *Transformation* for each. For *Return,* starting at the mid-point of the *Growth-Return* axis, for each tick mark in column 1, move one mark to the right. For each tick mark in column 2, move one

TABLE 25.1   **Change Questions**

	Today (√)	2 to 4 Years (√)
1. We will engage in an acquisition.		
2. Our industry will see a fundamental change in the products or services we provide.		
3. We will likely have financial challenges.		
4. We expect moderate to high turnover of our top leaders.		
5. We will see a significant change in our market share (positive or negative).		
6. We will attempt to shift the culture of our company.		

mark to the right. Write "Today" where these two points intersect (see Figure 25.2).

Repeat the exercise for the three- to five-year question, writing "Future" where those points intersect. Now draw a line between those two words.

Each quadrant in the Strategic Leadership Matrix demands a unique set of capabilities. The concept that one model of leadership competencies should somehow support all business situations will seem shortsighted after you have completed this exercise:

- *Upper right.* Transformational growth is where many companies strive to be. These firms tend to be dynamic, exciting places to work. Most dot-coms fell squarely in this quadrant but so did Microsoft and IBM in the 1990s and today.

  Capabilities needed from "growth" leaders in this environment include vision, speed, aggressiveness, risk-taking, managing change, and innovation, among others.

- *Lower right.* Steady growth is the focus of times in this quadrant. These firms often are comfortably established in their markets and innovating at a pace to keep them competitive. Colgate-Palmolive exemplifies this position, relying on strong products to drive growth but not seeing any fundamental changes in the marketplace for personal care products.

  Capabilities needed from "steady hands" include speed, aggressiveness, process management, risk-taking, planning, and task focus.

TABLE 25.2   Strategy Questions

Column 1	Today (√)	3 to 5 Years (√)	Column 2	Today (√)	3 to 5 Years (√)
Improving access to or exploring new markets.			Maintaining share in existing markets.		
Creating new businesses or products.			Selling existing products.		
Developing alliances and partnerships.			Focusing on core business.		
Expanding headcounts.			Consolidating functions and reducing staff.		
Growing top-line revenue.			Reducing expenses and finding efficiencies to reduce costs.		

- *Upper left.* This is "crisis corner," which normally means a firm is struggling mightily to transform itself. As this book goes to press, Xerox is still in this quadrant, as are energy firms such as Dynegy.

  Capabilities needed here from "turnaround artists" include vision, decision-making, financial acumen, managing change, risk management, and cost control, among others.
- *Lower left.* Quiet efficiency is needed from firms in this quadrant; these companies are seeking strong earnings based on a low-cost or efficiency-based strategy, with little company or industry turbulence. An

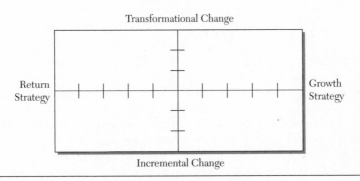

FIGURE 25.2   Results Graph

CASE STUDY: ABC UTILITY

Assume that you manage an electric and gas utility (ABC Utility), which is moving from a regulated to a deregulated environment. If you were asked the questions concerning strategy today, you might say that you are focused on ensuring a consistent rate of return for your stockholders by focusing on controlling the cost of raw materials and other general and administrative costs. Your strong preference is for a dollar of bottom-line (earnings) growth versus an additional dollar of top-line (revenue) growth. In fact, revenue growth, if driven by new customers, might actually be undesirable if it strains the capacity of your existing power plants to supply their customers.

The degree of change in your utility, which was formerly regulated, is likely very small. Your leaders are probably skilled at responding to the underlying level of change in their business, and it is unlikely that a competitor will emerge with a new low-cost power source that will demand that you aggressively change. If you map each of these measures on the matrix, you end up in the lower left-hand corner (see box figure).

Results Graph 2

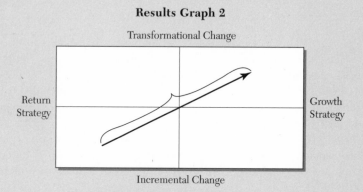

Transformational Change

Return Strategy

Growth Strategy

Incremental Change

Now, forecast your world three to five years from today when you are a fully deregulated company. Your strategy is to provide as much power to as many customers as possible (industrial, commercial, and residential) by providing power from your own power plants and by acquiring power through trading on the free market. You are clearly pursuing more of a growth strategy at that time, perhaps not completely willing to trade a dollar of earnings for a dollar of revenue but moving strongly in that direction.

On the *Change* axis, you need to fundamentally transform your business into a free-market organization focused on existing customers, leading in a growth environment, and aggressively marketing your services.

This seems like a much more significant change environment, not complete upheaval, but likely 75 percent of the way along the spectrum.

Thus, in the new environment, your firm is in the upper right-hand box. Your leadership strategy, the types of leadership behaviors, and leadership systems needed are much different from what you have today, and the path from today to tomorrow is the degree of change you will experience.

The leadership skills and behaviors needed in this environment will differ greatly from before, and the leadership systems will need to reinforce your ability to attract, engage, and retain leaders who "fit" with that environment.

ideal example here is ExxonMobil, which is largely constrained by the additional value it can extract from a barrel of oil.

Competencies needed from "efficiency kings" include risk management, process management, financial acumen, cost control, rule orientation, and task focus.

Crafting Your Leadership Strategy

Your *Future* position on the graph speaks volumes about the types of leaders and competencies you will need to realize your business strategy. As important, it provides clear direction about the types of leadership systems (sourcing, assessing, developing, and rewarding) you should use to reinforce those competencies. The combination of your competency model and the leadership systems forms your leadership strategy.

We use the Leadership Life Cycle (LLC; see Figure 25.3) to help clients map out the programs that reinforce their business strategy. The LLC includes the four key leverage areas for building leadership quality and depth:

1. *Sourcing.* How to obtain the leaders you need to meet your business goals. This includes the balance between "making" leaders (develop them internally) or "buying" them (recruit externally) and the processes for doing each. At a practical level, it includes succession planning, search firm relationships, and building a leadership brand, among others.
2. *Aligning.* How to ensure leaders are aligned with business goals and engaged with their jobs. Alignment means how well you are building expectations with leaders, what business results they are expected to accomplish, and how to accomplish, in addition to how well you've built a leadership environment that fully engages these leaders with the challenges you've established for them.

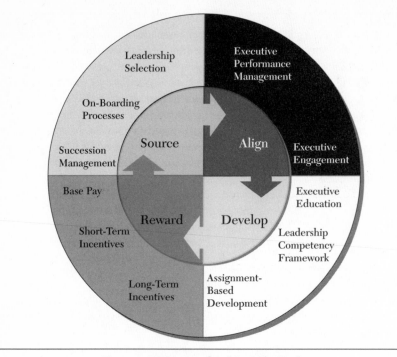

FIGURE 25.3   Leadership Life Cycle

3. *Developing.* How to build the capabilities, knowledge, and self-awareness of your leaders. This includes the assignment matching process that should flow from succession planning, executive coaching, mentoring, and any formal development programs.

4. *Rewarding.* How to compensate leaders to incent performance, reward success, and differentiate high performers. Rewarding includes base pay, annual incentives, and long-term incentives.

After completing the mapping exercise, consider the implications of each of these areas on your leadership practices. Are your current practices aligned with the business strategy that you plan to achieve? Which practices provide the most leverage and which need to be realigned? Most importantly, do the pieces mutually reinforce each other, sending consistent messages about the behaviors that you will encourage and reward?

Revisiting our case study company, ABC Utility, an overview of their leadership strategy might look like that shown in Figure 25.4.

The battle for top leadership talent will only intensify as more companies realize the value that great leaders deliver. Taking a planned, strategic approach

Critical Competencies

We've identified the following five competencies as most important for our executives given our business strategy and our change environment:

1. Grows the business.
2. Drives change.
3. Builds commitment.
4. Maximizes talent quality.
5. Focuses on the customer.

Sourcing Leaders

Make/buy mix. We will balance the ratio of internal hires/external hires in leadership at 70/30, to encourage new ideas and challenge our culture while providing opportunities for internal development.

Succession planning. Our succession planning process will be the exclusive method for placing leaders into jobs. We will identify candidates and match them with opportunities based on this process, using the competencies as a primary screen.

On-boarding leaders. Retention and success of leaders in new roles (from inside or outside the company) will be increased through a process that provides guidance and coaching around both personal performance and relationship building.

Aligning Leaders

Performance management. We will set aggressive goals for all leaders in our performance management process, ensuring that stretch goals are a key component and that a balanced measurement of business performance and individual behaviors occurs.

Engaging leaders. Executive engagement will be actively monitored through yearly surveys, with HR and the Executive team jointly held accountable for identifying and improving deficiencies.

Executive coaching. Providing select executives with coaching to further performance will be a core aspect of our strategy.

Developing Leaders

Assignment-based development. Job assignments will be the primary method for developing leaders and a process to match individuals and jobs will flow from succession planning. Support of internal coaches will be provided to leaders in developmental assignments to help ensure success.

High potential development. Our highest potential employees will receive a disproportionate share of developmental resources. We will develop group activities for them, increase their exposure to the senior team and board, and review their performance on a semi-annual basis.

Executive development. We will provide group-based sessions for our leaders to develop capabilities in serving customers, communicating a clear vision, and business acumen.

Rewarding Leaders

Base pay. We will set the 50th percentile as the goal for base pay, with high potential employees identified through our succession process being paid at the 60th percentile.

Annual incentive. We will provide a 75th percentile target for annual incentive, strongly differentiating between median performers and high performers in distributing rewards.

Long-term incentives. We will use a combination of performance-vesting stock and regular stock options to provide incentives for consistent leader behavior. We will target the 75th percentile for these awards, strongly differentiating between median performers and high performers.

FIGURE 25.4   ABC Utility—Leadership Strategy Summary

to attracting, motivating, and retaining leaders will result in stronger, more effective talent delivering superior business results.

For HR leaders, this provides a clear opportunity. It is debatable whether we have really proven ourselves a "strategic partner" despite our protestations to the contrary. By delivering to the organization the solution to the most challenging people issue of our day, the perception of HR's lasting value can finally be set aside and your "seat at the table" truly earned.

CHAPTER 26

⪻⬥⪼

Convergence of HR
Leadership and Change Management

WAYNE BROCKBANK

THIS CHAPTER ARGUES that three separate strands of business knowledge, activities, and roles are converging. These strands are leadership, change management, and human resource management. The convergence of these strands mandates that HR professionals add greater value in the future than they have in the past. This chapter begins with a brief summary of some of these key changes in the business environment and their implications for HR. The major section of the chapter compares themes and activities of leaders, change managers, and HR professionals and examines their convergence. The concluding section suggests some future implications for the HR profession.

Emerging Trends in the Business Context

Most contemporary business trends require that leadership, change management, and HR be effectively leveraged as major sources of competitive strength. These trends include globalization, speed, service economy, workforce composition, declining customer loyalty, and demands for financial results. A brief description of each follows:

- *Globalization.* Several factors have contributed to the substantial growth of globalization. Since the mid-1960s, the level of global tariffs has dropped by approximately 50 percent.[1] Since the mid-1970s, more than $2 trillion of economic activity has been deregulated. Globalization has been facilitated by substantial reductions in communications and transportation costs. The globalization of business is one of the primary factors that has increased the intensity of business competitiveness to an all-time high.[2]

- *Speed.* Time compression has become a major factor behind the mandate for change in many corporations. During the past decade, the time required to bring a car from concept to product has been cut by 78 percent. Companies have learned to synchronically engineer, reengineer, and reverse engineer products and processes at an ever-increasing rate.[3] Getting people to think differently, to relinquish old fiefdoms and hierarchical assumptions, and to continually question more traditional ways of doing things is a way of life.

- *Service economy.* In North America and Europe, the past twenty years have seen a marked increase in the proportion of gross national product (GNP) that is accounted for by the service sector. As people accumulate many of the physical goods they desire, quality of life becomes marginally more enhanced by services provided from the helping professions. In addition, the percentage of revenues from service after sales is growing faster than the percentage of sales of products. For example, 41 percent of IBM's revenues come from service—with hardware at 39 percent.[4] Given that people are the company's face to the consumer, companies are increasingly recognizing the importance of more effective management of the human side of business.

- *Workforce composition.* Changes in workforce demographics place additional pressure on employers to focus on "people management." The ethnic mix in North America is moving toward a greater proportionality of Spanish-speaking citizens. The birthrate of minority ethnic groups substantially outpaces that of groups of European ancestry. Women have established their presence in the workforce.[5] Loyalty has dropped from the top 15 business values, and the "What's-in-it-for-me?" factor has risen sharply. Increasingly, employees have increased their desires for greater time with families. Each of these changing trends mandates that the human side of business receive relatively greater emphasis and that leaders lead differently.

- *Customer loyalty.* With the extensive availability of competitive products and services, customer loyalty is increasingly undermined. The only way to ensure customer loyalty is to consistently provide the highest quality products and services at the lowest prices with the most attractive features. This trend mandates that employees engage in developing new products, finding and eliminating obvious as well as hidden costs, and maintaining the highest quality of products and services. They must accomplish these tasks with an unrelenting focus on present and future customers.

- *Financial performance.* Capital markets are placing higher demands on corporate financial performance. These higher demands have direct implications for the HR agenda. Companies must be more productive. Whereas a decade ago corporate creative energies focused heavily on product innovation, today the mandate is toward greater focus on creative ways of controlling and cutting costs. The continued explosion in mergers and acquisitions is heavily driven by the expectations of enhanced financial performance.[6] As is well documented, the preponderance of failures in mergers and acquisitions occurs because of leadership, change management, and HR-related issues.[7] Finally, the investment community has never before been more focused on corporate intangibles. Do they trust the leaders? Do they trust the integrity of the employees who must deliver on promises that they make to customers and shareholders?[8]

Each of these trends in the global business environment mandates that the human side of business be better managed as a fundamental source of competitive advantage. Given the acceleration of these trends over the past decade or so, the urgency around effective human resource management has likewise accelerated. In this new world of globalization, fast innovation, service, diversity, demanding customers, and demanding owners, HR professionals need to provide substantial intellectual leadership in better leveraging people for competitive advantage. As these trends increasingly accelerate, HR professionals need to be masters of change management. In this world of greater demands on the human side of business, HR professionals need to more powerfully design and implement HR practices and capabilities that create more powerful human organizations.

Convergence of Leadership: Change Management and Human Resource Management

Analytical Methods

The previous section suggests that leadership, change management, and HR are becoming more central to business success. This section provides an overview of the major activities and capabilities required for successful HR management, leadership, and change management. It establishes the premise that these three elements of business success are converging. It concludes that the convergence of HR management, leadership, and change management has important implications for the future identity and activities of HR professionals.

To identify the major themes and activities for HR professionals, this chapter relies predominantly on the 2002 "Human Resource Competency Study" from the University of Michigan's School of Business.[9] Because of the heavy reliance on this source of information about HR professionals, a brief overview of the study methodology is warranted. The 2002 iteration includes more than 7,100 respondents from 241 companies across Asia/Pacific, Latin America, Europe, and North America and across a variety of industries. The study uses a 360° feedback instrument that includes a self-assessment of HR participants, an assessment of the participants by the participants' internal HR colleagues, and an assessment of the participants by the participants' non-HR internal clients. This chapter relies exclusively on data provided by the non-HR internal clients.

Five major categories of HR activities and competencies emerge from the data:

1. *Strategic contribution.* Consists of culture management, fast change, strategic decision making, and market-driven connectivity.
2. *Personal credibility.* Consists of relationship skills, delivering results, and communication skills.
3. *HR delivery.* Consists of staffing, performance management, development, and organization design.
4. *Business knowledge.* Consists of knowledge of the integrated value chain, firm's value proposition, and labor relations.
5. *E-HR.* Consisting of delivering HR practices through information technology.

These activities and capabilities of HR professionals are compared to those of leaders and change managers in Tables 26.1 through 26.6. Only those HR activities and capabilities that are statistically significant predictors of high levels of firm financial performance are given; that is, these HR activities and capabilities are those that differentiate the HR professionals in high-performing firms from those in low-performing firms. (*Performance* is defined as the firm's financial performance compared to its major competitors over the last three years.)

The review of the leadership and change management literature reveals six major themes of leadership and change management activities and capabilities. These themes are:

1. Direction setting.
2. Leadership integration.
3. Support system design.
4. Engagement of implementers.
5. Measurement and learning.
6. Persistence to results.

In each of these six themes, key activities for leadership and change management are reviewed and compared to empirical data on the active involvement of HR professionals from high-performing firms in these major activities.

Direction Setting

Leaders bear primary responsibility for ensuring that the firm has a compelling and strategically accurate vision based on external market realities. They ensure that the vision balances the requirements of multiple stakeholders and that it functions as a precise road map with measurable outcomes. Change managers bear responsibly for facilitating each of these phases of direction setting. The

TABLE 26.1   Direction Setting

	Leaders	Change Managers	HR Professionals
Direction setting	Shape a powerful vision.	Facilitate establishment of vision and direction.	Help establish the business strategy.
	Develop a strategy for the future based on marketplace reality.	Bring external perspective and provide avenues for internal input.	Set the direction of change.
	State clear measurable objectives.	Establish process parameters for planning intervention.	Identify problems central to business strategy.
	Develop precise road map and timeline to make it happen.	Confront inconsistencies in strategy and key stakeholder demands.	Provide alternative insights on business issues.
	Balance the contradictions of multiple stakeholders while maintaining focus.	Coach senior executives on framing the strategy formulation process.	Bring intellectual rigor to business decision making.
			Are proactive in contributing to business decisions.
			Frame complex ideas in useful ways.
			Facilitate the change process.

HR professionals in the high-performing firms are centrally involved in these activities. They facilitate the setting of strategic direction. They "walk into the strategy room" with a point of view about what the strategy should be and how the strategy process and content should be framed. In high-performing firms, HR professionals bring intellectual rigor to business decision making, whereas the HR professionals in the low-performing firms do so, but at a significantly lower level (see Table 26.1).

Leadership Integration

For effective action to occur on a large scale, leaders must first achieve a substantial level of cohesion in the leadership team around key directional issues. In this context, *leadership team* refers not only to the leadership team at the top of the business, but also to the leadership team as it is integrated through the multiple layers of management. Leaders need to make decisions quickly and accurately as a result of their ability to work together. HR professionals in high-performing firms have credibility and chemistry with the management team.[10] With that credibility and chemistry, HR professionals help ensure that decisions are made quickly and with cohesiveness (see Table 26.2).

Table 26.2   Leadership Integration

	Leaders	Change Managers	HR Professionals
Leadership integration	Sponsor the change in a visible and public manner. Build coalition of support within the leadership. Communicate directly with key leaders at lower levels.	Build senior management team around the vision. Ensure support of senior executive who personally sponsors and dedicates time to the change and has gone public in support of it. Ensure that middle- and lower-level leaders are on board with the vision. Maintain and coordinate all leadership layers as implementation proceeds.	Focus on how to get decisions made quickly. Work well with management team. Have "chemistry" with key constituents.

Support System Design

For effective leadership and effective change management to occur, strategic direction must be supported by the resource allocation systems. Leaders must ensure the availability of the right people with the right information and adequate capital. They must ensure that the organization is exposed to the optimal quality and quantity of information through multiple media, including the visible and personal behaviors of key leaders. They must ensure that adequate funding is available so that the measurement and incentive systems are designed to bring about alignment between employee behavior and the specified business strategies.[11] HR professionals in high-performing firms conceptually and operationally translate strategic direction into resource support systems. They ensure the availability of people and information and that funding options are consistent with the desired outcomes. They also ensure that the physical environment in which strategy is implemented is consistent with prespecified outcomes (see Table 26.3).

Engagement of Implementers

A key activity of leaders and change managers involves the engagement of implementers. They enhance the understanding and commitment of key implementers so that execution occurs efficiently and effectively. HR professionals in high-performing firms likewise have a high degree of skill in building employee commitment to the culture that is required for financial success. They do this by exposing employees to key customer data, by encouraging employees

TABLE 26.3 Support System Design

	Leaders	Change Managers	HR Professionals
Support system design	Allocate right people to the right place at the right time with the right information and the right technical and cultural capabilities. Allocate information quickly to the decision makers and implementers; vision is clearly communicated; back-up information is available; lead the way as role models. Communicate the vision clearly and powerfully through words and personal behavior. Allocate money for high-priority agendas; eliminate funding for low-priority agendas. Allocate incentive funds that are linked to performance relative to targeted change. Hold people individually and personally accountable for appropriate results.	Apply multiple media to communicate the vision of change. Ensure that leaders role model behavior. Ensure the availability of human, financial, and informational resources. Reinforce direction of change through aligned measurements and reward systems. Remove obstacles to change. Provide training in newly required technical and cultural capabilities.	Ensure the availability of resources (money, information, people, that make change happen fast). Align HR with the desired culture. Design development programs that facilitate change. Facilitate the design of internal communication processes. Attract, promote, retain, and outplace appropriate people. Design measurement systems that distinguish high-performing individuals from low-performing individuals. Design performance-based compensation systems. Assist in restructuring of the organization. Encourage executives to behave consistently with the desired culture. Manage the arrangement of physical environment.

to exhibit the behaviors that are necessary for business success, and by providing employees the opportunity to be involved in challenging and valuable work[12] (see Table 26.4).

Measurement and Learning

To track success that can result in learning and improvement, effective leaders and change managers ensure the presence of robust measurement systems. They ensure that small wins occur and are systematically tracked and that

TABLE 26.4   Engagement of Implementers

	Leaders	Change Managers	HR Professionals
Engagement of implementers	Communicate rationale for change that is relevant for business success and personal well-being.	Ensure that those whose support is needed express it publicly, voluntarily, and irrevocably.	Frame culture in a way that excites employees.
	Leverage the voice of customers and shareholders to enhance the need to change.	Involve key action-takers in implementation decisions.	Identify the culture required to meet the business strategy of "your business."
	Involve coalition of key implementers in design and execution of implementation plan.	Answer the "what's-in-it-for-me?" question for key implementers.	Encourage employees to behave consistently with the desired culture.
	Need to change is widely and urgently shared.	Integrate the whole organization around key change initiatives.	Design high value-added and challenging developmental work experiences.
		Negotiate new and required behaviors among implementers.	Facilitate the dissemination of customer information.

measurement processes track behaviors and results and compare progress against competitors whenever possible. They apply these measured learnings to develop improvements that may then be communicated and applied throughout the organization. HR professionals perform the same measurement activities and are highly skilled at sharing learnings across the organization for further business success[13] (see Table 26.5).

TABLE 26.5   Measurement and Learning

	Leaders	Change Managers	HR Professionals
Measurement and learning	Take behavioral and results pre-measures at the beginning of change.	Create small wins and ensure visible communications of those wins.	Monitor process of change.
	Gather measures from both internal and external sources about reality and perceptions.	Ensure the availability of quantitative and qualitative measurements and use measurement to accelerate improvements.	Adapt learnings to new change initiatives.
	Ensure relevant comparisons against preset time, behavioral process, and output requirements.	Compare performance with major competitors.	Facilitate the integration of different business functions.
		Capture learnings about change for application in future change efforts.	

TABLE 26.6 Persistence to Results

	Leaders	Change Managers	HR Professionals
Persistence to results	Remove competing diversions. Leaders and implementers maintain a relentless passion to succeed. Factor learnings into future visions and agendas. Achieve success within the boundaries of moral and legally accepted practices.	Reinvigorate change initiatives with new themes, projects, and people. Work with key sponsors to ensure continuation of change initiatives until desired results are achieved.	Have track record of results. Meet commitments. Remove low value-added or bureaucratic work. Demonstrate high integrity.

Persistence to Results

Effective leaders have a relentless drive to achieve results: They have little tolerance for irrelevant, low value-added activities that deter them from achieving desired results. They take the learnings from each cycle of strategic initiatives and factor them into future visions and agendas. To achieve results with consistency and persistence, change managers recognize the importance of reinvigorating change initiatives with new ideas and people. They work with key sponsors to ensure continuity to results. In a related manner, HR professionals in high-performing firms have a track record of meeting commitments and achieving results. The variables having to do with "achieving results" factor together with the variables having to do with integrity. Thus, HR professionals are expected to be persistent in achieving results, but they must do so with a high degree of integrity. They also take a leadership role in ensuring the removal of low value-added work that may deter the organization from achieving its desired results[14] (see Table 26.6).

Conclusions

From the previous analysis, three conclusions may be deduced. First, there are far more similarities than differences in the key activities of leaders, change managers, and HR professionals. The great preponderance of what effective leaders do is the same as what effective change managers do and vice versa. Furthermore, the activities of HR professionals in the high-performing firms have substantial overlap with the activities of effective leaders and change managers. HR professionals in high-performing firms are centrally involved in the same activities with the same capabilities as effective leaders and effective change managers. Thus, the activities and capabilities of HR professionals, change managers, and leaders are converging.

Second, today's world of business requires much greater levels of globalization, service, innovation, efficiency, and speed. Each of these, in turn, requires that companies pay greater attention to enhancing their leadership, change, and human resource management capabilities. Thus, in today's business environment, the roles, themes, and agendas of leadership, change management, and HR will continue to converge as long as the world of business continues its trajectory of accelerating change.

Third, the challenges before HR professionals are that of identity and aspiration. The research from the University of Michigan indicates that HR professionals in high-performing firms are increasingly functioning as leaders and as change agents. The fact that HR professionals can do so has been clearly shown. Two personal decisions remain:

1. Do we HR professionals aspire to move into the activities and capabilities of leaders and change managers, and are we willing to pay the development price to do so?
2. Do we aspire to have leadership and change management as essential features of our professional identity?

The world of business is asking HR professionals to do so. If we are to add the value of which the HR profession is capable, these will be our aspirations and our identity.

THE HR PROFESSION: COMING DEMISE OR NEW BEGINNING?

———⟫•◇•⟪———

IN THE PRECEDING sections of this book, the notion that people are an organization's most important asset was reconfirmed. This isn't new, cutting-edge thinking; business professionals around the world have heard this mantra for years. Why, then, isn't HR an organization's most important function? HR has had a number of previous lives and is currently taking on yet a new shape. What *does* the future hold for our profession? As the function faces the most challenging forces it has yet to encounter, will it endure or cease to exist?

In this final section, the authors tell the story of the human resource function from the beginning and highlight the challenges and implications for HR as a profession in the coming years. They make predictions about the changes HR will face and suggestions for HR executives as they work to reinforce their significance and value for the businesses they serve. The following pages are a glimpse of the exciting and challenging future of HR.

CHAPTER 27

Is This the End of HR?

STAN DAVIS

NOT LONG AGO, I spoke at a conference for HR people from a *Fortune* 100 firm. First, the new CEO, an ex-General Electric star, laid out his strategy. Then, the experienced head of HR spoke about changes coming in the function. Touching all the appropriate bases (technology, outsourcing, globalization, etc.), he said the traditional metric of one HR person for every 100 employees was likely to slip to one for every 200, 300, or even 500 employees. He moved on to other matters, finished his speech, fielded a few innocuous questions, and then introduced me.

I was stunned. He had just said the equivalent of "Most of you in this room won't be here much longer," and it hardly caused a ripple. (As of this writing, the CEO has quit and the company is in play.) Which was the more extraordinary, the changing ratio and what it meant or the signal the audience missed and what that meant?

The Next Thing for the "People" Function

The field known as HR has had previous lives, and it is likely undergoing another transformation right now. Before the end of this decade, we may be seeing the end of HR and the birth of yet another generation of the "people" function.

I say "may" because I'm not certain. I care about the HR function very much, and I lay out my thinking here, not so much to predict the future as to stimulate debate. If I'm right, the life cycle change may not be a bad thing. It may just be the *next* thing for the people function.

Although HR as we know it may cease to exist, the needs it addresses are perennial and real. Some new form for addressing those needs will come into existence. However, there is no guarantee that the new form will have a place

239

for the HR professional; inevitably, some HR professionals will find the upcoming changes threatening, while others will see opportunities.

Past Lives of HR: Industrial Relations and Personnel

When my career first began in the mid-1960s, *industrial relations* was morphing into *personnel*. The title change suggested great expectations of a more enlightened era in companies' approaches to their employees. Industrial relations was born in response to the trade union movement of the 1920s and 1930s, and it lasted until the 1960s. In the early 1950s, about a third of the total U.S. workforce belonged to unions. Today, that number is only about 13 percent. The concerns in the spotlight during this time were "labor relations" issues. In the 1960s, this focus broadened and mellowed into personnel, which emphasized the administration of what had become entitlements (essentially, pensions and benefits) and "human relations" (essentially, training and development).

The *personnel* function had its life cycle, too. Ending in the 1980s with its replacement by *human resources*, this shift was also meant to be much more than a mere name change. The new underlying ethos was that employees were recognized as tremendously important to the success of the corporation. Trust, cooperation, and Theory Y replaced confrontation, negotiation, and Theory X.

The Birth and Death of HR

The birth of HR coincided with the passing of the industrial economy and the rise of both services and the information economy. Like agriculture before it, manufacturing had shrunk to a lower percentage of the economy, and the service sector was experiencing explosive growth. The spotlight shifted from factories to offices. Blue-collar issues dwindled from the spotlight; white-collar concerns multiplied. Phrases such as *knowledge worker* began to creep into the business vocabulary.

Since Karl Marx, land, labor, and capital have been the three factors of production. Land lost its supremacy with the shift from the Agrarian to the Industrial Age. In the Information Age, capital lost some of its grip to the human factor, or so the story went. Money was cheap; talent was scarce. HR became a player, and those who cared about people finally had a shot at the executive table. Some even reported directly to the CEO.

Many, if not most, HR professionals feel respected and esteemed by the big guys and gals at the top. The hard truth, however, is that HR has only partially lived up to its promise. Now, its moment may have passed and HR's days may be numbered.

Let's go back a few decades and contrast what happened to the two support functions, personnel and purchasing. If the personnel stereotype was that it was teachers and social workers who wanted to earn more, the purchasing stereotype was the back-office guy in a flannel shirt and suspenders, chomping on a cigar. Both types were necessary; neither was top management.

Between then and now, and using information technology, purchasing reconfigured itself into supply chain management (SCM). Distribution had already transformed itself into the broader function of logistics. SCM added a more completely integrated vision, which absorbed the much larger and more central manufacturing with logistics. By the time the integration was complete, the new SCM included the old purchasing, manufacturing, distribution, and delivery processes.

Customer relationship management (CRM) is currently attempting the same thing from the other end of the supply chain, integrating back up the value chain, creating a seamless flow of the company's essential purpose throughout the corporation. Horizontal processes, such as SCM and CRM, now dominate the pulse waves where vertical lines of structure and control once ruled.

Purchasing started calling itself SCM about a decade after personnel started calling itself HR. Both were tapping into fundamental shifts in how business would be conducted. Purchasing, more completely than personnel, however, used technology to integrate itself directly into the heart of the business. Using speed, connectivity, and intangible information, it exploded its old self out of existence and its new self into the business core.

Unlike purchasing, HR has not had comparable success fundamentally reorienting the corporation and how it runs or, in the process, fundamentally reconfiguring itself. Consequently, some of its activities are being outsourced, others completed by software, and an attenuated nontechnical portion of the function continues working valiantly to relate more directly to the business, its strategy, and policy matters.

Unrealized Opportunities

Jack Welch, the most esteemed executive of the second half of the 20th century, was noted for the managerial bench strength he created at General Electric. "I believe that a company's competitive advantage," he said, "is its ability to raise the intellectual capital of the organization every single day."[1] General Electric also happens to be the exception proving the rule when it comes to corporate longevity. This correlation between the success of a company and the depth of its management has long been a central belief on which HR is founded. It leads, though, to an obvious question: *If talent is the most important resource in today's economy, why isn't HR the most important function (or, more narrowly, the most important support function)?* Three possible reasons come immediately to mind, and each spells unrealized opportunities:

1. Perhaps talent is not the most important resource. Maybe it has been overrated and overpaid. The overpayment of top executives who cashed

in just before their companies crashed suggests there may be something to this interpretation. Of course, being talented and being at the top are not always the same thing, though our compensation systems are built on this assumption. Remember, the financial community, not HR, created the stock-option reward. HR merely climbed on the bandwagon, and it has the opportunity to lead the reevaluation but may not take it.

2. Since the Enron, WorldCom, and other scandals, there have been calls for greater accountability of senior executives, for treatment of stock options as expense items, and for the shift away from compensation systems that focus attention only on quarterly returns. These developments could also, but probably will not, be led, owned, and redressed by a vibrant HR function.

3. While belief in the importance of HR for corporate performance is almost universally held, it can never be decisively and definitively proven that it causes it. Correlation is not causality, and this has always been the Achilles heel of the HR function. The belief suffers when times get rough, and a cost-cutting focus usually replaces the more nurturing approach. What is treated as talent in an up market becomes an expense in down markets. Quantifying HR's direct value and financial contribution still remains elusive.

As long as this is the case, HR's original aspirations and promises go unfulfilled. Despite good work and meaningful respect, the function's status will inevitably backslide. The prize is to be had by methods and entities that link HR to profit and revenue growth, not just to cost and efficiencies. This need persists, and because it is not met internally, external forces such as new software technologies and outsourcing are evolving to do so.

Outsourcing HR

When you can't figure out how to measure something, put it out in the marketplace and let the market put a measure on its worth. We may never be certain how the market does it, what it is actually measuring, or whether the measure is just or right. But measure it, it does. This is key to the new moves toward outsourcing certain HR functions. It's a classic case of competition coming from outside the industry that uses new technology to redesign the activity. It suggests that the marketplace, and not HR departments, will create the new paradigm.

HR departments are too internal to the organization and too removed from marketplace rules to run their activities as profitable businesses. They are more a part of a company's organization than of its business. (Your *business* is what you do; your *organization* is how you do it.) This is the difference between ends and means. When HR functions are outsourced, however, they change from means into ends. When they cross that line, one-time expenses miraculously become revenues to someone else. What one company did as peripheral (staff) support, the other now does as its full-time business. In addition, technology speeds up not only the process, but also the evolutionary life cycle itself.

In November 2000, for example, Exult, Inc. signed a 10-year contract with Bank of America to take over the bank's HR function. For the client, outsourcing is a way to save money and focus on its business. It leaves a vastly pared-down internal HR to focus on strategy and policy rather than on transactions and administration. The agreement is expected to generate 10 percent or more in cost savings to the client and revenues for Exult of approximately $1.1 billion over the life of the contract. Noting Bank of America's move, Prudential outsourced its HR "piece of the rock" to Exult in January 2002. This deal is expected to be worth $700 million over 10 years. The two deals will service the HR needs of 150,000 and 47,000 employees, respectively. They are only two of many such agreements. The people function is migrating to those who manage it as a revenue-producing activity, which is something internal HR organizations do not do.

Some companies that outsource HR may invest in the contracting company or forge an alliance with it. From the employees' perspective, many will be let go in the transfer, but even more may only change the name of their employer, as they do the same job working for the external HR purveyor. This nominalizes the adjustment they have to make, but they may also end up with a significantly reduced benefits package.

Eliminating HR people through outsourcing and disintermediating them through IT software has another profound impact whose consequence has yet to be fully appreciated. The new approach treats customers and employees the same way. Outsourced contracts and services such as these rely heavily on IT—software and Web-based systems designed to eliminate organizational, transactional, and communications barriers, as well as bottlenecks and inefficiencies. Such self-service systems are being applied to customers as well as to employees for much the same reasons. Also in 2002, CIGNA Corporation, for example, an $85-billion employee benefits company, partnered with Yahoo! Corporation to provide its 16 million customers with personalized portals to track their claim status, benefit services, and health and retirement plans directly.

What's Next for the People Function?

Back in the heyday of the corporate culture craze, I remember that all vision and value statements (the ones in Lucite on desks and on cards in wallets) included one commandment about "customers" and another, usually the last, about "people" (employees). It always struck me that the distinction implied customers are not people and, more importantly, that they were to be managed differently. The reasons for managing them differently are readily apparent, but the reasons for managing them all as people are not. Whatever the next generation of the people function is, it is likely to articulate the gains to be made by leveraging the similarities. This is more likely to happen by making HR into a business itself, and it is very unlikely to happen as long as HR remains exclusively part of an internal overhead organization.

The self-help orientation of the information technologies is also speeding up the end of HR. For instance, just a generation ago, spreadsheets, another product of IT, "deskilled" financial analysis. The most junior people equipped with a PC and the right software could manipulate and organize data that was once reserved for skilled professionals. The same deskilling is now happening to several HR activities, as in the previous outsourcing examples, and a generation from now, it may well happen to strategy and planning, though that is beyond the scope of this chapter.

In summary, HR may be near the end of its life cycle, going the way of industrial relations and personnel before it. The people function, of course, will survive, though in other forms more suited to future needs. The current mantra, "Getting HR people to understand the company's business," will not be enough to rescue HR. The search to cut costs and improve efficiencies has already led to outsourcing and informationalization of HR activities. In part, HR is becoming a business in its own right. Externally, such businesses are emphasizing the similarities between how they handle their clients' customers and employees, more than they emphasize the differences between these two groups. What is being left internally is a highly trimmed, though more important, sliver, which is focused on strategies and policies that will be transformed in the next decade as well. For now, it may be only slightly premature to predict that the king is dead.

One final thought: What will we call the new baby? Some offspring are named before birth and others soon after. In a few cultures, including the corporate variety, naming waits until childhood ends and adulthood begins. Thus, we'll probably know the true new name within a decade, during which time everybody gets a chance at the naming game. But, then after all, what's in a name?

CHAPTER 28

Transforming Your HR
Department into a Start-Up
Professional Services Firm

WILLIAM BRIDGES AND
SUSAN MITCHELL BRIDGES

As AN ORGANIZATIONAL area and a professional field, human resources (HR) was created at the same time that *jobs,* as we know them, became the dominant way of organizing and assigning work. Organizations of one sort or another have been around for millennia, of course, but *jobs* were a 19th-century invention.[1] It was *the job* and not the steam turbine, the internal combustion engine, or the electric motor that was the great 19th-century invention, because *the job* totally restructured how work was done and how lives were lived. It made all the other inventions possible.

Before the middle years of that century, people worked awfully hard, and they were sometimes employed by large organizations. But they didn't have *jobs,* in the sense of fixed patterns of activity, regular hours, a boss, a predetermined salary, and a box on the organizational chart. They didn't have that thing that enables people to say (of some piece of work), "That's my job." (Or, sometimes, "That's *not* my job.")

Those things only came in with the factory system and the large government bureaucracies that grew up around the same time. Jobs were, in fact, invented to get the standardized, repetitive, and easily sequenced work of that age done. The assembly line and the huge office—and anywhere else where division of labor into constantly repeated tasks worked well—were the homelands of jobs. It is no accident that it was in the same settings, a few decades later, that what would ultimately be called "human resources" began to take shape. HR was created to make the world of jobs work.

245

Think of HR terminology: Hiring is *filling a job*—"How many *job openings* are there in marketing currently?" Pay scales are *job-based*. The candidate asks, "What does *the job* pay?" We urge the supervisor to see that people are really *doing their jobs;* it is, after all, *his job* to do that. The company's activity depends on an interlocking set of *job descriptions*. Periodically, we have *job evaluations*. Those who do well may get promoted to a *new job*.

The trouble is that jobs aren't such effective ways of doing work that is fast-moving, nonrepetitive, and knowledge-based, especially when constant change and novel situations are the order of the day. That is why start-up companies often do away with conventional job descriptions and assign people to *areas* or *projects,* and why many organizations shift their focus from *jobs* to *assignments*. To obtain the flexibility that these situations require, such organizations often utilize contingent workers, workers from a joint-venture partner, or freelancers. They often outsource work to another organization.

Information and communications technology have enabled (even encouraged) companies to use dispersed workers—who may not even be their own employees—to get their work done. Recently, an HR professional at one of our seminars showed us a list with eight categories of workers on a project that he was servicing. "Here are the people I have to look after," he said. "A few of them are employed by us, but most aren't. Some are temps, some are independent workers, and some belong to one or another of our joint partners: eight different groups of workers!" Welcome to the work world of the 21st century.

What is that world going to do to HR? Quite simply, it is going to change it beyond recognition. It is going to change the work (no, not "jobs"—those will go) of HR professionals completely. Let's run through some of what is likely to happen:

- Hiring is already changing, as the focus shifts to "talent" (which needn't be bought, since it can easily be rented from a variety of sources).[2] Furthermore, even if hiring does take place, why should HR do it? Managers themselves can do the hiring as they need it, especially with the kind of online help that is now available. There are, of course, problems here: Managers don't always pay the proper attention to effective assessment, gender and ethnic issues, pay equity, and other issues. However, with this shift, HR becomes an advisory function rather than the place you go to get something done.
- "Retention" is already coming to be an idea whose time is past. It's not that organizations won't want to retain their access to the very best talent that they can find, but they won't have to "employ" people for long periods of time to do that. In fact, an effective workforce policy is going to be as much about sending workers on their way after their work is done as it is about finding them in the first place. Forget retention of workers; manage the "talent flow" through the organizational system.
- If that is the case, then organizations are going to have to provide a new infrastructure to guarantee and regulate that flow. Transfer, relocation,

temporary assignment, overseas assignment—these things have always been important, but now they have to become part of a new organizational circulatory system that guarantees that when someone's work finishes *here*, it can resume somewhere else in (or around) the company without undue distress or delay.

- In this new workplace, career services are going to need to be reinvented. The "normal" career is not only going to move people around more than in the past—it is also going to carry people into, out of, and back into the organization several times during their careers. We suspect that the organizational "alumni groups" that exist at some big companies are the precursors to a shift from "employment" to "affiliation," as the basic relationship between organization and individual. What is this going to do to benefits?

- For some years now, there have been articles about the New Employment Contract. However, it's been mostly talk. HR has to step up to the table, as a partner in the executive suite, to articulate what the New Deal at its particular organization is—because the deals will differ from one organization to another. HR will have to help leaders learn how to explain, demonstrate, and utilize that New Deal to get the organization's work done. We know of no HR groups that have built the handling of fluid and fluctuating groups of workers into the leadership competencies around which they build executive development programs.

- Job descriptions were the heart and soul of any industrial operation. They were the puzzle pieces that locked into place the whole surface of the organization's work. In our results-driven age, however, job descriptions look disturbingly like excuses for paid activity that doesn't necessarily add value. Activities matter much less today than *outcomes*—which don't show up on job descriptions. Outcomes can be agreed on and time lined in advance by the worker and the manager. They give the worker a much clearer target to aim for, and they give the manager firmer control over the results.

- To construct those outcome-agreements, managers need to be able to modularize the work required by the project and to clump the modules into coherent packages that can be parceled out to employees, contractors, and supply chain partners. The ability to do that and to manage the different resulting work streams is going to be a critical skill for tomorrow's manager, but few management development programs reflect this new reality.

- That suggests that most of today's management development programs are a little out of date. No wonder: They were all about managing full-time employees rather than orchestrating the efforts of diverse groups of "talent." Today "managing" is more like the project-coordination work done on a construction site than it is like what yesterday's manager spent his days doing on the factory floor.

- How about communications? In the 20th century, they were largely one-way (top-down, center-out), and they were almost always initiated by the person at the top or the center. Those habits won't get very far into the 21st century. "Communication" will give way to "knowledge-access," which is initiated at the bottom or on the periphery of the organization— wherever the worker with a need-to-know is. Only the most general and generic communications will follow the old paths. In most other cases, the information will be sought out (online, in many cases) by the people who need to know it.

- That raises the larger question of whether the 21st century's HR services in general are going to be initiated from something called "HR," or whether (like communication—no, *knowledge-access*) they won't be de-livered primarily on-demand, at the convenience of the worker who needs them. Here, as elsewhere, power is shifting from the supplier to the user.

- This shift has important implications for the work of HR professionals. They've always been the people you went to see when you had a question. ("Let's go see what HR says about that.") Their status (and the satisfac-tion they got from their work) came from playing the role of the one-who-knew, sometimes the one-who-decided. But, increasingly, they'll be managing the systems that give employees access to the information and the answers, rather than giving it themselves. They'll more often be ex-pert at managing information systems than being the comp-and-benefits or communications or employee-relations experts that they have previ-ously been.

- There is a larger question here. HR has been the source, the referee, the repository of policy, the one who knew the-right-way-to-do-it. The word that describes what is happening to many such gatekeepers is *disinterme-diation*. Such middle-people are getting removed from the transaction. (Yes, we know that a new generation of information-based intermediaries has emerged, but that kind of intermediation—that tells you where to get the best Chinese food and which laptop is the neatest—is a very different business.) Much of the power and cachet of HR came from its old inter-mediary function—which is going to go away.

Start Planning for the Future

Although we believe that each of these statements is likely to describe the shape and functions of HR in the 21st century, we offer them not as detailed predictions, but as indicators of the direction that things are already taking. A particular HR group or an individual HR professional would do better to follow a strategy that capitalizes on the fact of change, rather than trying to guess what particular changes are going to take place.

That may sound like a rather vague jumping-off point, but it is actually the best available starting place for your planning—either as an individual profes-sional or as someone responsible for HR policy. A traditional HR department is just about guaranteed to be wrecked by the changes ahead. It is too inflexible and too slow to respond to change. It is like the big, old-line companies that get bypassed by the nimbler, newer, and more responsive ones. So, why don't you try this little exercise?

Take a group of HR folks away to a quiet place for a day. Tell them you are going to do a simulation. Talk a little about how as-if thinking helps us to get out of our mind-sets and explore new possibilities in a low-threat way. Then, distribute an official looking memo that says that, as a cost-saving measure, HR is going to be outsourced. The memo also says—with that queasy kind of kindliness that people always fall back on when they are saying something scary—that the company appreciates all the HR folks' fine work over the years, and it is going to give first consideration to an outsourcing proposal from any organization that is made up of former HR employees from dear old Employer Co. End of memo. Then tell them that you have called them here today to form such a company—a boutique HR firm that will bid on the old work (or as much of it as they really believe to be worth doing), plus any additional work that meets an unmet organizational need. Then, you spend the rest of the day planning your new start-up HR firm. At the end of the day, you take stock of what you have done, and you make one of the following statements:

- Did we come up with any good ideas? Do you want to try any of them in our present context?
- What's to stop us from doing some of these things within the context of our present department? This is what we'd do if we were trying to get the company's business. It's what we know they need. Let's spend the next week working out the details and then present it to the executive team.
- Hey, this was fun! Maybe we should leave the organization and bid back on our old work. The CEO is going to faint, but we can save him enough money to make him take notice. Sally and I will try to sell him on the idea and the rest of you start tomorrow morning putting together a marketing plan. Remember, we'll go after work wherever we can find it, so your task is to get us half a dozen new clients in the next six months.

The point is that HR is going to change in big ways in the 21st century. Your organization needs to put together a plan to capitalize on that change—and you, as an individual HR practitioner, need a plan, too.

CHAPTER 29

———❦———

What's Next for the People Function? A Missing Link for Delivering Value

DAVID ULRICH AND NORMAN SMALLWOOD

FOR MANY YEARS, HR professionals have sought answers to the question, "Do we matter?" In a quest to be strategic, be partners, or be at the table, HR professionals worked to earn respect. We believe that the HR profession now commands respect, not because HR declares it, but because line managers, customers, and investors affirm it. However, to deliver value, we start not with HR, but with the outcomes that line managers care most about. Value is defined by the receiver, not the giver. In HR terms, the receivers of HR work are employees, customers, investors, and the organization itself. All of these stakeholders care about the quality of HR because HR practices add value to their work.

Understanding and Delivering Value

For HR professionals to understand and deliver value, they need to start with understanding market or shareholder value because this is what investors, line managers, and other stakeholders care about. A senior executive we worked with claimed that there was no such thing as a "balanced" scorecard. He reasoned that if the firm failed to create sustainable market value for the investor, employees could not be retained, customers could not be served, and the organization would wither and fade away. If market value is the value many leaders, customers, and investors ultimately seek, HR professionals need to begin their journey of impact by understanding market value.

Why is a firm's stock price what it is? The easy, and some would say obvious, answer is that when firms make more money, their stock prices goes up. Market value follows financial performance. On the surface, this makes sense, but the facts refute it. Increasingly, a firm's market value is not fully explained by financial results such as earnings. A number of studies have shown that financial results explain 50 to 70 percent of a firm's market value. The rest of the value is explained by investors' perceptions of the firm's likelihood of achieving similar, greater, or lesser earnings in the future. This perception about future earnings is called *intangibles*. Intangibles describe the factors that drive the likelihood that a company will deliver on its promises for making money in the future.

The Importance of Intangibles

Baruch Lev, an accounting professor at New York University, has explored the importance of intangibles. He and his colleagues have found that the association (regression) of earnings and shareholder value of approximately 5,000 U.S. enterprises changed dramatically from 1980 through 1996. Earnings that once explained 80 to 90 percent of shareholder value now explain less than 50 percent. From a financial perspective, Lev has defined *intangibles* as "a claim to future benefits that does not have a physical or financial (a stock or a bond) embodiment."[1] He has shown the importance of intangibles as indicated through the market-to-book value (the ratio of capital market value of companies compared to their net asset value) of the S&P 500 from 1977 to 2001, which has risen from 1 to over 6 in the last 25 years—suggesting that for every $6 of market value, only $1 occurs on the balance sheet. This data shows that the value of many firms comes as much from perceived value as from hard assets. Firms such as Coca-Cola and Merck have high market value from brands and patents. Technology-based firms such as Amazon and Exult have high market value with relatively little in the way of either hard assets or patents. Even traditional companies such as General Motors and 3M are increasing market value by focusing on brands, leveraging the Web, and restructuring. Lev goes on to challenge traditional cost accounting systems that focus more on physical than on intellectual assets: "To claim that tangible assets should be measured and valued, while intangibles should not—or could not—is like stating that 'things' are valuable while 'ideas' are not."[2]

Some have argued that today's high price-to-earnings (P/E) ratios indicate that market values are inflated—a balloon waiting to pop rather than a reflection of predictable intangible value. We disagree. When the dot-com bubble burst, some firms' market values fell more than others. We believe that firms that survived the market credibility crisis did so because their leaders made the intangibles tangible. These leaders met financial goals, had a strategy for growth, created core competencies aligned with strategy, and ensured organization capabilities. Intangibles often exist within an industry, not across industries, so the patterns of P/E ratios of firms within an industry offer evidence of leadership intangibles in both up and down markets.

Harvard accounting professor Robert Eccles and his colleagues at PricewaterhouseCoopers (PwC) call for a "value reporting revolution" by changing financial reports to include more intangible information. They find that only 19 percent of investors and 27 percent of analysts "found financial reports very useful in communicating the true value of companies." They argue for changing the performance measurement game to better allocate capital and assess the true value of firms. In identifying better measures of firm performance, they focus on "key performance measures—both financial and nonfinancial—and how they relate to each other, how they are measured and reported on, and how they create real value."[3]

Ernst & Young's Center for Business Innovation also attempted to find out how investors use nonfinancial information in valuing firms. They interviewed and surveyed investors on both the buy and sell sides of equity transactions to assess the importance of nonfinancial intangible issues in decision making. They found that nonfinancial measures do matter to corporate executives and that investors consider these measures when valuing companies.[4] In the conclusion of their study, they found that nonfinancial criteria constitute, on average, 35 percent of the investor's decision. Sell-side analysts use nonfinancial data when evaluating companies and making buy/sell decisions, and the more nonfinancial measures analysts use, the more accurate their earnings forecasts prove to be.

Something other than earnings is playing a role in investor perception of market value. Understanding and being able to leverage intangibles is of enormous interest to leaders working to build market value. For these executives to deliver the shareholder value they desire, they have to learn to identify lead indicators of financial results or those intangible issues that affect investor perceptions of the firm.

We shared these ideas recently with a talented HR colleague. About ten minutes into the discussion, his eyes glazed over, and he wondered if we had lost our HR credentials. He wondered why we were so absorbed with the financial world and measures of market value. He did not see, nor did he want to understand, the link between investments in HR and shareholder value. We think he has mistakenly seen HR as a way for companies to care for people, not as a way to help executives build shareholder value. HR professionals who understand intangibles can demonstrate that their work affects market value, and that their commitment to caring for people endures because it builds market value. Caring for people is not a social agenda that depends on the goodwill of a particular leader or team, but it can be linked to an economic agenda that is sustainable over time.

The Next Phase for HR Professionals

Understanding intangibles is a next phase for HR professionals. As the HR profession developed from the 1930s through the 1980s, the focus was primarily on activities of HR. These activities ranged from labor relations to craft policies that dealt with unions; to staffing programs to place the right people in the right job at the right time; to training initiatives that ensured that employees acquire skills for future business demands; to compensation, benefits, and reward systems that offered incentives to employees and teams for good performance; to high-performing work teams; to organization redesign; and to flexible work/life policies. Each of these (and numerous other) activities has been the traditional focus of HR work.

The Shift from Activities to Outcomes

In the past decade, the HR profession has shifted focus from activities to outcomes, from doables to deliverables. The deliverables of HR are the outcomes from doing HR activities. Rather than measure the percentage of leaders who received 40 hours of training (an activity measure), the focus shifted to the impact or outcome of the training. What was the business impact of managers attending training, being hired with competence models, or being paid for performance?

The bridge between HR activity and business impact focused on organization capabilities. An organization's capabilities represent what the organization is good at doing, its DNA. HR professionals, as strategic or business partners, turn strategy into capability through an integrated set of HR practices. For example, we worked with a refinery manager of a large integrated oil company. His business goals were explicitly stated in financial and customer terms. As he performed an organization audit, he identified the key capabilities of collaboration (the ability to work across organization boundaries), speed (the ability to work fast), and engagement of all employees as critical to his business success. His professionals were then able to coach, architect, design, and facilitate the creation of capabilities.

Seven Critical Capabilities

Organization capabilities embedded inside a firm have intangible value to investors outside the firm. The missing explanation between earnings and shareholder value that finance colleagues call intangibles may be capabilities. Investors knowingly or unknowingly give a firm a market premium or discount based on their perception of the organization's capabilities. These capabilities become intangibles. We have posited seven critical organization capabilities that may now be seen as creating intangible shareholder value:[5]

1. *Talent* represents the ability of an organization to attract, motivate, and retain the employees it needs for peak performance. When HR professionals and leaders build systems that attract talent, they build the intellectual capital of their firm and assure that competent employees are

committed to firm goals and objectives. Talent implies that the organizations with the most competent and committed employees will most likely succeed over time. Winning the war for talent ensures that competent and committed employees are placed throughout a firm.[6]

2. A *shared mind-set* establishes the culture or identity of a firm. When a firm has a common identity or culture, customers identify the firm as a brand, and employees know what is expected of them. As an intangible, a shared mind-set increases customer value by confidence in the firm brand and increases employee productivity and commitment by reinforcing behavior in accordance with customer expectations.

3. *Speed* means that a firm manages change and moves quickly both into new markets and in adapting administrative innovations. When HR professionals can build agility, flexibility, or speed into their organizations, good things happen. Being right is not enough when being first is critical. Speed not only allows for first-mover advantage into new markets and products, but also excites and engages employees.

4. *Learning or knowledge management* becomes critical to an organization when it attempts to generate and generalize ideas with impact. HR professionals who build learning organizations encourage creativity and innovation of ideas within an organization unit and then build disciplined processes for sharing those ideas across organization units. Learning capacity is an intangible value when organizations have the ability to move ideas across vertical, horizontal, external, and global boundaries.

5. *Accountability* means that an organization has the ability to execute and deliver on its promises. Rhetoric needs to be replaced by resolve—and resolve comes when individuals in the organization are accountable for their behavior and outcomes. Leaders and HR professionals build organizations with accountability by setting clear goals and having consequences for meeting or missing goals.

6. *Collaboration* occurs when the whole is greater than the sum of the parts. Collaboration is required for companies that grow through mergers and acquisitions, for global companies, and for companies implementing shared services.

7. *Leaders at all levels of the firm* may also become an intangible asset. Effective leaders demonstrate competencies (knowledge, behaviors, and motives) and deliver results. A leadership brand may be established and integrated into a firm. As an intangible, investors who perceive a higher quality of leadership will have more confidence in a firm's future earnings opportunities.

As investors come to recognize these (and other) capabilities as intangibles, they gain confidence in the future value of the firm, and the market value gets a premium for cash generated. Building capabilities and increasing intangible value becomes a playbook for HR professionals who want to take the next step of shaping not only employee but also shareholder value. As HR professionals master the concepts and adapt the tools that build intangible value, they will be able to help executives deliver unbalanced scorecards, or market value, with current and pragmatic leadership actions. This requires that HR professionals do not fear or run away from their accounting and finance colleagues but partner with them. As the partnership evolves, all of these functions must change their traditional views of what builds value and find ways of working together to do a better job of building stronger organizations. This process drives intangible market value.

Building Intangibles

We have begun to see the cases of HR professionals who understand, know, and discuss capabilities that build intangibles. A senior HR executive we know joined a firm that had a remarkable history of financial performance. However, the firm's stock languished behind competitors. As he examined this situation, he felt that the company's rigorous financial accountability was not clearly shared or understood by either employees or executives. He helped the executive team craft a simple, clear strategy (or vision, mission, purpose, etc.) statement that focused the firm on growth, customer service, leadership development, and operating efficiency. All corners of the large organization were obliged to frame their goals and investments in these four themes. He also crafted a set of operating values that connected the pieces of the firm to one another through shared beliefs. As his simple story began to permeate employees, he took the story to the investment community. Working with the CEO, CFO, and other senior executives, he was able to craft a simple, clear message for investors. In a typical four-hour analyst meeting, he would spend 60 to 90 minutes talking about the firm's culture and how the organization was positioned to continue to deliver exceptional financial results. The stock doubled in two years, catching up to and eventually outperforming competitors' stock valuations.

The point of this story is simple, but not easy.[7] The simple message is that HR professionals add enormous value when they see their work connected to building the market value of a firm. However, it is not easy for HR executives to build this bridge. It requires that HR professionals understand how to weave HR actions into capabilities, that they are able to talk about market valuation models, and that they couple their work on organization capabilities with financial disciplines.

The intangibles we discuss in this chapter should become the deliverables of HR. HR professionals should be able to help define and deliver these intangibles through their collaboration with business leaders. Traditional measures of HR success (such as the percentage of managers who received 40 hours of training a year) are replaced with the outcomes of those activities (e.g., delivering one of the leadership intangibles we propose—learning, talent, speed, shared mind-set, accountability collaboration). The HR-led conversation focuses on intangible value when the capabilities we have presented become defined and real to the general managers who use them.

To our HR friend who feels such compassion about people, we say, "Make the link between people, capability, and intangible market value to ensure long-term people commitment." For the HR profession to fully engage line managers, we need to worry about what they worry about and help them with their problems, not ours. For those many executives who worry about market value, HR can be a business partner with them to build it.

CHAPTER 30

—≫◦≪—

Profession at a Crossroads

J. RANDALL MacDONALD

IT HAS BECOME virtually axiomatic that the global, interconnected, digitized world of e-business is driving levels of institutional and societal change not seen since the Industrial Revolution.

In the same way that all important relationships are being redefined—between businesses and consumers, governments and citizens, universities and students, physicians and patients—so are the fundamentals of the relationships between people and the enterprises in which they work.

We are all familiar with the changing demographics of the modern workforce. It is more diverse, older, and far more willing (and eager) to make multiple career changes. All of this drives an entirely new set of employee expectations in basic compensation, equity, benefits plans, the definition of job satisfaction, and what it means to be a "great place to work." And it is all happening in Web time.

This "fast-forward" redefinition of the compact between worker and employer brings with it a set of major implications for the role of the traditional human relations function, which, deserved or not, carries a reputation for bureaucracy and rigidity into this environment of speed and flexibility.

Our profession is at a crossroads. To understand what is next and what will characterize the effective, valued next-generation human resources function, it is important to first understand where the profession has been.

First, our profession is a fairly young one in terms of corporate organizational structures. Even in the days of the Roman Empire, the quaestor and the praetor were the equivalent of today's financial and legal functions. For all practical purposes, a career in *personnel* did not exist as recently as 100 years ago. As business has grown and transformed, changes in nomenclature have reflected the evolution of the role and responsibilities of the function—from *personnel administration* to *personnel* to *industrial relations* to *employee relations* and, in recent years, to *human resources.* I will be surprised if the next iteration does not include the word *workforce.*

The role of the modern HR function dates to roughly the 1930s, when the first signs of companies taking an interest in their employees for reasons other than productivity became apparent. The impetus was largely external. Depression-era workers started to demand different and more equitable treatment from their employers and in some cases to unionize. "Unique" benefits, such as cafeterias and recreation programs, were introduced, which in turn drove the requirement for a staff to manage them. Thus were born departments of *personnel administration*. Unfortunately for HR as a profession, these departments were typically staffed with people who did not have the skills to make it elsewhere in the organization. The principal qualification for one of these jobs was "being good with people," and the HR function was strictly administrative.

During the 1940s and 1950s, the role expanded in response to the tight labor market that resulted from World War II and the rise of mass manufacturing. Management gained new interest in issues, including pay practices and labor management, which drove a renewed "professionalizing" of the HR function. *Personnel departments* were formed with core disciplines around competitive pay, benefits, labor relations, and a far more strategic purview. This was the advent of what we now call human resources, and it was the first real opportunity (limited though it was) to have a voice in the corporation's matrix of authority.

The 1960s and 1970s saw the introduction of new governmental pressures on commercial organizations, which further elevated the role of the personnel function. Governments became more focused on social and legal issues in areas such as equal opportunity, wage controls, employee safety, and healthy workplaces, as well as pension reform. Suddenly, the necessity of having an effective HR function converted from "nice-to-have" to imperative, as the function assumed authority for regulatory compliance and some financial management.

Professional degrees in the area of personnel and human resources were awarded, which further legitimized the field. Personnel made the enormous leap from organizing company picnics and monitoring employee attendance to developing and overseeing complex workforce policies. Yet, even then, the function lacked credibility as a "value-added" contributor to the corporation's bottom line, and it suffered from a lingering perception that it was not an equal partner to other corporate units in terms of technical and operational excellence.

The corporate actions of the 1980s, characterized by takeovers, buyouts, and mergers and acquisitions, forced organizations to cut costs, improve productivity, raise quality standards, and focus relentlessly on the customer. Although still not actively invited to take a seat at the table of senior management, HR professionals were at least consulted more heavily and were expected to deliver leadership solutions to these complicated issues. The name *human resources* became more prevalent as the function inched closer to the seat of power. From putting out fires to overseeing legal proceedings and implementing control policies, the function was earning its first significant opportunity to add value in a period of rapid change.

The 1980s also saw the rise of a far more diverse and inclusive workforce composition—with females and other minorities competing for more jobs and more senior-level positions. The appeal of organized labor grew among workers in large corporations. HR executives were increasingly seen as key counselors to members of senior management. Their increased stature in business decision making reflected the broad-based transition from soft "people issues" to the management representative that best understood the "voice of the people."

I have no doubt that many in our profession would argue this point, but it is my opinion that the HR function did not truly "arrive" until the 1990s. Again, the change in stature was driven by the marketplace. CEOs who were forced to restructure, downsize, and cut costs assigned the management of workforce reductions to their HR leaders, with the expectation that these actions would be carried out with minimal disruption to the image, productivity, and morale of the organization. As a result, HR executives of vision and strong strategic thinking evolved from being the "voice of the people" to the "advocate of management." After approximately 100 years and several variations on the theme, we were at the table.

As I assess our position at the beginning of the 21st century, I think it's fair to say that HR has not only occupied its seat at the leadership table, but also fulfilled this major responsibility admirably.

We no longer have to evangelize our value to colleagues inside our own companies. In the information technology industry, for example, there are hundreds of thousands of open jobs for skilled professionals. IBM and every company we compete with (and every customer of the technology industry, for that matter) are engaged in a war for talent that is unlike anything we have ever seen. The ability to attract, motivate, and retain the best people is not just an aspiration, and it is not just a mantra recited by all well-meaning HR professionals. It is nothing less than a matter of competitive survival, co-equal to the ongoing mission to build leadership and organizational capability. Especially in periods of economic uncertainty, the HR function has a critical role to play in ensuring that an organization's most important asset, its people, is engaged and motivated.

Returning to the "What is next-generation HR?" question, we HR professionals have learned at least one obvious lesson over the past century: Our function will respond and adapt to the marketplace environment—employees' expectations, governmental influences, and competitive and economic pressures. So what are the marketplace indicators that can lead us to some conclusions about the next evolution?

In the broadest terms (accepting and allowing for variations within individual industries), the coming environment will continue to be characterized by customer consolidations in many industries, the inextricable linking of business strategy and networking technologies, and the growth of service-related organizations. Workforce diversity will increase. Company loyalty will decrease. Developed countries that have traditionally supplied the majority of the labor force are beginning to age. Emerging markets are building educational systems and training programs, which is creating new opportunities to "source" expertise from countries such as Russia, China, and India. Complex employer-employee issues will evolve around ethics, employee privacy, and genetic testing.

Creating the next generation work environment—highly collaborative and capable of not just fostering but also encouraging the instant, seamless movement of ideas and expertise—will present both intellectual and technical challenges for us as professionals. Just as obviously, the power of information technology, probably even more than we can imagine, will change our social, personal, and working lives.

For years, we have believed that successful companies are those that learned how to exploit their knowledge on behalf of their customers better and faster than their competitors. That has come to pass. The new paradigm is that to remain competitive and relevant, organizations will increasingly channel that intellectual capital toward the development of a concise set of core competencies, strengths, and capabilities.

Given all that, perhaps a more relevant question for us to spend time on is: "What are the characteristics of the next-generation HR professional?" rather than the next generation of the profession. Elements of the top performer's job description include:

- *Operational excellence.* Providing functional expertise to the business that is strategic and leading edge.
- *Creativity.* Developing breakthrough thinking to internal customers.
- *Accountability.* Being responsible, taking risks, and ensuring that we deliver on our commitments with speed and accuracy.
- *Quality.* Raising the bar and ensuring that organizational and individual performance improves day-to-day, month-to-month, and year-to-year.
- *Teamwork.* Collaborating and building relationships across all areas of HR and the line organization to deliver responsive solutions.

Beyond that "starter set" of personal attributes, do not forget that the environment we work in is less predictable than at any time over the past ten years. That's a statement of both the current economic uncertainty and the technology-driven change of the networked world. Thus, I conclude with a few observations on what it's going to take for us to consolidate and build on the position we've established as individuals and as a professional function:

- *Amass knowledge.* For us to hold our seat at the table, we need to be so steeped in knowledge of our businesses and our industries that we do more than respond to change; we anticipate the change and lead the response. We need to be truly strategic, we need to be more "high-touch" in our approach and in the development of new solutions, and we need to demand high-performing cultures.

  We will see HR professionals increasingly spending their time on understanding the organization's strategy, its competitors, the relevant technologies, and, most importantly, immersing themselves in customer expectations. We need to help our corporations gain competitive advantage by providing HR solutions and tools that continuously replenish the talent of the employee base.

In other words, we need to know the business, and then we need to apply our particular expertise to create value based on what's happening in the marketplace. HR theory is fine, but it's essentially meaningless when practiced apart from the market realities that drive our companies' strategic directions.

- *Be an agent for change.* Creating change is not easy, but it can happen. I believe that the most successful HR professionals in the next generation will define themselves as confident, decisive, and action-driven change agents and that they will be perceived as such by colleagues outside the HR function.

- *Rethink our value.* Knowing our business and our profession is one thing; being accountable is another. Typically, investments in its workforce are among the most significant expenditures any company makes. Thus, we must demonstrate our value by measuring it. The HR function's measurements must be tied directly to the attainment of the business plan of the enterprise. These measurements must relate to strategy and, even more importantly, to execution and marketplace performance.

  Our human capital results and our performance must be based on pre-determined, hard-edged business metrics and goals. We start by taking responsibility for the return on investment of essential HR programs, such as recruitment, retention, and turnover. Employee attitudes, compensation, health and safety, learning, workforce models, and productivity need to be evaluated based on the impact that they have on the organization's bottom line. After we set our targets and ensure that they are aggressive and aligned with the company's strategies, we need to communicate them to the business. Only in this way will we prove to the business that we hold ourselves accountable for delivering results and making the greatest possible contribution to an organization's success.

- *Innovate.* In addition to reinventing our intellectual contributions to the business, as previously discussed, a technology statement along two dimensions is needed:

  1. Embrace and exploit the full capabilities of information technology to deliver our services in a cost-effective manner. Many companies, including IBM, are aggressively pursuing the outsourcing of transaction-based aspects of their HR organizations to allow investment to flow to more strategic, high-impact initiatives. Key to our profession's future success is a continual focus on innovation in how we deliver our programs (i.e., driving out costs, reducing cycle times, and ensuring customer satisfaction with our services). We need to act and think like a business, not a staff function.

  2. Apply advanced technologies to drive high performance, to handle the realities of an increasingly mobile workforce, and to foster the rise of a truly knowledge-based learning culture in which people can contribute regardless of where they "sit" in the hierarchy. For any organization to

compete in this white-knuckle environment, employees have to develop skills faster than ever before, and the organization must tap into expertise wherever it resides in the enterprise.

Finally, we have to be smart about the application of advanced technologies in finding talent and then creating strong relationships with potential, current, and past employees. This means minimizing attrition among our best performers and at the same time dealing with low performers either by improving their contribution or managing them out of the business:

- *Create the future.* This is about restocking the talent pipeline, but it also includes focusing on the next generation of leaders, at all levels of the organization, and ensuring that we are developing a leadership team that is as diverse as our employees and customers. Our approach needs to do early career identification of those employees who have the potential to be leaders and who have the potential to hold senior executive positions. After we find them, we must provide programs and opportunities for these employees to develop both their skills and their understanding of their strengths and weaknesses.
- *Drive high performance.* This is about creating an organizational bias for action. It is about understanding the difference between a culture premised on obedience and one based on individual judgment. There is a specific and measurable correlation between the workplace climate and performance. The organization has to be crystal clear about the kinds of behaviors that will be recognized and rewarded and those that are discouraged.
- *Reward the winners.* The key word here is *differentiation.* The best performers need to know that if they deliver, they won't be treated as average. The top performers must take down the lion's share of the merit pay and variable incentives. Weaker performers need to know they have to raise their contributions before they will see an increase. As HR professionals, we have to help our managers make tough and fair decisions to drive a truly high-performance culture.

The next generation HR professional will be a hybrid. The profession is going to evolve by maintaining its heritage of focusing on people, but with a new emphasis on accountability for bottom-line business performance. We need to talk about HR with an attitude; turn knowledge into action; make informed decisions about the investments we make in programs and practices, always with a sharp eye on business results; and conduct ourselves with the confidence and decisiveness borne of deep understanding of our enterprise and the competitive pressures and opportunities it faces.

CHAPTER 31

Human Resources and Power

Oxymoron or Necessity?

JEFFREY PFEFFER

I N A WORLD in which intellectual capital and knowledge are considered *the* most important assets of companies or even countries, in which all work is increasingly knowledge work, and in which building an organizational culture that brings out the best in people and helps attract and retain the best is the focus of much senior management attention, you might think that human resources, a function that potentially touches all of these issues, would have great power. You would be wrong. Except in a few countries, such as Japan, human resources is neither the road to the top nor a function that often gets much respect from people inside—or outside—companies. At Stanford Business School, which has a core MBA course in human resources that has recently been among the top two or three core courses in popularity, the most frequent comment from students is that they had no idea that human resources was either so important or so interesting.

There are two unfortunate consequences from the low-power, low-status position of human resources. First, human resource professionals are disadvantaged. The function pays less, is more likely to be downsized or outsourced, and is less likely to be a road to senior general management positions than other staff functions, such as finance or line management activities. Second, and perhaps even more important, the perspective of human resources is not likely to be very influential in affecting important company decisions, such as business strategy, mergers and divestitures, decisions about business processes and management practices, or even topics presumably in the domain of HR, such as downsizing and outsourcing work. The absence of an influential human resource perspective on critical decisions is unfortunate because many decisions made without the benefit of relevant research and the HR perspective frequently wind up being value-destroying rather than value-creating. The words of a senior executive at a large, industrial gas and chemicals company, which had gone through a downsizing, ring in my ears: "It took us two months to decide to do it, two weeks to accomplish it, and two years to recover." You might wonder, given the extensive literature on the generally negative effects of downsizing, if this company would have made the same decision and implemented that decision in the same way had human resources had a more influential voice in the councils of power.

There are many reasons for the relatively low power position of human resources, but, in many instances, HR professionals have been at least partly to blame—"enablers," in the words of one senior marketing and sales executive. Many HR professionals believe that power remains, to use Rosabeth Moss Kanter's apt phrase, "the organization's last dirty secret," and want nothing to do with the activities of building and exercising power and influence. After a session on power and influence to a group of HR professionals, one individual approached me. "If I had wanted to engage in organizational politics, I would not have gone into HR," he said. HR practitioners frequently have a strong values orientation that sees power as "harmful" and engaging in influence as something that nice people—they—do not do.

However, for the human resources function to add significant value to organizations in the future, HR professionals need to become more comfortable with developing and wielding influence and more effective in doing so. Developing influence skills requires, first and most importantly, getting past our ambivalence about power. It also requires becoming knowledgeable about the sources of power and political strategies and tactics, as well as getting accustomed to thinking strategically about not only what to do, but also how to get it done.

Getting beyond Our Ambivalence about Power

Having taught a course on power and politics in organizations for more than 20 years, I have developed some understanding of why people resist the idea that decisions in organizations result from the exercise of influence and not just from everyone doing the "right" thing. First, the idea that decisions are based on power violates our belief in a just world. The just world hypothesis, originally articulated by the social psychologist Mel Lerner, maintains that people want to believe that the world in which they live is predictable, fair, and just. Therefore, when "unjust" things happen, individuals seek to make sense of what has occurred by finding ways of rationalizing the event to make it seem sensible and controllable. For instance, crime victims may be blamed for being in the wrong place, not taking sufficient precautions, or dressing too provocatively. In the context of organizational decision making, we don't want to believe that the powerful prevail, but that the just prevail. Admitting that power matters violates our sense of justice and the corresponding idea that events are controllable.

Second, many people, particularly in western countries, believe that people are either good or bad, that there is a consistency in behavior over time, and that people and organizations can be judged and categorized accordingly. For instance, it drives students crazy to confront someone like Lyndon Johnson.

For 20 years, Johnson threw his lot in with the Southern Democrats, was an acolyte of Senator Richard Russell of Georgia, and voted against every civil rights bill that came along, even one that forbade lynching. Then, beginning in 1957, first as majority leader of the Senate and then as president, he took the lead in passing the first civil rights bill since Reconstruction and, in 1964 and 1965, the most important civil rights bills ever passed. How do we reconcile these two views of Johnson? You don't if you see people as good or bad, instead of recognizing that all people are mixtures of motives and traits.

Third, the image of engaging in politics violates our self-image as nice people doing nice things. The self-enhancement bias suggests that we are motivated to see ourselves in the most positive light, which is why study after study finds that more than half of any population believes they are above average. To the extent that we have come to see power and politics as "not nice," we don't want to be associated with them because of guilt by association.

Fourth, beginning in school, we have been taught that the world presents problems that have right and wrong answers. It is our job as effective managers to find out what the right answer is and to advocate that answer. The problem here is obvious. In the first place, where you stand (on an issue) depends on where you sit (in the organization), and what is right and wrong is often a matter of judgment and perspective. Different people inside organizations have access to different information and have different points of view because of their roles and what they are rewarded for doing. It is naïve to believe that they will all see the world the same way. In the second place, as Peter Drucker pointed out a long time ago, anyone over the age of 21 can probably find the facts to support his or her position. Leaders are paid not just for doing straightforward analysis but also for exercising judgment. Unlike in school, the world does not come to us packaged with decisions that have clear right and wrong answers, at least at the time the decision needs to be made.

Ambivalence about power has at least two very adverse consequences. First, we don't take the opportunity to learn as much as we can from the people and situations we confront, because we are too busy making judgments about whom we like and don't like and with whom we agree and disagree. One of the first lessons is to not simply make judgments but learn from all of the situations and the people we encounter. Second, our ambivalence about obtaining and using power can make us reluctant to act, to get into the arena, and to *do* something. A line manager at a large defense electronics firm once commented to me that the human resources people in his company had what he called a *servant's mentality*. He noted that the function had been so derogated and beaten down that HR professionals were, for good reason, unwilling to take initiative and advocate forcefully their points of view. The implication of his comments are that anything that keeps human resource professionals from making their cases and pushing their perspectives, which includes being ambivalent about influence and the need to be proactive, is harmful to both the reputation of the function and to its ability to contribute to the organization's well-being.

Making Human Resources More Powerful

Based on decades of research on power and influence, there are a number of recommendations that can help make human resource professionals more powerful and effective, thereby enhancing their ability to get their expertise and knowledge used in organizational decision making:

1. *Take the initiative.* As many observers have noted, power is most often taken, not given or granted. If HR is to exercise influence, it cannot simply wait to be invited to do so. HR professionals need to take the initiative, to insert themselves into discussions and decisions, and to forcefully advocate their points of view. Taking initiative and getting involved in discussions is also important because those who move first can frequently set the terms of the debate, the language used to discuss the issue, and the data that are relevant. For instance, from one perspective, raising wages, increasing training, and improving benefits can be seen as actions that increase costs and thereby diminish profits. Alternatively, these same actions can often be accurately viewed as initiatives that bring better quality people into the organization; help retain talent, knowledge, and experience; enhance customer service and retention; and retain organizational learning—all of which increase profits. How such actions are viewed depends importantly on how they are framed, and, in this framing, being preemptive often is crucial.

2. *Act as if you have power.* Research has shown that powerful people act differently because of their power. As analyses of conversations show, powerful individuals are more likely to interrupt and less likely to be interrupted. They are more likely to express anger and displeasure. They are less concerned at every moment about how others view their actions. Powerful individuals are more likely to express certainty in their opinions and use less tentative language. However, who has power is often ambiguous in social settings. Therefore, acting as if you have power can frequently convey power. In other words, HR needs to overcome the legacy of being downtrodden. One of the best ways to do this is to act as if HR is influential.

3. *Leverage control over crucial resources and decisions.* In many companies, human resources has at least some degree of influence, if not control, over critical resources and decisions, such as salary determination, advanced degree and executive education programs, performance-management and appraisal activities, internal training initiatives, and career development. These decisions and resources can potentially provide great power to the function. When finance was in the process of taking and solidifying its power at Ford Motor Company in the post-World War II period, finance

people made sure that other finance people got the best evaluations and the best job assignments. Because finance did well, not surprisingly, the most talented people wanted to join, thereby cementing its power. I have seldom seen human resource professionals recognize, let alone strategically use, the power that they have.

4. *Develop a broader range of contacts and expertise.* Whether defined in intellectual or social terms, it is natural for people to remain in familiar territory. Thus, we tend to associate with our friends and colleagues and to do tasks that we already know well. However natural, sticking with the familiar limits our ability to expand our reach and influence as well as to develop new competencies. Therefore, it is important to consciously seek to broaden our horizons. Some years ago when an HR executive entered Apple Computer, she knew she needed to know more people and more about the company. Therefore, she intentionally arranged coffees each Wednesday morning with four different people. After a few weeks, she had a much broader network and had learned much about the social structure and technology and business of the company. Similarly, when we run HR programs, we get many HR executives. It may seem counterintuitive at first, but HR executives would probably be much better served taking programs and training in marketing, finance, operations, and other business functions that are important and unfamiliar. It is only in this way that people can broaden and deepen their knowledge and skill base. Knowing more about more things contributes to your power and influence.

5. *Learn to use language and to frame issues effectively.* In the late 1980s, Marine Lt. Col. Oliver North testified in front of a joint committee of Congress about the Iran-Contra debacle and his role in both the events and the cover-up. His use of political language—language that evokes emotion, that beclouds or precludes analysis—was masterful. Everything he did was placed in the context of saving American lives, of ensuring national security, of keeping his superiors informed, and doing what they told him to do. What about the shredding of documents? North pointed out that he was shredding documents of national security sensitivity and that, after all, the government had given him a shredder! Vivid language, language that places things in context, language that creates feelings as much as thought, is persuasive language. HR needs to couch its arguments in effective political language and become increasingly skilled at doing so.

6. *Build coalitions of support.* Allies are important for getting things done in interdependent systems, which is what organizations are. Friends are invariably helpful. Many human resources units have built an alliance with the legal department around issues of compliance. If companies do not follow federal and state laws concerning hiring, dismissal, treatment of people with disabilities, and so forth, they will get into trouble. Although this may seem like a natural alliance, it may not be the most helpful one.

Keeping companies out of trouble is a worthy goal but not one that senior leaders may see as intimately and directly tied to success. Compliance may be good for the company, but not necessarily welcomed by many managers who see the imposition of rules as interfering with their ability to do what they need to do to get their jobs done. A more natural and potentially useful alliance is with operations, including sales and manufacturing. The efficiency gains from high-performance management systems mean much to operations people; and the attraction, retention, and motivation of talented individuals is crucial in both operations and sales. In building alliances, human resources needs to be able to offer support and help in return.

7. *Be willing to engage in conflict when necessary.* What political columnist Chris Matthews has called *porcupine power* is an essential element of building and exercising influence. I still remember the late John Gardner's comment on this issue. Gardner, Secretary of Health, Education, and Welfare (HEW) in the Johnson administration and later the founder of Common Cause, was as gentle and principled a person as you could ever hope to encounter. But in talking about his days at HEW and pushing a number of the Great Society programs, he remarked that he let it be known that people could oppose him in his efforts at reform and implementation, but he also made it clear there would be a price for doing so. A certain toughness and willingness to stand your ground is at once a signal of power and something that helps to create power and influence.

Each of these strategies has risks. Advocating an HR point of view risks not only opposition; it can even risk a person's job. Yet, in the end, job security predicated simply on not bothering anyone may not be worth that much to the individual or the function. It seems preferable to have your career premised on doing what you believe needs to be done, obviously as constructively as possible, rather than simply going along with decisions with which you disagree. If there is any lesson from the recent spate of business scandals, it is this: Being true to your information, values, and principles is a better path for both the individual and the organization than following what seems expedient.

The Power to Get Things Done

If organizational change were going to occur rapidly and easily, it would have already occurred. Getting things done invariably requires developing and mobilizing influence, and power skills are critical, particularly for staff departments such as human resources that typically do not have much formal authority. As the importance of people and culture for business success has increased, as contrasted with physical resources and capital equipment, it is imperative for organizational performance that human resources build both the will and the skill to develop and use power and influence. Otherwise, an important perspective will not be sufficiently heeded in organizational decision making.

In my experience, some, although obviously not all, human resource professionals and departments have been somewhat complicit in their own disenfranchisement. Some are more interested in programs and in being liked than in making changes and making things happen that have real impact on companies. Some believe that power is something that they cannot or will not do. Some have seen their role too much as compliance officers instead of business and strategic partners. Some have wanted too much to be liked, or to keep their jobs, and have been insufficiently concerned with being effective and remaining true to their data and beliefs.

For human resources to contribute in the way that it can and should for organizations to be successful in the 21st century, becoming a real player in internal organizational decisions is essential. This requires becoming more skilled at building influence and more willing to use that influence. For human resources, given its present position in most companies, it is almost impossible to conceive of it becoming too powerful or too effective. Hence, starting down the path I have outlined seems imperative. For human resources, building power is not something that contradicts what it is and what it stands for, but rather, it is the only thing that will ensure its ideas and values actually come to influence companies.

◆

CHAPTER 32

Managing for Execution

HR Delivery Imperatives for the 21st Century

JASON JEFFAY AND SANDY K. BICOS

POISED ON THE brink of the 21st century, HR stands at a crossroads. One path leads to the transactional role the function has traditionally played, while the other paves the way to a more strategy-driven existence, one focused on providing real business solutions, rather than merely reacting to circumstances. For the majority of HR professionals, the choice is simple, as the path less traveled is the one that will ultimately earn them the treasured "place at the table."

Flawless Execution: The Price of Admission

In its rush to contribute in more strategic ways, HR's customers still expect, in fact, they demand, that service delivery and other basics of the function be handled efficiently and effectively. Many HR professionals make the mistake of viewing strategy and delivery as an either/or proposition, rather than as mutually reinforcing elements. Designing new programs or initiatives must be undertaken with the ultimate delivery in mind. This is often overlooked, and, as a result, little attention is given to implementation budgets or resources during the planning process. The result is great ideas, underwhelming execution, and a perception among constituents that HR does not have the ability to deliver on its promises.

The consequences of such inattention could not be more severe as strategy becomes reality through execution and delivery. Even the most forward thinking of initiatives will fail to produce the desired outcomes if the delivery component is lacking. Consider this concept in a manufacturing setting. If a team of engineers were to come up with a means of boosting the mileage of an automobile, only to have the new design not make its way to the assembly line, the car's mileage potential would remain the same, even if the engineers' innovation was truly revolutionary. Delivery of a service is truly the enabling mechanism through which strategies become real and achieve their intended impact.

Delivery as an Engagement and Cost Lever

Service delivery presents a valuable opportunity to connect with employees in a consistent and compelling way. The way HR services are delivered tells employees a great deal about the organization for which they work. Therefore, delivery serves as far more than a means for giving employees the information and services that they need; it is also a valuable tool for reinforcing corporate culture, building loyalty, boosting retention, and ultimately impacting the bottom line.

Unfortunately, for many organizations, service delivery remains a challenge that is growing more prominent with each passing year. Cost pressures, an increasingly global workforce, demand for instant access to data, fuzzy organizational boundaries, and rising customer expectations are further complicating the issue and making it all the more critical for HR to reexamine its approach to service delivery as the 21st century continues to unfold.

Still, most HR functions spend the vast majority of their time on administrative processes, as both the cost and the rapidly changing nature of technology make it difficult to organize and deliver services. Just when users get comfortable with a particular system, it seems that it is branded obsolete and replaced by the new "latest and greatest."

Keeping up with such a rapid-fire pace of change can prove prohibitively expensive for HR, when you take into account the considerable cost of purchasing and installing technology, not to mention the associated training and change management initiatives. And as more organizations adopt the mantra, "Do more with less," senior management is unlikely to increase HR's budget simply to maintain the status quo.

Service Delivery across Borders

Globalization creates unique challenges for delivery of HR services. Even organizations that have done a reasonably good job of streamlining HR delivery in North America are struggling with how to consolidate their operations around the world. Despite their obvious commonalities, individual business units in most global organizations continue to operate in a highly decentralized manner, making it exceedingly difficult for HR functions to share information and deliver services in a consistent manner across borders, oceans, and continents. As the pressure mounts to manage human capital more seamlessly across national boundaries, HR strategies and programs will have an increasingly global span, which will challenge the function to be equally as global in its delivery mechanisms.

Using Delivery to Enable the Changing Role of HR

Service delivery is certainly nothing new to HR. On the contrary, the function can trace its origins back to the delivery-centric personnel departments of the 1960s, which in actuality did little more than plan social activities and hand out paychecks. Over time, HR's role evolved into that of technical specialist, charged with tracking and interpreting regulatory changes to ensure that the organization remained in compliance. Subsequently, HR took on more of a consultative stance, working with managers and supervisors to help implement policies and practices, as well as to facilitate a variety of undertakings, including layoffs, downsizings, and reorganizations.

Now, *strategic partner* takes its place as HR's most recent incarnation. HR managers are increasingly adopting a broader, more strategic approach, one that is focused on helping the business succeed, rather than assisting individual managers or employees with specific issues. Looking at the organization's demographics, for example, HR may discover that a substantial number of people in critical positions will become eligible for retirement within the next five years. The strategic approach dictates that HR evaluate what needs to be done to get the right people in place and trained, so that the organization does not miss a beat when those retirements take place.

Although the vast majority of HR professionals would enthusiastically affirm that they are eager to assume a more strategic role in the organization, most are hindered in their desire to step up to the plate because HR is viewed as a function that focuses on the basics. And to be accepted by business leaders, they must continue to do the basics well. Thus, to streamline HR processes and free up time for staff to focus its attention on more strategic matters, organizations are moving to a shared services model, where transactional work and basic customer service is handled in an administrative service center. Similarly, design and more strategic, consultative work is done through *centers of expertise,* which coordinate with the service center to ensure effective delivery of these programs. Consolidating the components of service delivery allows the organization to make better decisions over process design, technology deployment, and service level standards.

Where Delivery Breaks Down

Today, there are many inefficiencies in how HR services are delivered. Though HR departments get things done, they often must apply extra resources or develop "workarounds" to overcome poorly designed processes and nonintegrated technology. All too often, data or transactions must be entered twice because systems do not talk to one another. Inordinate amounts of time frequently must be spent reconciling data in the company's HR systems or performing manual interventions because there are special rules for one part of the population that do not apply to the rest of the workforce. Far more than inconveniences, all of those issues add cost, time, and frustration.

Many service delivery problems stem directly from how HR is managed. Most HR organizations simply do not have a clear definition of effective service delivery. Is the goal to meet customers' stated needs or to get to their desired outcomes? Do we respond to their individual requests or do we do what is right for the greatest number? Do we move heaven and earth to get it done, or is there a cost/benefit analysis to how far we go?

The concept of *customer service* often is interpreted as making executives, managers, and employees happy with every transaction, even if that entails customizing programs and processes on demand. While the underlying goal may be admirable, it does not lend itself to efficient or cost-effective service delivery. It serves to perpetuate a "one-off" or crisis-driven approach to HR management.

Service delivery also suffers from an ineffective use of technology, which holds great potential for streamlining much of the function. Unfortunately, many HR organizations are not technology savvy. HR may be unaware of what the existing technology offers or may use it to simply do the wrong things faster. Consequently, the desired return on investment is not realized, and HR service delivery continues to be less efficient and effective.

Understanding How HR Spends Its Time

Although delivery of HR services is typically the largest single cost incurred by the function, few organizations truly have a handle on how much they spend in this area because the people involved frequently cross functional lines. In addition, service delivery typically comprises only a fraction of someone's total responsibilities. Thus, it becomes necessary for HR to evaluate its service delivery costs to ensure that this huge expenditure is being spent appropriately and that the right people are focused on the right tasks.

Many organizations would be alarmed to learn how much of their service delivery budget is being spent on the wrong things. In a recent activity analysis of a large electronics manufacturer, for example, it was discovered that the largest delivery expenditure was in the area of recruiting and staffing, despite the fact that a hiring freeze had been in place for more than a year. Another company found that some of its HR staff members were spending a portion of their time on payroll administration, even though the payroll function had been outsourced for several years. This could point to a duplication of work, poor performance on the part of the vendor, or a lack of communication concerning the transition to outsourcing.

It is also not uncommon to find the wrong people performing delivery-oriented tasks. In the spirit of customer service, for example, many organizations task their managers or directors with handling routine administrative questions. One organization determined that its managers were spending 45 percent of their time performing "level one" customer service tasks—providing forms to associates and responding to questions about basic benefits issues. In another situation, it was discovered that nonexempt associates with no specialized training were spending significant amounts of time addressing diversity questions and complaints. This not only fails to provide employees with the expected level of service but also leaves the company open to expensive litigation.

As these kinds of situations continue to become known, HR organizations are increasingly reevaluating their existing processes in the struggle to get their arms around the delivery challenge. While they acknowledge the need to do more with less, they also recognize the need to balance budgetary considerations with the proverbial "personal touch." The underlying goal may be to attain greater efficiencies but not at the risk of making delivery impersonal and clinical.

In determining the proper approach, HR must take care to align its value proposition or employer brand with the delivery mechanism. It is critical to deliver services in a manner that is consistent with the message the organization conveys—either explicitly or implicitly—about the employment relationship. If a company's value proposition centers on being a caring and helpful environment with many opportunities, for example, the delivery mechanism needs to reflect that by ensuring that transactions and requests are processed with the appropriate degree of care and concern. An organization that presents itself as employee-focused, only to consistently foul up people's transactions, will quickly be deemed a fraud by the workforce and, thanks to word of mouth, by potential employees and customers as well.

Treating the Employee as a Customer

Increasingly, HR organizations are embracing *employee relationship management* as a means of reinforcing their value proposition and strengthening the bond between the company and its workforce. Centered around the concept of *employee as customer*, employment relationship management presents the ultimate vision of delivery in which the organization uses everything it knows about employees to market services and benefits to them that better ties individuals to the company, while increasing their personal productivity.

Employees' growing comfort level with technology has only served to make this proposition more feasible. In recent years, employee self-service has emerged as an effective means of reducing transaction costs, while improving the accuracy of data collection. Employees and managers alike have exhibited their willingness to go to the Web or the intranet for answers to basic questions about benefits or company policies.

Over time, they have also grown accustomed to conducting transactions over the Web. Increasingly, employees can be found initiating the processing of basic HR transactions, applying for internal jobs, modeling retirement options, and initiating expense reports. Immediately after accepting a job offer, for example, a new associate may log on to a special employee orientation Web site, where he or she can review information about the new employer, enroll in benefits programs, and complete a new-hire survey, all before the first day on the job.

Meanwhile, managers may be greeted with a personalized portal featuring all the tools needed to do their jobs. This could include metrics relating to turnover and overtime, reminders of performance reviews that need to be completed, and cues to initiate job requisitions for new hires. The portal may also include links to internal or external sites, where the manager may access information and expertise to aid in handling difficult people-management issues or evaluating decisions such as setting base pay rates or incentive targets.

Portals for HR professionals can provide similar conveniences and quick access to tools and information. When they log on to the intranet, they may see a list of e-transactions awaiting approval. With a quick click of the mouse, the transactions are approved and electronically routed to the next person in the approval chain. HR can also access special alerts on tasks such as changes to the FMLA policy or the status of recruiting efforts for open requisitions.

In the employment relationship management vision, HR takes the power of technology to new heights to proactively serve and engage the workforce. Much the same way as Amazon.com tracks customers' past purchases and then makes recommendations for future purchases based on the interests they have exhibited, an organization tracks employees' job responsibilities, career aspirations, and life events to prompt them to take specific actions.

When an employee logs on to his or her personal portal, the system automatically makes recommendations of training courses that might pique his or her interest, based on courses taken in the past. Just as Amazon provides customer reviews of books, videos, and music items, the organization's system is set up to present customer reviews of training courses, so that an employee can see what his or her coworkers thought of the experience before signing up.

Employees are also automatically informed of internal job openings that match their competency profiles and encouraged to prepare for their next performance reviews. On returning from his or her honeymoon, an employee may even be prompted to make necessary changes to his or her personnel file and to ensure that the spouse is included in the appropriate benefit plans. The idea is to get employees so tied in to the organization that leaving becomes difficult because it's just so comfortable and effortless to stay onboard and further their careers with their current employer.

Outsourcing Noncore Functions

To achieve the highest degrees of self-service, however, substantial investments are required to get to the next generation of delivery mechanisms. The kinds of people, process, and technology investments necessary to produce a state-of-the-art delivery mechanism do not make sense for most organizations because that would divert mission-critical resources from the core business. As HR considers these means of providing a higher level of delivery, a critical question becomes whether to keep such administration in-house or turn to outsourcing.

By *insourcing*, or keeping the program in-house, an organization maintains ownership of the people and technology and, therefore, can exercise more flexibility over how the program is delivered. Insourcing remains a valid option for organizations that feel that they simply are not ready to move toward an outsourcing solution, either because of their size or because they believe they can be efficient taking advantage of the tools currently available to them.

More often, however, organizations are considering outsourcing as a viable means of HR service delivery. In a 2002 Hewitt Associates study of more than 500 chief financial officers from companies with $1 billion or more in revenue, 41 percent indicated that they had either partially or completely outsourced the HR function.[1] Outsourcing allows companies to dramatically improve service delivery by turning to companies who invest in the requisite technology and process design to maintain a high standard and whose core competencies are in service delivery. Additionally, outsourcing often reduces costs by providing economies of scale. The decision to outsource benefits administration saved East Coast utility PSE&G $3.3 million in 1997, its first year, and a total of $17 million year-to-date.

While outsourcing may not be the right solution for every organization, company leaders are challenging HR to learn what it can from the experiences of other functional areas that have exited certain activities in this way. More and more organizations are reaching the conclusion that it makes sense to turn to a specialized service provider in their efforts to become a state-of-the-art 21st-century HR function. However, each company needs to come to its own decision, based on its own scenario. To do that, an organization must chart its current costs, service level, and effectiveness against those same three metrics in an outsourcing scenario.

Though cost is an important driver, it should not be used as the sole determinant in deciding whether to outsource. It becomes HR's responsibility to ensure that services are delivered in a manner that is both appropriate and in line with the company's employee value proposition, in addition to reasonable cost.

Competencies for Excellence in Execution

As HR advances further into the 21st century, it will become apparent that a new set of skills, capabilities, and competencies are required among its own staff. To gain credibility with senior management, HR professionals must demonstrate greater business acumen so that they can better understand the business and balance creativity and business realities in the solutions that they present.

They will also need much stronger customer relationship management skills and a better understanding of technology and the role it can play in attaining more effective HR service delivery. For organizations that choose to outsource, an emerging skill is the ability to negotiate contracts and set performance standards with vendors. HR managers need to be able to not only strike a deal that benefits the organization, but also monitor vendors' performance and hold them accountable for meeting established standards.

Thinking Differently about HR in the 21st Century

Effective service delivery truly is the key to becoming the strategic HR function of the 21st century. Even if an organization feels that it is miles away from achieving the level of delivery that will earn it the credibility that ultimately equates to a place at the table, it is important to begin building that future vision today. To begin the transition to exceptional service delivery, HR needs to clearly define its strategy, painting a picture of how it adds value to the business.

A careful evaluation of the HR organization itself also helps map the path toward more effective delivery. With speed and agility as guiding principals, HR needs to examine major administrative processes and not be afraid to ask the tough questions, such as whether these processes add value to the business, if technology could help take out time and money, and if outsourcing would provide a better solution.

HR service delivery in the 21st century represents a dramatic shift for many HR associates because it demands a new way of thinking about the function. No longer are HR associates focused on mere transactional work; their attention is on a means of demonstrating HR's business focus, cutting costs, and elevating the level of services delivered to its customers.

CHAPTER 33

<hr>

HR as a Trusted Partner

JAMES B. DAGNON

"WE WERE GOING into a period when mergers and acquisitions were going to play a big role in the company's future, and his experience with the issues raised in mergers and acquisitions was invaluable. I think more than anything else, I needed a trusted partner. Jim saw that opportunity and I got a good partner."—Phil Condit, chairman and CEO, The Boeing Company.[1] This quote appeared in an article covering my retirement as Boeing's chief human resource officer. To me, being called a "trusted partner" by the CEO was one of the most satisfying compliments I, or any human resource professional, could receive.

For years, human resource professionals have sought a place at the table as true partners with senior management. The pressures most companies face today, such as mergers, globalization, and a sluggish economy, are bringing people issues to the forefront. When something is in short supply, it gets moved to the top of the corporate agenda. When capital was short, it was the era of the chief financial officer. Now, talent has replaced capital as the most critical success factor. With key skills in short supply for the foreseeable future and the need to change corporate cultures to meet today's competitive pressures, it is the era of the chief human resource officer.

A Source of Competitive Advantage

Human resources is a source of competitive advantage that is hard to replicate. For example, outsourcing human resource services may help a company be more competitive by reducing cost; however, your competitor can easily do the same and your competitive advantage may not last long. By creating a unique corporate culture, Southwest Airlines achieved a sustained competitive advantage. Its competitors have tried to copy Southwest's success by buying the same 737s, and imitating its approach to routes and operations, but they haven't been able to replicate Southwest's "color outside the lines culture." Harley-Davidson is another employee-involvement success story, in which a hard-to-build partnership with a major international union was one factor of its current competitive success that is hard to duplicate.

Because our profession can make a difference, CEOs today are looking for their HR professionals to be trusted partners. In the introduction to their book *Straight from the CEO*, William Dauphinais and Colin Price ask how a CEO can achieve innovation without leadership or respond to globalization without knowing a great deal about corporate culture?[2] The overriding theme that they distilled from the more than 30 CEOs represented in their book was not anticipated. "Today's CEOs have, sometimes consciously and sometimes not invaded the field of human relations and imposed their own stamp on it."

What they found that was new was the CEO's enthusiasm and passion for taking charge and pumping up results through changes in behavior. The CEOs are ready for us. How do we get ready for them? How do we get ready to meet their appetite for a trusted partner?

Creating Trusting Relationships

Merriam-Webster's Dictionary defines *trust* as: "Assured reliance on the character, ability, strength, or truth of someone . . . To place confidence: Depend . . ." That same dictionary defines *partner* as: "One that shares . . . One associated with another esp. in an action: associate, colleague . . ."[3]

We delegate decision making to trustworthy leaders of character. Shouldn't we expect our leaders to do the same?

Creating a trusting relationship with your CEO or line manager creates an environment where you can stand up and say, "You can count on me." It creates a bias for action. In these highly competitive and chaotic times, what a company needs most is agility, and the group best positioned to help a company become more agile is the human resource team.

The Path to Trusted Partnerships

Being a trusted partner means not only that we help shape business strategy, but also that we help our partner translate those strategies into human resource priorities. As such, we take on four distinct roles: strategic partner, administrative expert, employee champion, and change agent.[4] If we fail to balance these roles, it should not surprise us if we are asked, "Whose side are you on?" Thus, there are some basic questions that we can ask ourselves that will help provide a solid foundation for the partnerships we seek:

1. *Purpose.* What is the common mission and shared vision that we are both working toward?
2. *Expectations.* What do we expect of each other?

3. *Working together.* How can I best complement and fit into my leader's style of working?
4. *Expected results.* What does the CEO want from me if the objectives of our company are to be achieved?

As a trusted partner, we must be able to successfully execute multifarious roles. Balancing the roles of business partner, human resource consultant, smoke detector, mentor, listener, straight talker, confidant, catalyst for action, and change agent, as well as board resource, is a continuous juggling act. However, the business-partner role is the foundation on which the rest of the relationship should be built. Your CEO wants you to know how the fundamentals of the business work in your company. In *What the CEO Wants You to Know,* Ram Charan defines *business acumen* as "the ability to understand the building blocks of how a one-person operation or a very big business makes money."[5] This book should be mandatory reading for every human resources professional! It will help you understand the key business success factors of cash, margin, velocity, growth, and customers.

In his book, Ram points out that as we learn to see our company as a total business and make decisions that enhance its overall performance, we will help make meetings less bureaucratic and more focused on the business issues. As our suggestions and decisions help the business grow and prosper, we'll become more excited about our jobs. In addition, when we learn to speak the universal language of business, we can have meaningful discussions with anyone in the company. Equipped with business acumen in our tool bag, we can take our role as coach beyond behavioral coaching; we can coach on the business side and help the person we are coaching execute the company's business plan.

Effective Execution

Effective execution is the key to business success. Ram aptly summarizes that "An edge in execution comes from having the right people in the right jobs, synchronizing their efforts, and releasing and channeling their energy toward the right business priorities." He continues with the following point, "It takes insight into people and the organization to get the energy aligned." What an opportunity for human resource professionals to add value! Linking business values and people is our bag.

Having the best people is critical to any company's success; however the added challenge for us is that talent will be in short supply for the foreseeable future.[6] This is where our role as human resource consultant comes to the forefront. We must apply our HR expertise in three essential areas:

1. Attracting, retaining, and developing key leaders who give us a competitive edge.
2. Helping the organization adapt to change.
3. Removing the human resource roadblocks to company agility.

Upward Mentoring

While mentoring is a critical skill that must also be in our toolkit, it is upward mentoring that will give us another major step along the path to being a trusted partner. Jeffrey Steele captured this concept in a special report to the *Chicago Tribune*. His article, "Master the Art of Coaching the Boss—with Discretion," was a review of Michael Useem's book, *Leading Up: How to Lead Your Boss So You Both Win*. In the article, Jeffrey reports on three important principles from Useem's book.[7]

First, make sure that you're not usurping your superior's authority. Second, build trust between your boss and yourself based on your own reliability, respect for your superior, and your ability to help him or her recognize the quality of your thinking. Third, be able to persuasively express and explain your ideas to your supervisor.

Chief executives feel the pressures of isolation, and since they are already at the top, what they need is a sympathetic listener and a straight-talking, honest friend. "The critical issue is how to master the art of upward mentoring without it becoming a career-shortening move."[8]

The Smoke Detector

A trusted partner has a knack for anticipating and forecasting. This is what I call the "smoke detector" role. A smoke detector does not just fight fires, but forecasts and helps prevent them. As human resource professionals, we must see the potholes in the road ahead if we are to steer around them. In this world of exponential change, being ahead of the power curve is key if the executive team is to stay focused on business results. Nothing sends a clearer message that you are on the leading edge than by being "early adapters" of effective technology. We need to constantly scan the environment and not only anticipate and prevent, but aim ahead of the trends. We must see the organizational implications of competitive challenges, and then dedicate the time and energy to the capabilities the organization needs to meet them. When your CEO wants to see you about a future problem he senses, when he discovers that you saw it coming and have an action plan in place, you will have taken one more step toward being a trusted partner.

We all want to win but that is not enough. We must go beyond the mastery of cash, margin, velocity, growth, customers, and new manufacturing processes. An organization must be able to change, learn, move, and act faster than its competitors. A trusted partner helps the CEO develop a strategic plan for the culture that will lead to winning in the marketplace. The trusted partner becomes a catalyst for rapid change. We bring the tools to help the line managers lead the changes, and then we help them deal effectively with the consequences that always come from change.

We need to help see that the right things happen. One good example is dealing with mismatched executives. Too often we avoid dealing with this issue, especially at the senior-executive level. There are a variety of reasons that executives and managers avoid this issue, such as hoping the person will turn around, feeling obligated to the person for past help, or just wanting to avoid conflict. By helping the CEO realize that a change is needed and by handling the outplacement with style (and with the executive's dignity intact), we can eliminate a huge energy drain on the company. Helping the CEO to confront and deal with the mismatch will earn his or her trust.

Often we are called on as a resource for the board's compensation committee or, in some situations, the full board of directors. When the board members go into executive session and ask the CEO to leave and you to stay, you are presented the opportunity to walk the tightrope of integrity one more time. Handling that responsibility by considering the needs of the company, the role of the board, and the trust that your CEO has in you, is essential to finding the right balance between the needs of these potentially competing stakeholders and responding to board questions.

It Takes Personal Credibility to Lead Change

Setting aside your own personal desires, ambitions, and agendas when giving advice and counsel to your CEO is critical to your acceptance as a trusted partner. I've found that when a CEO learns that you have no personal axe to grind and that you have set aside your personal motives, he or she is quick to recognize and understand that your advice is untainted. The same will hold true when it comes to delivering bad news or something that he or she does not want to hear. The CEO's respect for you will grow when you have built a reputation as someone who tells people what they need to hear.

In the final chapter of Dave Ulrich's book, *Human Resource Champions,* he describes the model for future HR competences:[9]

- Business mastery.
- Human resource mastery.
- Change and process mastery.
- Personal credibility.

All are critical to reaching the goal of trusted partner. However, personal credibility clinches your place as a trusted partner. Becoming a trusted partner means to appreciate what the CEO needs from you if the objectives of the organization are to be realized. As a trusted partner, you can truly make a difference.

CHAPTER 34

The HR Head as Trusted CEO Advisor

Six Strategies for Becoming a Valued Partner to Senior Management

ROBERT GANDOSSY AND ANDREW SOBEL

IN THE AFTERMATH of the September 11, 2001, terrorist attacks, American Airlines' CEO Don Carty faced a crisis that few corporate leaders have ever confronted. During this difficult period, Carty's executive vice president of human resources, Sue Oliver, served not just as a functional expert representing HR but as a trusted top-management advisor. She participated, as part of American's executive team, in virtually every major business decision affecting American's people, from the difficult layoffs and cost-cutting that followed the decline in air travel to the revamping of security, and she was instrumental in working with the rest of the management team to restore morale to a devastated organization.

In a very different industry that has faced its own difficult challenges, J. Randall (Randy) MacDonald, senior vice president of human resources at IBM, has played a similar role with recently retired CEO Lou Gerstner, one of the smartest and toughest bosses in corporate America. "You don't become an advisor who can influence the CEO overnight," MacDonald says with understatement. "At first, you do a lot of listening, get the lay of the land, observe, learn the business, and then deliver with great quality. You focus on the business

---

"Trusted oldvisor" as it first appeared in the October 20, 2002 edition of *Human Resource Executive*.

issues. You always act with persistence and determination, but you learn when to hold them and when to fold them and walk away."[1]

Behind every great leader you'll probably find at least one great advisor. Alexander the Great's tutor and counselor was Aristotle, ancient Greece's famed philosopher and scientist. King Henry VIII chose as his chief advisor Thomas More, who precipitated his own demise when he stood by his principles and publicly defied his royal client; President Franklin D. Roosevelt had the services of the trustworthy Harry Hopkins as well as the great General George Marshall. Today's CEOs have an equal or greater need for trusted individuals who can act as sage counselors and discreet sounding boards. Even compared to just 10 years ago, the pace of decision making is faster, there are more strategic choices available, and the amount of information executives have to absorb has grown dramatically.

Ironically, it's not easy for CEOs to find individuals who can fulfill this role. Outside professionals must tread a thin line between their own and their client's interests; corporate insiders also have their own biases and agendas. Bob Galvin, the former chairman of Motorola, comments that "When it comes to the CEO's direct reports, where you sit is where you stand. It is difficult to find truly objective insiders who can serve this important trusted advisor role to the CEO."[2]

Human resources executives are in an ideal position to play the role of trusted counselor to top management. In fact, if you want to truly stand out from the pack, you've got to learn to play this role *and* do a standout job of managing the HR function itself. The HR head does not represent a particular business unit, nor is it a highly specialized staff function like investor relations. By dint of training and experience, he or she is also uniquely equipped to help the CEO with one of their most important and difficult tasks—identifying and cultivating leaders. Mike D'Ambrose, executive vice president of human resources for Toys 'R Us, echoes other top HR executives in saying, "One of my key roles is to help the CEO make judgments about people and develop our leaders."[3]

How do you build this type of relationship and become a trusted advisor to the CEO? How do you go beyond your "HR expert" label and become viewed by top management as a critical partner in making the corporation's most important decisions? To find out, we spoke with a dozen of the world's top HR heads. They have advised some of the smartest, most demanding CEOs in business today—Lou Gerstner of IBM, John Reed and Sandy Weil of Citigroup, Ivan Seidenberg of Verizon, Chuck Lee formerly of GTE and Verizon, Michael Capellas at Compaq, and Don Carty at American Airlines—and they have both the scars and the wisdom to show for it. In addition, co-author Andrew Sobel interviewed 30 leading CEOs about their most valued, trusted advisors, during the research for his book, *Clients for Life*. Together, these conversations have given us a unique understanding of the ingredients of the trusted advisor role.

The bottom line is that HR "experts" are a dime a dozen. Professionals who have great expertise *and* who are able to bring wisdom, insight, and perspective to bear in the context of a trusted personal relationship, on the other hand, are irreplaceable resources who are highly valued by top executives.

The secret to the success of these leading HR executives, we discovered, lies in a blend of six strategies that can be developed and cultivated by other HR professionals. It's not an easy prescription, but it is one that will serve you well if you aspire to evolve from an HR "expert" to a trusted partner to senior management. These experienced hands talk about advising the CEO, but the principles they exemplify have served them throughout their entire careers, whether their "client" was an assistant plant manager, a division executive, or the chairman.

These top HR heads also acknowledge that developing these relationships is a never-ending process. They must be continuously worked to add value and to maintain the appropriate balance of CEO confidant versus member of the CEO's team, of directness and challenge versus respect and deference.

Strategy One: Become a Deep Generalist— A Business Advisor as Well as an HR Professional

America has become a nation of specialists, and we revere the "expert." It's no surprise, then, that some human resources professionals spend their entire careers digging deeper into their core specialty, driven by a corporate emphasis on specialization and a perception that this is how you get ahead. If you want to manage the HR function effectively and also be a trusted advisor to top management, however, you need depth *and* breadth—you need to become a *deep generalist*.

Randy MacDonald at IBM, for example, has always assiduously cultivated his business breadth: "I was always protective of my generalist background," he says, "and I managed my career to acquire a breadth of experience. When I was the VP of organization development at GTE, for example, I also had responsibility for HR in several business units. I wouldn't accept certain positions if they weren't broad enough."[4]

Steve King, head of HR for Hewitt Associates (not an easy job—being the HR chief for a firm of HR consultants!), says, "I don't really think of myself as an 'HR guy.' I actually have a master's in economics. My interest in the business itself, and how we really make money, helps me win credibility from business leaders. By understanding the business, you will get your best clues about your people issues."[5]

How do you become a deep generalist? Fight hard to get broad exposure early in your career. Invest time to become intimately familiar with your company's strategy, organization, and operations. Read general business publications, not just HR magazines, and get out of your office—make sure you spend ample time in the field. One HR leader requires HR staff to be out of the office—in the trenches—at least 50 percent of the time, "If you're not out of the office 50 percent of the time meeting with leaders, managers, employees—even our customers, then you're not doing your job. It's the only way to really understand the business."

Strategy Two: Listen Deeply—Then Act

When a journalist asked the great Spanish artist Picasso what he thought of mainframe computers, Picasso replied, "Computers are useless. They can only give you answers."[6] Indeed, when we think of ourselves as experts possessing an authoritative body of knowledge, we are inclined to *tell* and to provide *answers*. Trusted advisors, however, begin by asking great questions and listening. Ezra Singer, executive vice president of human resources for Verizon, puts it this way: "You have to listen well and let people air their views. Try to understand the reasoning for an initial 'No' and see if there is a way to reach common ground. Remember that an initial 'No' doesn't mean no forever."[7]

Several of our HR heads recalled their early days as labor negotiators, and how those experiences trained them in the art of listening. "I can remember sitting through the first four hours of a meeting without saying a word, just listening and trying to understand the other side's point of view," recalls IBM's MacDonald.[8] Yvonne Jackson, former senior vice president of HR at Compaq, used listening as an important means of building her knowledge base about the company: "I hold frequent meetings with employees at our field locations. I ask three questions: What do you do? What's the one thing that keeps you up at night? What do you like about Compaq? These sessions, in conjunction with survey data, give me a clear sense of the culture and of what works and doesn't work."[9]

To listen well you need self-knowledge, a bit of humility, and a learning attitude. If you don't understand your own hot buttons and biases, you'll never be able to accurately tune in and listen empathetically. If you don't feel you truly have something to learn from others, you'll shut them out.

Once you've listened, however, you've then got to formulate a strong, well-reasoned point of view. As Toys 'R Us' D'Ambrose says, "A trusted advisor is not neutral—you're more than just a sounding board. In the end, you have to have an opinion and the courage and the ability to express it."[10]

Strategy Three: Always Make the Business Case

"Value-added" and "measurable results" have become mantras for CEOs who are under ever-more pressure from shareholders to deliver revenue and profit growth. Not surprisingly, our top HR heads have all learned to put HR programs and policies solidly in the context of how they will help achieve business results.

Mike D'Ambrose, currently executive vice president of human resources for Toys 'R Us, was previously Citigroup's HR chief under John Reed and Sandy Weil. He says, "At Citigroup I developed a real bottom-line orientation—I learned to quickly focus on those things that would improve our financial performance and drive the business forward." He adds, "Some students of HR don't understand how companies make money. They don't know how to read a balance sheet."[11] Verizon's Singer comments, "My job is not to introduce lots of new programs, but to tie everything I want to do to our business objectives."[12] John Raffaeli, senior vice president of human resources for The Thomson Corporation, a global e-information and solutions company with 40,000 employees, echoes these comments, adding, "I recall once I hadn't yet understood the bottom-line impact of a benefits proposal I made in a large budget meeting—I hadn't put it firmly in the context of a business case. It didn't fly because I hadn't yet done the necessary homework. When I came back with solid facts about the positive business impact, however, it was easily approved. What gives me credibility are the facts."[13]

How do you ground yourself in the business? Tom Bouchard, who recently retired as IBM's HR head under Lou Gerstner, says flatly, "You have to really work to stay in touch with the business. All corporate HR staff, for example, should regularly be rotated into the field."[14] A good start is to give yourself a solid grounding in your company's strategic, operational, and financial objectives, and to thoroughly examine both the hard and soft impacts of every recommendation that you make to management.

Strategy Four: Straight with Integrity and Conviction

Walter Wriston, Citibank's legendary CEO during the 1970s and now a member of half a dozen boards, talks about the role of the trusted advisor as honest broker and grounding agent: "The CEOs of large corporations tend to get insulated from reality. You have your own jet, people make your coffee, and those around you hesitate to give you the tough messages. You need advisors who will tell you exactly how things really are."[15] Another CEO, the head of a large bank, commented that "I divide all the professionals I work with into two groups: those who do exactly what I tell them to, and those who are truly independent. Those are the ones I really value."

Toys 'R Us' D'Ambrose recalls a seminal experience in this regard: "Right after college I worked for Ingersoll-Rand at a major nonunion site. I learned quickly that the only way I could have influence was if I was very direct—if I always told the truth and was direct with it. People liked to talk to me because of this. 'Straight talk' became my secret weapon."[16] Many people mistakenly believe that shooting straight will hinder your progress inside the organization. Most of these HR leaders believe the opposite is true. Shooting straight and having bold confidence is a prerequisite to being a trusted advisor. Thomson's Raffaeli says, "In your relationship with the CEO you must have the freedom to say what you need to say—what *you* want to say not what *he* wants you to say."[17] You also have to be willing to admit your mistakes. Tom Bouchard adds, "You also must have the guts to walk in and say, 'Hey, we screwed up in Peoria.' "[18]

What enables you to be a straight-shooter? You have to be willing to take risks. Underneath your straight talk has to be integrity and conviction—you have to be clear about your principles and willing to stick to them. Senior corporate executives can be pretty strong-minded individuals, and convincing them of your point of view requires dynamic communications, persistence, and a rock-solid belief system.

By being open and honest with your boss, and demonstrating consistent integrity—reliability, discretion, and strong values—you'll also build trust, which is the foundation of any successful advisory relationship.

Strategy Five: Be the CEO's and the Team's Confidant

When asked to describe the characteristics of their most trusted advisors, many corporate leaders we have spoken to first mention *discretion*. Big-picture thinking skills and objectivity are high on their lists, but often not as high as the ability to keep confidences. HR heads face a dilemma in this regard: They must simultaneously be the trusted confidant of the CEO and also of other line executives. How else can they understand the organizational dynamics and politics that are at work or the developmental needs of these top managers? If they don't have strong relationships with the CEO's direct reports, how can they be helpful to the CEO when it comes to questions of succession planning and leadership development?

Gerrit Klaassen, the head of HR for Philips Electronics' $6 billion medical systems business, gives us some wise advice in this regard: "You are in a peculiar role here—as a member of the management committee you have to have good relationships with the other executives, yet there are times when you also have to talk about them with the CEO. It works if you have complete integrity. In any conversation I have, both sides know that I cannot repeat what is said. Sometimes I will add, 'Did we have this discussion or not?' If it's an issue that I feel must eventually reach the CEO, I will say, 'I advise you to open this up now.' But it's their decision."[19]

The head of HR cannot be a lone-ranger advisor to the CEO—to be truly effective, they have to build trusted relationships upward, laterally with peers, and below with subordinates. They can only do this if they have consistently demonstrated rock-solid integrity and discretion.

Strategy Six: See the Big Picture—Don't Trip Over the Blades of Grass

Any competent HR professional can provide top management with solid analysis. It's the person who can also bring big-picture thinking to the table, however, who is truly invaluable. Big-picture thinking—synthesis—is the ability to see patterns, to discern connections, to create new ideas out of old data, to reformulate problems, and to grasp the essential issues in complex situations. Many of our top HR heads are moving in this direction and spending more of their time on this type of problem solving. American Airline's Sue Oliver, for example, tells us, "Right now, 10 percent of my time is focused on my strategic, advisory role with other company leaders, where I have the opportunity to function as a sounding board and strategist on cross-functional issues and leadership development. I intend to grow that proportion to 25 percent because the greatest value added in my current role is to promote the future success of American through the creativity and vision of its leaders."[20] Verizon's Ezra Singer adds, "Where I can really add value is around strategic issues—leadership development, making the workforce more productive, and so on."[21]

How do you develop big-picture thinking skills? First, you've got to become a deep generalist, which is the very first strategy we outlined in this article. Knowledge breadth gives you the ability to make connections. There are other techniques that you can use as well. Here are a few to consider:

- Use simplifying frames to help highlight the key issues.
- Strive to understand multiple perspectives—tap into the points of view of each major constituency.
- Get your hands dirty—make sure you have a first-hand understanding of the details of the problem, as opposed to just a 50,000-foot view.
- Take time for reflection. Creative insight most often develops during a period of rest and reflection that follows intense work.

As Mike D'Ambrose tells us, "When I was 16, I had a New York City fireman as my football coach. On my desk, I still have something he said: 'Don't trip on the grass blades on the way to the goal line.' I am always looking for the big idea. I am always thinking about how an event may impact our company. If you want to be viewed as a partner to the CEO, you've got to act like one."[22]

What does all this mean for you if you're not yet the head of HR for your company? The six strategies outlined here can be effectively applied right at the very start of your career. In addition, we asked our top HR heads what specific advice they would give to young professionals who aspire to play this valuable trusted advisor role with management. Here is a summary of their recommendations:

- Build credibility early on by consistently delivering. You'll never become a trusted advisor if you don't do a great job at your core function.
- Don't specialize too early—get as many experiences as you can early on. Learn how to tie your HR knowledge to other disciplines like sales, marketing, and operations.
- Take chances—go out on limb occasionally and be willing to admit your mistakes.
- Don't just talk about the problem—always come up with solutions.
- Be available. Schedule time with people without setting any particular agenda. You've got to invest in relationships to make them grow.

- Be assertive in defining and shaping your role. Take on assignments that are outside the scope of what you were asked to do.
- Seek out organizations and leaders who care about the HR function.
- Get out of the office! Invest time getting to know your company's operations and people.
- Assiduously cultivate your reputation for integrity and being a straight-shooter. Never point fingers and don't badmouth people.

Finally, trusted advisor relationships are often forged during crises—what we call *breakthrough moments*. Almost all of the top HR heads we spoke with could recall one or two critical events that provided the opportunity to take their contribution, and their relationship with top management, to the next level. For some, the catalyst was a major acquisition; for others, such as Sue Oliver at American Airlines, it was a crisis precipitated by external events. Recognize these moments and be prepared to truly stretch yourself to meet the challenge. You may find your relationships transformed as a result.

As companies increasingly scrutinize the contribution of every business unit and every function, human resources executives need to demonstrate their value day in and day out. By utilizing these six strategies, you'll earn the trust and respect of top management and truly distinguish yourself.

NOTES

Chapter 1: Getting Extraordinary Results from Ordinary People

1. F. R. Reichheld, *Loyalty Rules!* (Boston: Harvard Business School Press, 2001), p. 15.
2. R. Levering and M. Moskowitz, *The 100 Best Companies to Work for in America* (New York: Doubleday Dell Publishing Group, A Currency Book, 1993), p. xiii.
3. A. Ciancutti and T. Steding, *Built on Trust* (New York: Contemporary Books, 2000), p. 209.
4. J. R. Katzenbach, *Peak Performance* (Boston: Harvard Business School Press, 2000), p. 186.
5. A. Raskin, "What's an MBA Worth?" *Business 2.0* (July 2002).
6. Jeffrey Pfeffer, Stanford management professor, found there is almost no data to support the assumption that a business degree leads to business success. Available from http://www.business2.com/articles/mag/0,1640,41346,FF.html?ref=bonus.
7. M. Finney, "From Working Wounded to Working Joyfully," *Across the Board* (September 1998), p. 28. Publisher: David Vidal.
8. R. Barrett, *Liberating the Corporate Soul, Building a Visionary Organization* (Boston: Butterworth-Heinemann, 1998).

Chapter 2: Looking North on the Leadership Compass: Effective HR Management for the New Century

1. *American Heritage Dictionary* (Boston: Houghton Mifflin, 2001).
2. *Webster's College Dictionary* (New York: Random House, 1992).
3. P. Drucker, "Not Enough Generals Were Killed!" *The Leader of the Future,* eds. Frances Hesselbein, Marshall Goldsmith, and Richard Beckhard (San Francisco: Jossey-Bass, 1996).
4. J. MacGregor Burns, *Leadership* (New York: HarperCollins, 1978).
5. First Inaugural Address by President Abraham Lincoln (March 6, 1861).
6. From John F. Kennedy's 1961 speech, delivered before a joint session of Congress, which first proposed landing a man on the moon.
7. J. M. Citrin, "A Conversation with eBay's Meg Whitman: Leadership Lessons from America's Most Successful Internet Company," *Business 2.0* (October 3, 2001).

Chapter 3: The 21st Century Workforce: Implications for HR

1. Bureau of Labor Statistics 2000–2010 Employment Projections, Issued December 3, 2001, News Release USDL 01–443, Specifically Table 4. Employment and total

job openings, 2001–2010, by education or training category, and Table 5 Civilian Labor Force by sex, age, race, and Hispanic origin, 1990, 2000, and projected 2010 BLS RELEASES 2000–2010. EMPLOYMENT PROJECTIONS Web: www.bls .gov/news.release/ecopro.nr0.htm.

2. *The Quotable Woman,* Inspirations Series (Philadelphia: Running Press, 1991), p. 149.

Chapter 5: Globalization: How Real Are the People Challenges?

1. J. Clarkson, "American Graffiti," *The Sunday Times Magazine* (June 9, 2002).
2. N. Klein, "No Logo: Taking Aim at the Brand Bullies," *Flamingo* (2001).
3. G. Dyke, Speech to Television Society Conference (Edinburgh, Scotland, 2001).
4. AA Gill, "Star Spangled Bender," *The Sunday Times Magazine* (2002).
5. B. Lindsey, *Against the Dead Hand* (New York: Wiley, 2002).
6. S. Rhinesmith, *A Manager's Guide to Globalization* (Chicago: Richard D. Irwin, 1993).
7. J. P. Jannet, *Managing with a Global Mind-Set* (Edinburgh, Scotland: Prentice Hall, 2000).
8. C. A. Bartlett and S. Ghoshal, *Transactional Management,* 3rd ed. (New York: McGraw-Hill International, 2000).
9. See note 6.
10. M. Gould and A. Campbell, *Designing Effective Organizations* (San Francisco: Jossey-Bass, 2002).
11. See note 8.

Chapter 6: Understanding Referent Groups and Diversity: A Key Challenge for Human Resource Leaders

1. Information based on in-depth interviews with more than 200 specially chosen, high-potential leaders from 120 of the world's premier organizations recently conducted by Accenture with Alliance for Strategic Leadership. For a more in-depth look at this research and its implications for global leadership, see Marshall Goldsmith, Cathy Greenberg, Alastair Robertson, Maya Hu-Chan, and Warren Bennis, *Global Leadership: The Next Generation* (New York: Prentice-Hall, 2003).
2. Marshall Goldsmith and Iain Sommerville, "Coaching Free Agents," *Coaching for Leadership,* eds. Marshall Goldsmith, Laurence Lyons, and Alyssa Freas (San Francisco: Jossey-Bass, 2000).
3. See note 2.

Chapter 7: Putting Pride to Work: Recapturing the Power of the Most Effective Motivational Force

1. Thomas A. Peters and Robert H. Waterman, *In Search of Excellence* (New York: Warner Books, 1982), p. 10.

Chapter 8: Leveraging HR: How to Develop Leaders in "Real Time"

1. J. Kouzes and B. Z. Posner, *The Leadership Challenge* (San Francisco: Jossey-Bass, 1998); Morgan N., Jr., McCall, *The Lessons of Experience: How Successful Executives Develop on the Job* (San Francisco: Free Press, 1989); and C. Argyris, "The Executive Mind and Double Loop Learning," *Organizational Dynamics,* vol. 11, no. 2 (1982): 5–22.

Chapter 9: Strategic HRM Measurement: From Justifying HR to Strategic Talent Leadership

1. Brookings Institute. Understanding intangible sources of value: Human capital subgroup report. Retrieved 2000, http://www.brook.edu/es/research/projects/intangibles/doc/sub_hcap.htm.
2. J. W. Boudreau and P. M. Ramstad, "Human Resource Metrics: Can Measures Be Strategic?" *Research in Personnel and Human Resources Management,* suppl. 4 (1999): 75–98.
3. J. W. Boudreau and P. M. Ramstad, "Strategic I/O Psychology and the Role of Utility Analysis Models," *Handbook of Industrial and Organizational Psychology,* eds. W. Borman, R. Klimoski, and D. Ilgen (New York: Wiley, in press). See also J. W. Boudreau and P. M. Ramstad, "From Professional Business Partner to Strategic Talent Leader: What's Next for Human Resource Management." Working Paper 02–10 (Ithaca, NY: Cornell University, Center for Advanced Human Resource Studies, 2002).
4. See note 3.
5. J. W. Boudreau and P. M. Ramstad, "From Professional Business Partner to Strategic Talent Leader: What's Next for Human Resource Management." Working Paper 02–10 (Ithaca, NY: Cornell University, Center for Advanced Human Resource Studies, 2002).
6. N. Tichy, "The Teachable Point of View," *Harvard Business Review* (March/April 1999), pp. 82–83.
7. J. W. Boudreau, B. B. Dunford, and P. M. Ramstad, "The Human Capital 'Impact' on e-Business: The Case of Encyclopedia Britannica," *Pushing the Digital Frontier: Insights into the Changing Landscape of e-Business,* eds. N. Pal and J. M. Ray (New York: AMACOM, 2001). See also, J. W. Boudreau and P. M. Ramstad, *Supply-Chain Measurement for Staffing,* Working Paper 01–16 (Ithaca, NY: Cornell University, Center for Advanced Human Resource Studies, 2001).
8. A. J. Rucci, S. P. Kirn, and R. T. Quinn, "The Employee-Customer-Profit Chain at Sears," *Harvard Business Review* (January/February 1998), pp. 83–97.
9. J. W. Boudreau and P. M. Ramstad, "Strategic I/O Psychology and the Role of Utility Analysis Models," *Handbook of Industrial and Organizational Psychology,* eds. W. Borman, R. Klimoski, and D. Ilgen (New York: Wiley, in press). See also, J. W. Boudreau and P. M. Ramstad, "From Professional Business Partner to Strategic Talent Leader: What's Next for Human Resource Management," Working Paper 02–10 (Ithaca, NY: Cornell University, Center for Advanced Human Resource Studies, 2002).

10. For a more detailed application of the HC BRidge™ Framework to the strategic challenges of the Internet, see J. W. Boudreau, B. B. Dunford, and P. M. Ramstad, "The Human Capital 'Impact' on e-Business: The Case of Encyclopedia Britannica," *Pushing the Digital Frontier: Insights into the Changing Landscape of e-Business,* eds. N. Pal and J. M. Ray (New York: AMACOM, 2001).

11. For more details, references, and a discussion of several other categories, see J. W. Boudreau and P. M. Ramstad, "Strategic I/O Psychology and the Role of Utility Analysis Models," *Handbook of Industrial and Organizational Psychology,* eds. W. Borman, R. Klimoski, and D. Ilgen (New York: Wiley, in press).

12. J. Fitzenz, *How to Measure Human Resources Management* (New York: McGraw-Hill, 1995).

13. B. E. Becker and M. A. Huselid, "High Performance Work Systems and Firm Performance: A Synthesis of Research and Managerial Implications," *Research in Personnel and Human Resource Management,* vol. 16 (1998): 53–101; and B. Pfau and I. Kay, *The Human Capital Edge: 21 People Management Practices Your Company Must Implement (or Avoid) to Maximize Shareholder Value* (New York: McGraw-Hill, 2002).

14. P. Cappelli and D. Neumark, "Do 'High-Performance' Work Practices Improve Establishment-Level Outcomes?" *Industrial and Labor Relations Review,* vol. 54, no. 4 (2001): 737–775.

15. B. A. Gerhart, P. M. Wright, G. C. McMahan, and S. Snell, "Measurement Error in Research on Human Resources and Firm Performance: How Much Error Is There and How Does Its Influence Effect Size Estimates?" *Personnel Psychology,* vol. 53, no. 4 (2000): 803–834.

16. R. S. Kaplan and D. P. Norton, "Using the Balanced Scorecard as a Strategic Management System," *Harvard Business Review* (January/February 1996), pp. 75–85.

17. B. E. Becker, M. A. Huselid, and D. Ulrich, *The HR Scorecard: Linking People, Strategy, and Performance* (Boston: Harvard Business School Press, 2001).

18. G. Walker and J. R. MacDonald, "Designing and Implementing an HR Scorecard," *Human Resource Management,* vol. 40, no. 4 (2001): 365–377.

19. A. J. Rucci, S. P. Kirn, and R. T. Quinn, "The Employee-Customer-Profit Chain at Sears," *Harvard Business Review* (January/February 1998), pp. 83–97.

20. D. Shelgren, "HR Outsourcing," *Journal of Business Strategy,* vol. 22, no. 4 (2001): 4.

Chapter 10: Human Resource Management and Business Performance: Lessons for the 21st Century

1. See as examples: R. Batt, "Work Organization, Technology, and Performance in Customer Service and Sales," *Industrial and Labor Relations Review,* vol. 52 (1999): 539–564; C. Ichniowski, K. Shaw, and G. Prennushi, "The Effects of Human Resource Management Practices on Productivity: A Study of Steel Finishing Lines," *American Economic Review,* vol. 87 (1997): 291–313; M. B. Lee and N. B. Johnson, "Business Environment, High-Involvement Management, and Firm Performance in Korea," *Advances in Industrial and Labor Relations,* eds. D. Lewin and B. E. Kaufman (Greenwich, CT: JAI Press, 1998), pp. 67–87; T. M. Welbourne and A. O. Andrews, "Predicting the Performance of Initial Public Offerings: Should

Human Resource Management Be in the Equation?" *Academy of Management Journal,* vol. 39 (1996): 891–919; J. P. MacDuffie, "Human Resource Bundles and Manufacturing Performance: Organizational Logic and Flexible Production Systems in the World Auto Industry," *Industrial and Labor Relations Review,* vol. 48 (1995): 197–221; M. A. Huselid, "The Impact of Human Resource Management Practices on Turnover, Productivity, and Corporate Financial Performance," *Academy of Management Journal,* vol. 38 (1995): 635–672; M. Morishima, "Information Sharing and Firm Performance in Japan," *Industrial Relations,* vol. 30 (1991): 37–61; and D. J. B. Mitchell, D. Lewin, and E. E. Lawler III, "Alternative Pay Systems, Firm Performance, and Productivity," *Paying for Productivity,* ed. A. S. Blinder (Washington, DC: Brookings Institution Press, 1990), pp. 15–88.

2. See J. Pfeffer, "Seven Practices of Successful Organizations," *California Management Review,* vol. 40 (1998): 96–124. The omissions from this listing are especially notable and include "leadership," "organizational culture," and "change management," all of which are claimed by other scholars and many practitioners to be key success factors in business performance. This implies that the HRM and organizational behavior research communities operate in isolation from one another, that is, in "silos" of the type they frequently counsel businesses to avoid or eliminate!

3. J. Pfeffer and J. F. Viega, "Putting People First for Organizational Success," *Academy of Management Executive,* vol. 13 (1999): 37–48.

4. M. L. Tushman and C. A. O'Reilly III, *Winning through Innovation* (Boston: Harvard Business School Press, 1997).

5. D. Lewin and D. J. B. Mitchell, *Human Resource Management: An Economic Approach,* 2nd ed. (Cincinnati, OH: South-Western, 1995).

6. D. Lewin, *HRM and Business Performance Research: Empiricism in Search of Theory,* Paper presented to the 62nd annual meeting of the Academy of Management (Denver, CO, 2002).

7. See note 6; and D. Lewin, "Low Involvement Work Practices and Business Performance," *Proceedings of the 53rd annual meeting, Industrial Relations Research Association* (Champaign, IL: IRRA, 2001), pp. 275–292.

8. The original sample sizes were 525 companies, 540 business units, 1,115 manufacturing plants, and 445 sales and service field offices. Two survey mailings, a telephone follow-up, an e-mail follow-up and, in the case of the insurance company, a letter from a senior official that accompanied the survey, helped achieve response rates of 55 percent, 58 percent, 41 percent, and 65 percent, respectively, among these four samples of business entities. Additional detail on the design of the surveys and sampling frames is provided in notes 6 and 7.

9. For the four samples as a whole, peripheral employment accounted for just less than 32 percent of total full-time equivalent employment in 1998, closely approximating the extent of peripheral employment at that time in the U.S. economy. Between 1995 and 1998, peripheral employment increased by about 14 percent in the company sample, 15 percent in the business unit sample, 16 percent in the manufacturing plant sample, and 15 percent in the insurance sales and service field office sample. For further details, including changes in specific categories of peripheral employment in these four samples of business entities, see note 6.

10. Details of the rationale for specification of the business performance variables and control variables as well as definitions of these can be found in Lewin, see notes 6 and 7.

11. Together with the aforementioned argument by Pfeffer and Viega (see note 3) that only about one out of eight business entities adopts and sustains usage of the "full complement" of high-involvement HRM practices, these data can be interpreted to mean that business entities are relatively more receptive to and thus more likely to adopt and sustain usage of low-involvement HRM practices. Further supporting this interpretation is the argument that low-involvement HRM practices (applied to peripheral employees) are intended primarily to contain or reduce labor costs, whereas high-involvement HRM practices (applied to core employees) that are intended primarily to add value to a business nevertheless also require additional costs.

12. Not included in this "calculation," however, is the potential or hidden cost to a business if its (relatively low-cost) peripheral workforce becomes so large that it seeks to become part of its (higher-cost) core workforce.

13. G. Hofstede, *Culture's Consequences: Comparing Values, Behaviors, Institutions, and Organizations Across Nations* (Thousand Oaks, CA: Sage, 2001).

14. See note 4.

15. D. Lewin, "IR and HR Perspectives on Workplace Conflict: What Can Each Learn From the Other?" *Human Resource Management Review*, vol. 11 (2001): 453–485.

16. D. Lewin, D. J. B. Mitchell, and M. A. Zaidi, "Separating Ideas and Bubbles in Human Resource Management," *The Human Resource Management Handbook, Part I*, eds. D. Lewin, D. J. B. Mitchell, and M. A. Zaidi (Greenwich, CT: JAI Press, 1997), pp. 1–31.

17. B. E. Becker and M. A. Huselid, "Overview: Strategic Human Resource Management in Five Firms," *Human Resource Management*, vol. 38 (1999): 287–301.

Chapter 11: The Icarus Syndrome: Talent Management and Derailment in the New Millennium

1. I. Deary, L. Whalley, H. Lemmon, J. Starr, and J. Crawford, "The Stability of Individual Differences in Mental Ability from Childhood to Old Age: Follow-Up of the 1932 Scottish Mental Survey," *Intelligence*, vol. 28 (2000): 49–55; P. R. Costa and R. McCrae, "'Set like Plaster?' Evidence for the Stability of Adult Personality," *Can Personality Change?* eds. T. Heatherton and J. Weinberger (Washington, DC: American Psychological Association, 1994), pp. 21–40.

2. C. Cox and C. Cooper, *High Flyers: An Anatomy of Managerial Success* (Oxford, England: Basil Blackwell, 1988), p. 160.

Chapter 12: Maximizing the Probability of Success of Newly Recruited Executives

1. "The War for Talent," *McKinsey Quarterly*, no. 3 (McKinsey & Company, 1998): 44–57.

2. Jenny C. McCune, "Sorry, Wrong Executive," *Management Review* (October 1999).

3. Martha H. Peak, "Welcome to Your Job: You're Fired!" *Management Review*, vol. 82, no. 1 (January 1996). See also, Amy Newman Korn, "Gotcha!" *Across the Board*, vol. 35, no. 8 (September 1998).
4. For a discussion of this assessment process see Cora Daniels, "Does This Man Need a Shrink?" *Fortune* (February 5, 2001).

Chapter 15: Free to Choose: Fostering the Innovative Organization

1. For an overview of agility and flexibility, see L. Dyer and R. Shafer, "From Human Resource Strategy to Organizational Effectiveness: Lessons from Research on Agile Organization," *Research in Personnel and Human Resources Management* (Supplement 4: Strategic Human Resource Management in the 21st Century), eds. P. Wright, L. Dyer, J. Boudreau, and G. Milkovich. (Stamford, CT: JAI Press, 1999), pp. 145–173.
2. David Held has explored the issues of democracy in *Models of Democracy* (Cambridge, MA: Polity Press, 1996).
3. For deeper analyses of the rise of mass customization, see *Markets of One: Creating Customer-Unique Value through Mass Customization,* eds. J. Gilmore and B. J. Pine (Boston: Harvard Business School Press, 1988).
4. The description of the situations and actions in the companies which follow are all based on case research in each of these companies, and all quotations in this chapter are derived from these interviews. I have also had access to documents from both public sources and the companies themselves.
5. For a description of the internal labor market and the impact of job posting, see P. Cappelli, *The New Deal at Work: Managing the Market-Driven Workforce* (Boston: Harvard Business School Press, 1998); and P. Cappelli, *The Path to the Top: The Changing Model of Career Advancement.* Paper presented at the Harvard Business School Conference on Career Evolution (June 2002).
6. Many authors have seen project structures as the foundation of the agile company. The role of projects in the accumulation of knowledge has been described by K. E. Weick, "Enactment and the Boundaryless Career," *The Boundaryless Career,* eds. M. B. Arthur and D. M. Rousseau (New York: Oxford University Press, 1996), pp. 40–57. See J. Galbraith, *Designing Complex Organizations* (Reading, MA: Addison-Wesley, 1973) for a conceptual overview; and S. L. Brown and K. M. Eisenhardt, *Competing on the Edge: Strategy as Structured Chaos* (Boston: Harvard Business School Press, 1998) for examples in practice.
7. See J. Burgoyne and M. Reynolds, *Management Learning: Integrating Perspectives in Theory and Practice* (London: Sage, 1997), for a thoughtful exploration of the impact of significant work experience on building knowledge and capability. Cross-boundary experiences as a key builder of the deep relationships of social capital have been described by M. Granovetter, "The Strength of Weak Ties," *American Journal of Sociology,* vol. 78 (May 1973): 1360–1380.
8. The impact of mentoring and coaching on performance was highlighted by R. M. Kanter, *When Giants Learn to Dance* (New York: Simon & Schuster, 1989); and R. J. DeFillippi and M. B. Arthur, "The Boundaryless Career: A Competency-Based Perspective," *Journal of Organizational Behavior,* vol. 15 (1994): 307–324.

9. Edward E. Lawler has traced the rise of customization in remuneration packages. See *Rewarding Excellence* (San Francisco: Jossey-Bass, 2000); and "Individualizing the Organization: Past, Present, and Future," *Organizational Dynamics,* vol. 29, no. 1 (2000): 1–15.

10. There is a growing body of evidence that location and time choice are crucial to well-being and performance. For a summary, see the Ford Foundation's report by R. Rapoport and L. Bailyn, *Rethinking Life and Work: Toward a Better Future* (1997).

11. A broader discussion of the integration processes can be found in S. Ghoshal and L. Gratton, "Integrating the Enterprise," *Sloan Management Review* (Autumn 2002).

12. The impact of these side deals is explored by D. Rousseau in "The Idiosyncratic Deal: Flexibility versus Fairness?" *Organizational Dynamics,* vol. 29, no. 4 (2001): 260–273.

13. M. Wheatley and M. Kellner-Rogers, *A Simpler Way* (San Francisco: Berrett-Koehler, 1996); and R. Axelrod and M. D. Cohen, *Harnessing Complexity: Organizational Implications of the Scientific Frontier* (New York: Free Press, 1999) provide useful description of these aspects of complexity theory.

14. Author interview with Greg Grimshaw (February 2002).

Chapter 16: Building a New Partnership

1. This point is elaborated in Allan R. Cohen and David L. Bradford, "Power and Influence in the 21st Century," *Organizations 21C,* ed. Subir Chowdhury (London: Financial Times Prentice Hall, Forthcoming).

2. See Chapters 9–12 in David L. Bradford and Allan R. Cohen, *Power Up: Transforming Organizations Through Shared Leadership* (New York: Wiley, 1998).

Chapter 18: Accommodating Change in the 21st Century

1. John P. Kotter and Dan S. Cohen, *The Heart of Change: Real-Life Stories of How People Change Their Organizations* (Boston: Harvard Business School Press, 2002).

2. Jim Collins, *Good to Great: Why Some Companies Make the Leap . . . and Others Don't* (New York: HarperCollins, October 2001).

3. James Kouzes and Barry Posner, *The Leadership Challenge* (San Francisco: Jossey-Bass, November 1996).

Chapter 19: Managing Global Total Rewards

1. Geert Hofstede, *Culture's Consequences: Comparing Values, Behaviors, Intuitions, and Organizations across Nations,* 2nd ed. (Thousand Oaks, CA: Sage, 2001), p. 9.

Chapter 20: Globalization of HR: 21st Century Challenges

1. www.corporateleadershipcouncil.com, 1/20/2003.

Chapter 22: When Change Is Out of Our Control

1. All quotes in this article are from personal interviews conducted in July 2000 by the author.
2. Ibid.

Chapter 23: Mother's Work Is Never Done: Myths and Facts about Organizational Change

1. J. O'Toole, *Leading Change* (San Francisco: Jossey-Bass, 1995), p. 53.
2. See note 1.
3. R. G. Ackerman and G. L. Neilson, "A Case Study of Re-Engineering, the Corning Way," *Strategy + Business*, no. 2 (1996): 56–64.
4. See note 3.
5. See note 3.

Chapter 24: Unilever's Path to Growth: Reflections on a Journey in Progress

1. Available from http://www.unilever.com/company/ourpurpose.

Chapter 25: Finding the Missing Link: Connecting Your Business Strategy and Leadership Strategy

1. Bruce A. Pasternack and James O'Toole, "Yellow-Light Leadership: How the World's Best Companies Manage Uncertainty," *Strategy + Business*, no. 27 (2002), p. 3.

Chapter 26: Convergence of HR: Leadership and Change Management

1. T. Friedman, *The Lexus and the Olive Tree* (New York: Farrar, Straus and Giroux, 1999).
2. R. D'Aventi and R. Gunter, *Hypercompetition: Managing the Dynamics of Strategic Maneuvering* (New York: Free Press, 1994).
3. M. Hammer, *Beyond Reengineering* (New York: HarperBusiness, 1996).
4. See the 2001 Annual Report from the IBM Corporation.
5. "As Leaders, Women Rule," *BusinessWeek* (November 20, 2000). Rochelle Sharpe.
6. M. Clemente and D. Greenspan, *Winning at Mergers and Acquisitions* (New York: Wiley, 1998). See also, J. Krallinger, *Mergers and Acquisitions: Managing the Transaction* (New York: McGraw-Hill, 1997).
7. P. Mervis and M. Marks, *Managing the Merger* (Paramus, NJ: Prentice Hall, 1992).
8. See Baruch Lev, *Intangibles: Management, Measurement, and Reporting* (Washington, DC: Brookings Institution Press, 2001). See also "Measures that Matter," The Ernst and Young Center for Business Innovation. Available from www.ey.com. Cambridge, MA.

9. "Human Resource Competency Study" is an ongoing study since 1988 by David Ulrich and Wayne Brockbank at the University of Michigan School of Business. For more information go to http://webuser.bus.union.edu/programs/hrcs.

10. M. Goldsmith, L. Lyons, and A. Frees, eds., *Coaching for Leadership: How the World's Greatest Coaches Help Leaders Learn* (San Francisco: Jossey-Bass/Pfeiffer, 2000).

11. S. Kerr, ed., *Ultimate Rewards: What Really Motivates People to Achieve* (Boston: Harvard Business School Press, 1997).

12. R. Ashkenas, D. Ulrich, T. Jick, and S. Kerr, *The Boundaryless Organization* (San Francisco: Jossey-Bass, 2002).

13. B. E. Becker, M. A. Huselid, and D. Ulrich, *The HR Scorecard: Linking People, Strategy, and Performance* (Boston: Harvard Business School Press, 2001).

14. See note 11.

Chapter 27: Is This the End of HR?

1. Charlie Rose, "Leadership through Change." *E-volve,* vol. 3, no. 1 (Spring 2002): 15.

Chapter 28: Transforming Your HR Department into a Start-Up Professional Services Firm

1. Before that time, the word "job" just meant "a task" or "a piece of work to be done." Ironically, it was applied more often to what today we would call a "temp" situation than to long-term, full-time employment. For more on that and a description of the rise of what we today recognize as "jobs," see William Bridges, *JobShift* (Cambridge, MA: Perseus, 1994), pp. 1–53.

2. The CFO of the exploration arm of one of the largest international oil companies asked us to guess recently what the core competence of that part of the corporation was. We guessed that it involved the technologies of finding oil and gas, as well as those of extracting them from the ground, and also transporting the product, we suggested. "Wrong," he said. "Our core competence is writing and managing contracts." The people who did the actual oil and gas work were no longer company employees!

Chapter 29: What's Next for the People Function?
A Missing Link for Delivering Value

1. Baruch Lev, *Intangibles: Management, Measurement, and Reporting* (Washington, DC: Brookings Institution Press, 2001).

2. Cited in study by Ernst & Young, "Measures that Matter," The Ernst and Young Center for Business Innovation. Available from www.ey.com.

3. Robert G. Eccles, Robert Herz, Mary Keegan, and David Philips, *Value Reporting Revolution* (New York: Wiley, 2001), pp. 4, 5, and 6.

4. See note 2, p. 3.

5. Clearly, the seven capabilities we posit as intangibles are not conclusive, but indicative of what intangibles might be. We know that other capabilities and other

intangibles may be delineated. We pick these seven as a starting point for debate and dialogue.

6. The "War for Talent" was the topic of a study by the McKinsey consulting organization. See Charles Fishman, "War for Talent," *Fast Company*, no. 16 (August 1998): 104.
7. We are grateful to Marshall Goldsmith for the "simple but not easy" insight.

Chapter 32: Managing for Execution: HR Delivery Imperatives for the 21st Century

1. *"CFOs' Views on Outsourcing"* (Lincolnshire, IL: Hewitt Associates, January 2002), p. 3.

Chapter 33: HR as a Trusted Partner

1. Maureen Jenkins, "Dagnon Retires, 'People' Remain His Lifelong Passion," *Boeing Frontiers*, vol. 1, no. 1 (May 2002), p. 1.
2. G. William Dauphinais and Colin Price, of Price Waterhouse, *Straight from the CEO* (New York: Simon & Schuster, 1998), pp. 16, 17.
3. *Merriam-Webster's Collegiate Dictionary,* 10th ed. (Springfield, MA: Merriam-Webster, 2001).
4. David Ulrich, *Human Resource Champions* (Boston: Harvard Business School Press, 1997).
5. Ram Charan, *What the CEO Wants You to Know* (New York: Crown Business, 2001), pp. 12, 119.
6. I base this statement upon my 35 years of experience in human resources and my review of current population demographics. I am convinced that there will be a shortage of qualified talent until the time that those children who are nine years old in 2002 are graduated from college.
7. Jeffrey Steele Special to the *Tribune, Chicago Tribune* (January 20, 2002), p. 5.
8. See note 7.
9. See note 4.

Chapter 34: The HR Head as Trusted CEO Advisor: Six Strategies for Becoming a Valued Partner to Senior Management

1. Author interview with Randy MacDonald, IBM, Armonk, NY (January 29, 2002).
2. Interview with Bob Galvin (August 1997).
3. Interview with Mike D'Ambrose, conference call (March 6, 2002).
4. See note 1.
5. Interview with Steve King, conference call (January 15, 2002).
6. Pablo Picasso, 1881–1973.
7. Interview with Ezra Singer, conference call (January 3, 2002).
8. See note 1.
9. Interview with Yvonne Jackson, conference call (January 9, 2002).
10. See note 3.

11. See note 3.
12. See note 7.
13. Interview with John Raffaeli, conference call (February 8, 2002).
14. Interview with Tom Bouchard, conference call (January 9, 2002).
15. Interview with Walter Wriston (August 1997).
16. See note 3.
17. See note 13.
18. See note 14.
19. Interview with Gerrit Klaassen, conference call (April 4, 2002).
20. Interview with Sue Oliver (January 17, 2002).
21. See note 7.
22. See note 3.

ABOUT THE CONTRIBUTORS

SANDY K. BICOS leads Hewitt Associates' North America Human Resource Effectiveness consulting. She specializes in helping organizations reduce their HR function's operating costs. She consults in the analysis and improvement of human resources delivery strategies and effectiveness, process improvement, measurement, and e-HR applications for the human resources function. Prior to joining Hewitt Associates, Sandy was the director of human resources for World Book, Inc., an international publishing company. She has held human resources positions with Avery Dennison and Helene Curtis, and, while working as an independent consultant, she was an adjunct instructor at the University of Notre Dame's Graduate School of Management. Contact: skbicos@hewitt.com; www.hewitt.com.

JOHN W. BOUDREAU, PhD, is professor of human resource studies and director of the Center for Advanced Human Resource Studies (CAHRS) at Cornell University, John is recognized worldwide for breakthrough research on the bridge between superior talent and sustainable competitive advantage. His research has received the Academy of Management's Organizational Behavior New Concept and Human Resource Scholarly Contribution awards. John consults and conducts executive development with companies worldwide that seek to maximize their employees' effectiveness by quantifying the strategic bottom-line impact of superior people and human capital strategies. He is a Fellow of the National Academy of Human Resources and has published more than 40 books and articles, including *Human Resource Management*. Contact: jwb6@cornell.edu; www.ilr .cornell.edu/CAHRS/boudreau_john.html.

DAVID L. BRADFORD, PhD, is currently a senior lecturer in organizational behavior at Stanford University's Graduate School of Business. David has conducted workshops and seminars and served as an organizational consultant to a variety of industrial, educational, governmental, and service organizations. He has also developed training programs on performance management, interpersonal skills, and dealing horizontally and upwards in organizations. David has published numerous articles and books, including *Managing for Excellence: The Guide to Developing High Performance in Contemporary Organizations; Group Dynamics; Influencing Without Authority;* and his most recent, *Power Up: Transforming Organizations through Shared Leadership*. Contact: bradford_david@gsb.stanford.edu; www.gsb.stanford.edu.

SUSAN MITCHELL BRIDGES has spent more than 20 years consulting on executive development and leading change. She held senior management positions with international consulting firms prior to forming her own company. She is co-author with William Bridges of "Leading Transition: A New Model for Change" included in *On Leading Change: A Leader to Leader Guide* by The Drucker Foundation. Contact: susan@wmbridges.com; www.wmbridges.com.

WILLIAM BRIDGES is a speaker, author, and organizational consultant in the field of managing change. He is the author of *JobShift, Transitions, Managing Transitions,* and most recently, *The Way of Transition.* His clients have included Intel Corporation, Hewlett-Packard Company, McKesson HBOC, BankBoston, and Delta Airlines. The *Wall Street Journal* has called him one of the top 10 executive development presenters in the country. Contact: bill@wmbridges.com; www.wmbridges.com.

WAYNE BROCKBANK, PHD, is clinical professor of business at the University of Michigan Business School. He is faculty director of the Strategic Human Resource Planning Program and the Advanced Human Resource Executive Program at the school's Executive Education Center. He is director of the Human Resource Executive Program in China and of the Global Program in Executive Development in India. Wayne's research focuses on conceptual and process linkages between human resource practices and business strategy, creating performance-based organizational cultures, and implementing business strategy through people. He has published articles and book chapters on these topics, and, in 2001, the Society of Human Resource Management selected "If HR Were Really Strategically Proactive?" as paper of the year. Contact: Wbrock@umich.edu.

JEFF BROWN is vice president of organizational effectiveness within Bank One. His experience is in the areas of organizational design, workforce planning, learning strategy, career development, and program measurement. He was a recipient of the Workforce "Optimas" Award in 2001, as well as the American Society for Training and Development's "Excellence in Practice" award in 2000. In addition, he was named one of *Training Magazine's* "Movers and Shakers" for 2001. Jeff has published articles and made presentations on a number of OE topics related to human resources' impact on business effectiveness. Contact: jbdrums24@hotmail.com.

NIKO CANNER is a founding partner of Katzenbach Partners LLC, a management consulting firm specializing in leadership, team, and workforce performance. Niko leads the firm's work on frontline workforce productivity and the application of quantitative tools to organizational performance. Formerly a manager with Mitchell Madison Group and co-founder of MMG's Organization Practice, he has managed numerous engagements in financial services and pharmaceuticals and was the architect of MMG's "executional excellence" methodology for achieving breakthrough improvements in frontline performance. As an associate with McKinsey & Company, Inc., he was a founding member of the McKinsey Change Center. Contact: niko.canner@katzenbach.com; www.katzenbach.com.

ALLAN R. COHEN, PHD, is the Edward A. Madden Distinguished Professor of Global Leadership at Babson College and director of corporate entrepreneurship, recently completing seven years as chief academic officer. Co-author of the best-seller, *Managing for Excellence and Influence Without Authority*, his latest book, with David Bradford, *Power Up: Transforming Organizations through Shared Leadership*, was selected as one of the best leadership books of 1998 by the Management General Web site. Among his many publications is the co-authored textbook, *Effective Behavior in Organizations*, which has had a major impact on the teaching of organizational behavior, and the award-winning *Alternative Work Schedules: Integrating Individual and Organizational Needs*. He recently edited *The Portable MBA in Management*. Contact: cohen@babson.edu; www.babson.edu.

JAMES B. DAGNON has more than 35 years in the human resources and labor relations fields, having served as senior vice president for two leading companies. James is an experienced leader in the human resources profession. He started his career as a union representative for what is now the Transportation and Communication Union. He joined the human resources management team when a merger formed Burlington Northern in 1970 and advanced to executive vice president, employee relations. As the company head of HR, he was involved in accomplishing the successful merger that created BNSF. He joined the Boeing Company as senior vice president, people, and was instrumental in the successful mergers of Rockwell and McDonald Douglas into the new Boeing Company. Contact: JamesDagnon@msn.com.

STAN DAVIS, PHD, is a highly respected commentator on business in the future. He is author of 12 books, including *Blur, 2020 Vision*, and *Future Perfect*. His next book, *It's Alive: The Coming Convergence of Information, Biology, and Business*, with Christopher Meyer, will be released in 2003. Stan's creative thinking makes practical connections to new business opportunities. Stan spent two decades as an academic, mainly on the faculty of the Harvard Business School. For the last 20 years, he has been active in research, writing, consulting, public speaking, seminars, training, and video. He is also senior research fellow at Cap Gemini Ernst & Young's Center for Business Innovation, Publication board advisor at the *New England Journal of Medicine*, and board member of Opera America. Contact: stanmdavis@aol.com; www.stanmdavis.com.

KATE DCAMP is a senior vice president of human resources at Cisco. Kate leads a global team of HR professionals responsible for the design and implementation of business strategies, programs, and tools that focus on recruitment, retention, leadership, development programs, and productivity. Before joining Cisco, Kate served as Global Leader, Compensation and Executive Programs for General Electric Capital. Recognized as a "General Electric Best Practices Expert" on international compensation and benefits and sales and team incentives, Kate designed and managed all executive, compensation, and recognition-related programs for the company's 130,000 employees and 28 businesses. Prior to joining General Electric, Kate held several other human resource leadership roles, including director of executive programs at The Associated Group in Indianapolis. Contact: kdcamp@cisco.com; http://newsroom.cisco.com/dlls/tln.

BEN E. DOWELL, PHD, is vice president, Center for Leadership Development for the Bristol-Myers Squibb Company. He is responsible for leading a group that provides coaching and consulting to the senior management of the company and is focused on the identification, selection, and development of senior leaders in the company. Prior to this, Ben held a number of management development and human resource generalist positions in various divisions of PepsiCo. Prior to joining PepsiCo, he was assistant professor of administrative sciences at the Graduate School of Business at Kent State University and managing partner of The Kent Group, a consulting firm he co-founded. Contact: Ben.Dowell@bms.com.

MARC EFFRON is the global leader for Hewitt Associates' Leadership consulting practice. His work centers on helping organizations attract, develop, and retain top leadership talent. Marc's recent experience includes developing corporate leadership strategies, senior team succession-management processes, executive performance management programs, and executive engagement strategies. Marc guides Hewitt's research efforts on leadership, creating and managing Hewitt's Top Companies for Leaders on-going global research, which was the cover story of *Chief Executive* magazine in June 2002 and the subject of a forthcoming book in 2003. Marc specializes in managing the leadership challenges during mergers and acquisitions integration. His prior experience includes serving as senior vice president, leadership development for Bank of America and director of organization effectiveness and learning for Oxford Health Plans. Contact: marc.effron@hewitt.com; www.hewitt.com.

MARC A. FEIGEN is managing partner and co-founder of Katzenbach Partners LLC. Marc combines expertise in strategic, analytic problem solving with published expertise in organizational performance. He helps clients focus on organizational transformation, information technology effectiveness, and frontline performance improvement. His work has immersed him in health care, pharmaceuticals, financial services, telecommunications, and transportation. Previously a consultant with McKinsey & Company, Marc co-founded and led the McKinsey Change Center, an office chartered to lead

McKinsey's efforts in change management and organizational performance. Co-author of *Real Change Leaders: How You Can Create Growth and High Performance at Your Company,* he has contributed to the *Wall Street Journal* and has been a regular commentator on the WCBS Small Business Report. Contact: Marc.feigen@katzenbach.com; www.katzenbach.com.

ADRIAN FURNHAM is a professor of psychology at the University College London. He is an expert in selection methodology, the assessment of potential, and the management of performance within organizations. His proposition that individuals can be assessed by their motivation, intelligence, and organizational fit is an intriguing one that a number of companies have used to significant benefit. Contact: a.furnham@ucl.ac.uk.

ROBERT GANDOSSY is a global practice leader for Talent and Organization Consulting in Hewitt Associates' Connecticut Center. A member of Hewitt's Global Council, Bob has special expertise in improving organizational effectiveness, human resource strategy, reengineering, managing large-scale change, mergers and acquisitions, and increasing growth through innovation. He was co-project manager of a major research effort, "The Changing American Workforce," and has written articles and books on subjects including HR strategy, mergers and acquisitions, pay-for-performance, productivity improvement, innovation and change, and business ethics. His book, *Bad Business* was deemed a "masterful job" by Tom Peters and "high drama and a fascinating story" by Rosabeth Moss Kanter. Bob has been a speaker for Harvard Business School, Human Resources Planning Society, The Wharton School, Tom Peters Group, Yale Law School, Yale's School of Organization and Management, American Compensation Association, American Management Association, and The Conference Board. He is also co-author of the forthcoming book, *Best Companies for Leaders.* Contact: robert.gandossy@hewitt.com; www.hewitt.com.

MARSHALL GOLDSMITH is widely recognized as one of the world's foremost authorities in helping leaders achieve positive, measurable change in behavior: for themselves, their people, and their teams. In 2002, Marshall became the first consultant in his field to be featured in a *New Yorker* profile and was interviewed by *Harvard Business Review.* He was listed in *Forbes* as one of five top executive coaches and in the *Wall Street Journal* as one of the "Top 10" executive educators. His work has received national recognition from the Institute for Management Studies, the American Management Association, the American Society for Training and Development, and the Human Resource Planning Society. Marshall's 15 recent books include: *The Leader of the Future, Coaching for Leadership, Partnering: The New Face of Leadership,* and *The Leadership Investment.* Marshall is a founding director of A4SL (Alliance for Strategic Leadership). Contact: Marshall@A4SL.com; www.A4SL.com.

LYNDA GRATTON is associate professor of organizational behavior at London Business School and dean of the full-time MBA program. She directs the school's executive human resource strategy program and is research director of The Leading Edge Research Consortium. Lynda developed and co-directed, with Sumantra Ghoshal, the Global Consortium Program. She has a dynamic research portfolio, including The Leading Edge Research Initiative, which focuses on identifying and articulating how business strategy is developed through people. Her main field of interest is human resource strategy where she is acknowledged as one of the world's leading authorities. Lynda's focus is helping senior executives consider the people implications of business strategy. Her most recent book is *Living Strategy: Putting People at the Heart of Corporate Purpose.*

PAUL HOWES is Hewitt's Market Manager for 200 associates in four offices in the Netherlands and is based in Amsterdam. Paul has previously worked for the firm in Brussels, Lincolnshire, Connecticut, Hong Kong, where he managed operations in the Asia-Pacific Region, and most recently in New Jersey as a Managing Consultant, working with some of Hewitt's larger clients.

Originally an actuary (in three countries), Paul has consulted with large multinational clients across all the fields of human resource management on six continents. His current specialties are helping clients take a more global approach to people management and applying business strategy to people management. Paul speaks four languages and a little Mandarin Chinese.

During his career, Paul has been involved with more than 100 acquisitions, including four as a manager for Hewitt. Paul has a BSc (Econ.) honors degree in Statistics from the London School of Economics and has published articles and spoken in many different countries.

YVONNE R. JACKSON joined Pfizer Inc. in November 2002 as Senior Vice President, Corporate Human Resources. She is responsible for setting the overall strategy for Pfizer's Corporate Human Resources division, as well as overseeing the development of company-wide HR policies, plans, and procedures. Jackson also heads the company's leadership development and HR service delivery initiatives that reach the company's 90,000 employees and is a member of the Pfizer Management Council (PMC), a senior-level executive advisory team.

Most recently, Jackson was head of human resources for Compaq Computer Corporation in Houston, Texas, a position she held for three years. In that capacity, she was responsible for managing and implementing human resource strategies, organizational effectiveness, development, safety, security and environmental policies, and procedures for Compaq on a worldwide basis.

Prior to joining Compaq, Jackson held senior human resources positions at Burger King Corporation and Avon Products, Inc. She earned her Bachelor of Arts degree from Spelman College in Atlanta, Georgia, and holds a Management Development Certificate from Harvard Business School in Cambridge, Massachusetts. Contact: yvonne.jackson@pfizer.com.

JASON JEFFAY leads Talent and Organization Consulting for Hewitt Associates' southeast region. In addition, he is a member of the global leadership team for Hewitt's Human Resource Effectiveness practice responsible for developing Hewitt's Internet strategy for the HR consulting business. Jason consults in the area of human resource strategy, talent management (competencies, strategic staffing, career development, and performance management), organizational alignment, and HR service delivery. Some of Jason's clients include BellSouth, Capital One Financial Corporation, Ernst & Young, First Union Corporation, GTE, Rhone Poulenc Rhorer, and United Parcel Service. Jason has published on a number of topics including: *Fundamentals of Flexible Compensation, HR Issues in Mergers and Acquisitions, Outsourcing the HR Department*, and *Improving HR Service Delivery*.

ROBERT J. JOY is senior vice president, global human resources, at Colgate-Palmolive and has been responsible for Colgate's global human resources since 1996. His primary focus has been to improve the capability of Colgate people around the world, to deliver the company's ambitious growth objectives, and to develop the next generation of leaders. Bob was the recipient of the Human Resources Executive of the Year award presented by *Human Resources Executive* magazine in 1992. He earned this award because of his work to forge a business partnership between human resources and line executives throughout the Colgate organization. Bob has made many significant contributions to the organization, including the initiation of a career planning system that serves as the model for the current global competency initiatives. Contact: bob_joy@colpal.com; www.colgate.com.

RICHARD KANTOR is a senior consultant in Hewitt's Talent and Organization Consulting group and leader of Hewitt's Global Total Rewards Consulting area. He consults with clients on all aspects of worldwide organizational performance, cross-cultural management, and global total rewards strategy and design. He has experience working with organizations on five continents to: set global human resource and total reward strategies that are aligned with business objectives; evaluate performance and reward systems for strategic and cultural consistency; and design and implement performance and reward systems. Richard has gained experience from living and working abroad. Prior to his return to Hewitt's Connecticut office, Richard managed Hewitt Associates' Paris and Madrid offices, and Hewitt's Compensation practice in the West Region of the United States. Contact: richard.kantor@hewitt.com; www.hewitt.com.

JON R. KATZENBACH is a founder of Katzenbach Partners LLC, a firm specializing in organization, leadership, team, and workforce performance. Formerly a director of McKinsey & Company, Inc., Jon's areas of competence include leadership, organization, motivation, and change. He has served executives of leading companies, as well as public institutions. Jon regularly conducts independent research efforts on new approaches to organizational performance. His perspectives on these topics have been presented to numerous executive leadership groups throughout the world. Jon's published works include *The Wisdom of Teams, Real Change Leaders, Teams at the Top, Peak Performance,* and *The Discipline of Teams.* In addition, he is editor of *The Work of Teams* (a *Harvard Business Review* compendium). His newest book, *The Greatest Motivational Force in the World: Why Pride Matters More Than Money,* will be published later this year. Contact: jon.katzenbach@katzenbach.com; www.katzenbach.com.

BEVERLY KAYE, PHD, is a world authority on career development, talent retention, and mentoring. As president of Career Systems International, Inc., corporations including American Express, Dow Corning, Chevron, Chrysler, Marriott International, and Sears use her management and career development programs. She is a prolific writer, popular lecturer, and management consultant. In the early 1980s, Beverly published her book, *Up Is Not the Only Way.* Her latest research is on management strategies for retaining knowledge workers, and she has recently co-authored *Love 'Em or Lose 'Em: Getting Good People to Stay.* Kaye has received many honors and awards, including the National Career Development Award of the American Society for Training and Development. Contact: www.careersystemsintl.com; www.keepem.com.

DAVID LEWIN is the Neil Jacoby Professor of Management, Human Resources and Organizational Behavior in the Anderson Graduate School of Management at UCLA. Prior to joining UCLA in 1990, he was professor, director of the PhD program, director of the Human Resources Research Center, and director of the Senior Executive program at the Columbia University Graduate School of Business. A specialist in human resource management and industrial relations, Professor Lewin has published 16 books and more than 150 articles in academic and business journals.

Two of Professor Lewin's books have won "best book" awards and several of his papers have received comparable awards. In 1995, Lewin was elected a Fellow of the National Academy of Human Resources. He previously served as a member of the executive board of the Industrial Relations Research Association, president of the University Council on Industrial Relations and Human Resource Programs, vice-dean and faculty director of the UCLA MBA program, and co-chair of Los Angeles Mayor Riordan's Task Force on General Manager Compensation and Performance. He presently serves as a member of the Research Advisory Board of WordatWork, is senior editor of *Advances in Industrial and Labor Relations,* and is a member of the editorial boards of *Industrial and Labor Relations Review, Industrial Relations* and *California Management Review.*

He is a member of the board of directors of K-Swiss and serves as faculty director of the UCLA Anderson School Advanced Program in Human Resource Management and of the Strategic Leadership Institute.

J. RANDALL MacDONALD joined IBM in August 2000 as senior vice president, human resources. In this position, he is responsible for the human resources practices and policies of the organization. Prior to joining IBM, Randy was the executive vice president of human resources and administration for GTE (now Verizon Communications). He serves on the board of directors of Covance. He is a member of Cornell University's Center for Advanced Human Resources Study and is chair of its executive board; the Cowdrick Group; the Personnel Roundtable; the Labor Policy Association; and serves on its board of directors as vice chairman.

THOMAS W. MALNIGHT is professor of strategy and international management at IMD. His fields of interest are global strategy and management, evolutionary organizational change in multinational corporations, and internal growth and renewal. Thomas has written for the *Strategic Management Journal,* the *Journal of International Business Studies,* and the *Academy of Management Journal.* He has also authored more than 30 case studies on various aspects of global strategy and organization. Prior to joining IMD, he was on the faculty of the Wharton School, University of Pennsylvania, and he worked for 10 years at Mitsubishi International Corporation, which included two years in Japan. Thomas has consulted extensively with numerous U.S., European, and Asian companies. Contact: malnight@imd.ch.

ELLIOTT MASIE is an internationally recognized speaker, futurist, humorist, author, and consultant on the critical topics of technology, business, learning, and workplace productivity. Elliott is editor of *TechLearn Trends,* an Internet newsletter read by over 41,000 business executives worldwide, and *Learning Decisions,* a subscription newsletter. He heads The MASIE Center, a think-tank focused on how organizations can absorb technology and create continuous learning and knowledge within the workforce. He leads a consortium of Fortune 500 companies exploring the future of technology in the workplace, has developed models for disseminating technology throughout organizations, providing workforce development with technology, and making sense of the buzz and hype of the "e" and "dotcom" world. Elliott is considered one of the leading experts in the emerging field of digital collaboration. Contact: emasie@masie.com; www.masie.com.

D. QUINN MILLS consults with major corporations and teaches leadership, strategy, and human resources at Harvard Business School. A member of the Panel of Thought Leaders of the Peter Drucker Foundation, he has consulted for governmental agencies. A prolific author, Quinn recently published *Buy, Lie, and Sell High: How Investors Lost Out on Enron and the Internet Bubble* and *e-LEADERSHIP: New Ideas for 21st Century Business.* Other books include *Broken Promises,* which examines the business strategy of the IBM Corporation, and *Staying Afloat,* which examines business strategy in the world's construction industry. *The GEM Principle* provides a practical method of empowerment. In addition, Mills has written the leading text in labor relations, *Labor Management Relations*. In the past decade, Mills has concentrated his scholarly attention and business activities on start-up firms, several of which he is a director.

HOWARD MORGAN is a director of Leadership Research Institute and a member of the Alliance for Strategic Leadership (A4SL). Since joining the firm in 1988, he has led a variety of international organizational change initiatives on behalf of his clients. Howard specializes in executive coaching as a strategic change management tool leading to improved customer/employee satisfaction and overall corporate performance. His recent achievements include the development of an internal coaching model for a large international organization and coaching executives on the art of managing managers. He has worked with many executive committees of the world's largest organizations on improving corporate and executive performance. Howard sits on several boards of directors and has taught business courses at leading universities. He is known for providing strategic business/leadership solutions in a practical manner. Contact: howardmo@att.net; www.lri.com.

NEVILLE OSRIN is a consultant in the Talent and Organization Consulting group at Hewitt Associates. Previously, he was vice president of strategic development and marketing at Financiere Strafor. Neville has written, consulted, and lectured on organizational effectiveness and business strategy. He consults across a broad range of strategic business issues, particularly in the areas of competitive positioning, business transformation, leadership, and corporate restructuring. Neville advises several leading companies on the impact of national culture on cross-border alliances and transnational management. He is a consultant to a number of leading-edge global leadership programs and is an executive coach to senior business leaders. He has been a visiting professor at the Universities of Glasgow and Rotterdam and at the Graduate School of Business (Witwatersrand) and a visiting consultant at the NPI Institute for Organization Development in the Netherlands. A chartered psychologist and associate fellow of the British Psychological Society, Neville is a full member of the International Association for Applied Psychology. Contact: neville.osrin@hewittbaconwoodrow.com.

JAMES O'TOOLE is research professor in the Center for Effective Organizations at the University of Southern California (USC), where he has held the University Associates' Chair of Management and served as executive director of the Leadership Institute. Previously, Jim served as editor of *New Management* magazine and director of the Twenty-Year Forecast Project. Among his 13 books and numerous articles, *Vanguard Management* was named "One of the best business and economics books of 1985" by the editors of *Business Week*. His latest book, *Leadership A to Z,* received an enthusiastic review in *Fortune.* Jim served as a special assistant to Secretary of Health, Education and Welfare, Elliot Richardson; as chairman of the Secretary's Task Force on Work in America;

and as director of field investigations for President Nixon's Commission on Campus Unrest. He served most recently as chair of the Booz-Allen & Hamilton Strategic Leadership Center academic board of advisors.

ARJAN OVERWATER was born in Amsterdam, grew up in a quiet, old town called Hertogenbosch in southern Holland. He began his career at Shell headquarters in the mid-1980s. He worked internationally for logistics (Shell equivalent of "MAST") and computing in career development, remuneration, and organization in Aberdeen, Scotland. He taught human resources at Webster University in Leiden, Holland. After leaving Shell, Arjan worked for two years with Hay, an HR consultancy firm, managing their business in Holland for oil and gas and FMCG companies. He moved on to Brussels to work for Coca-Cola as its HR director for northwestern Europe, before joining Unilever as vice president for reward and organization. Contact: arjan.overwater@unilever.com.

JEFFREY PFEFFER is the Thomas D. Dee II Professor of Organizational Behavior at the Graduate School of Business at Stanford University. He is the author or co-author of more than 100 articles and book chapters and 10 books, including: *Managing with Power: Politics and Influence in Organizations; Competitive Advantage Through People: Unleashing the Power of the Work Force; The Knowing-Doing Gap: How Smart Companies Turn Knowledge into Action;* and *Hidden Value: How Great Companies Achieve Extraordinary Results with Ordinary People.* Jeffrey has served on the faculties of the business schools at the University of Illinois and the University of California at Berkeley. He is a member of the visiting committee for the Harvard Business School and on the advisory boards of EarlyBird and Connet and Company. During the 1990s, Jeffrey served as Stanford Business School's director of executive education during which time he was responsible for the school's executive education activities. Contact: Pfeffer_Jeffrey@gsb.stanford.edu; http://faculty-gsb.stanford.edu/pfeffer.

PETER RAMSTAD is executive vice president for strategy and finance at Personnel Decisions International (PDI). Having held leadership positions within PDI for the last 12 years, Peter has had many opportunities to work first-hand with the core tools of business strategy, organizational effectiveness, and talent development. Peter has formed two research partnerships with faculty from Cornell and Texas A&M universities to study how people create value and how that value can be measured. As part of this research, he has worked with clients to understand and measure the financial implications of employee development and effective management. Clients view Peter's breakthrough thinking in this area as fundamental to an organization's ability to implement the systems and techniques required to fully manage human resources as assets, rather than merely expenses. Peter's work goes beyond traditional HR system analysis to the core issues of how organizational capabilities create value and the implications this has for business strategy in the knowledge-based economy.

LIBBY SARTAIN is responsible for leading Yahoo! Inc.'s global human resources efforts and managing and developing the human resources team focusing on attracting, retaining, and developing Yahoo!'s employees who promote and strengthen the company culture, as well as represent the powerful Yahoo! brand. Prior to joining Yahoo! in August 2001, Sartain was "vice president of people" at Southwest Airlines, where she led all human resources functions, including employment, training, benefits, and compensation. She also played a key role in developing an employment brand strategy, which helped double employee growth during her tenure as HR Chief. Sartain also served as chairman of the Society for Human Resource Management in 2001 and was named fellow of the National Academy of Human Resources. She is the author, with Martha Finney, of the recently released AMACOM Book, *HR from the Heart: Inspiring Stories and Strategies for Building the People Side of Great Business.*

DEVON SCHEEF is president of Scheef Organizational Development and Training, Inc. and co-founder of The Learning Café. Devon assists clients in making peace with multiple workplace generations, leadership development, succession planning, talent-retention strategies, and mentoring initiatives. Devon spent 17 years in the corporate world in careers of market research, sales, and organizational development. She is a frequent and popular speaker at leadership meetings and conferences on bridging the generation gap, developing talented leaders, how to get the most out of mentoring initiatives, and leading in uncertain times. Author of *The Personal Learning Model,* she is also co-author, with Beverly Kaye, of *Mentoring: A How-To Guide.* Her unique leadership development work has been showcased in *Borrowing from the Best: Best Practices Resource Guide for Training and Continuous Learning.* Contact: www.careersystemsintl.com; www.keepem.com.

LINDA SHARKEY is responsible for the design and launch of the executive leadership development effort for General Electric Capital. She is also human resource manager for Six Sigma. Prior to joining General Electric, Linda was corporate vice president for leadership and organizational development at PaineWebber, where she established an integrated system for developing leaders. Additionally, she led the launch of their diversity effort. As vice president of professional development for Chemical Bank, she created a global leadership initiative aimed at increasing the capacity of the salesforce to segment and improve customer accounts and to increase sales. Linda also established a core curriculum to sustain the quality effort. Linda assisted New York State in launching the Excelsior Award (the state's equivalent of the Malcolm Baldrige Award). She has published several articles on leadership, including "A Case of Leadership Transformation in Financial Services" in the *Organizational Development Journal.*

NORMAN SMALLWOOD is co-founder of Results-Based Leadership Inc. The company provides education and consulting services to increase leaders' capability to deliver business results consistent with the organization's values. Norm was managing director (and co-founder) of Novations Group Inc., a strategic change management and career development-consulting firm. He also held positions at Procter and Gamble (P&G) and Esso Resources Canada Ltd. (Imperial Oil). At P&G, he participated in the start-up of a successful manufacturing plant. At Esso, he worked in research and development and then in exploration as an organization effectiveness consultant. Norm is co-author of *Results-Based Leadership,* which was named book of the year by the Society for Human Resource Management, and of *Real Time Strategy,* which was part of the Portable MBA series. His upcoming book, *How Leaders Build Market Value,* will be published in 2003. Contact: nsmallwood@rbl.net; www.rbl.net.

ANDREW SOBEL is the leading authority on client relationships and the skills strategies required to earn enduring client and customer loyalty. A noted business strategist, he is the author of *Making Rain: The Secrets of Building Lifelong Client Loyalty* and the bestselling *Clients for Life: Evolving from an Expert for Hire to an Extraordinary Advisor.* A sought-after speaker on how to build long-term business relationships, Andrew has been featured on a variety of national media, such as CNBC and ABC. He is President of Andrew Sobel Advisors, Inc., an international consulting and professional development firm.

FRANCIS STICKLAND is a consultant with Hewitt Associates in Europe. He has expertise in the areas of organizational development, business restructuring, and facilitating complex business change. Prior to joining Hewitt Associates, he held positions within both the banking and manufacturing sectors. He has worked within several European countries engaged in corporate-wide performance improvement and pan-European business reengineering projects. Since then, he has consulted in North America, the Middle East, and Europe at board and top team levels. Author of the recent book, *The Dynamics of Change,* Francis has published, consulted, and lectured on organizational behavior, systems thinking, and business transformation. He has worked with a range of organizations across sectors and continents. He is a member of the International Society for the Systems Sciences. Contact: Francis.Stickland@hewitt.com; www.hewitt.com.

CHARLES G. THARP is professor of human resource management at Rutgers University and former senior vice president of human resources of Bristol-Myers Squibb. He holds a PhD in Labor and Industrial Relations from Michigan State University. Contact: charlie.tharp@mindspring.com.

DIANE THIELFOLDT is co-founder of The Learning Café. Her consulting expertise includes retention, mentoring, generational differences in the workplace, and experiential learning design and facilitation. She partners with clients to create environments that not only produce business results, but also support personal growth. She focuses on the human potential by helping people and organizations translate strategic direction into meaningful work for exceptional business people. She spent 20 years in the corporate world, where she created a dazzling array of events, experiences, simulations, and seminars carefully designed to reinforce a strategic message to employees about the value of learning. Her work at Xerox was featured in the 1997 special edition of *FAST Company* magazine and Chris Turner's book, *All Hat and No Cattle*. Contact: www .careersystemsintl.com; www.keepem.com.

R. ROOSEVELT THOMAS JR. has been at the forefront of developing and implementing innovative concepts and strategies for maximizing organizational and individual potential through diversity management. He serves as CEO of R. Thomas Consulting & Training, Inc. and is president of The American Institute for Managing Diversity (AIMD). Roosevelt is the author of five books: *Building a House for Diversity; Redefining Diversity; Differences Do Make a Difference; Beyond Race and Gender, Unleashing the Power of Your Total Work Force by Managing Diversity;* and his most recent, *Giraffe and Elephant—A Diversity Fable*. He is also author of several articles, including the *Harvard Business Review* article "From Affirmative Action to Affirming Diversity." Contact: rrthomasjr@aol.com; www.rthomasconsulting.com.

DAVID ULRICH is currently president of the Canada Montreal Mission for the Church of Jesus Christ of Latter-Day Saints, while on a three-year sabbatical from his position as professor of business administration, University of Michigan. Professionally, David studied how organizations change fast, build capabilities, learn, remove boundaries, and leverage human resource activities. He has helped generate multiple award-winning, national databases on organizations that assess alignment between strategies, HR practices, and HR competencies. A prolific author, David's books include *Organizational Capability: Competing from the Inside Out* (with Dale Lake); *The Boundaryless Organization: Breaking the Chains of Organizational Structure* (with Ron Ashkenas, Steve Kerr, and Todd Jick); and *Human Resource Champions: The Next Agenda for Adding Value and Delivering Results*. He was editor of the *Human Resource Management Journal,* is a fellow in the National Academy of Human Resources, and is co-founder of the Michigan Human Resource Partnership. In 2001, *Business Week* ranked David as the #1 management educator. Contact: dou@umich.edu; www.rbl.net.

MICHAEL USEEM is professor of management and director of the Center for Leadership and Change Management at the Wharton School of the University of Pennsylvania. Michael's university teaching includes MBA and executive-MBA courses on management and leadership in the United States, Asia, Europe, and Latin America. He also works on leadership development with many companies and organizations in the private, public, and nonprofit sectors. Mike is author of *The Leadership Moment: Nine True Stories of Triumph and Disaster and Their*

Lessons for Us All and, to experience such moments, he organizes teams of Wharton graduates, company managers, and other groups for treks up the slopes of Mount Everest, trips to Civil War battlefields, and other learning events for leadership development. He recently published *Leading Up: How to Lead Your Boss So You Both Win*. Contact: useem@wharton.upenn.edu; http://leadership.wharton.upenn.edu/l_change/index.shtml.

MARGARET WHEATLEY writes, teaches, and speaks about radically new practices and ideas for organizing in chaotic times. She works to create organizations of all types where people are known as the blessing, not the problem. She is president of The Berkana Institute, a charitable global foundation serving life-affirming leaders around the world, has been an organizational consultant for many years, and a professor of management in two graduate programs. Her latest book, *Turning to One Another: Simple Conversations to Restore Hope to the Future*, proposes that real social change comes from the ageless process of people thinking together in conversation. Meg's work appears in the award-winning books, *Leadership and the New Science* and *A Simpler Way*. Contact: info@berkana.org; www.margaretwheatley.com.

LINDY WILLIAMS is a senior consultant with Career Systems International, Inc. and founder of Futures in Focus, a human resources consulting firm concentrating on career and employee development, retention, and leadership effectiveness. She has more than 25 years' experience in human resources development, line operations management, career and leadership development, and change management. Her work has included design and delivery of development processes for management and associate level employees in businesses ranging from financial services to construction and engineering. Lindy's frontline leadership experience combines with her consulting expertise to offer a broad perspective of the realities of business issues and opportunities. She has previously presented at numerous international conferences, as well as published articles in a range of journals. Contact: FuturesinFocus@aol.com.

INDEX